Sint-Paulus

Corsendonk Monk's Pale

Corsendonk Monk's Dark

Judas

Campus

Pauwel Kwak

Mort Subite Gueuze

Jacobins Kriek

Brugse Tripel

Maes Pils

Petrus

Hapkin

ABOUT THE AUTHOR

Michael Jackson is the world's leading consumer-writer on beer, and is well known for his love of Belgian brews. In 1993 he was made an Officer of Honour in the Chevalrie de Fourquet, and in 1994 he won the André Simon Award and the Glenfiddich Trophy. He has lectured on Belgian beer at the Smithsonian Institution in Washington, D.C., is frequently a guest lecturer at Cornell University, New York, and is a professional member of the James Beard Foundation.

In 1994 the Belgian Ministry of Foreign Trade and European Affairs decided that he should receive The Mercurius Award for his contribution to the promotion of Belgian products (i.e. beer). The award was made with particular reference to *The Great Beers of Belgium* and *The Beer Hunter*.

His other books include *Michael Jackson's Beer Companion*, *The Pocket Guide to Beer* and *The Complete Guide to Single Malt Scotch*. Jackson writes regularly for *The Independent*, London, and contributes periodically to many other major newspapers and magazines ranging from *The Washington Post* to *Playboy*. His "Beer Hunter" television series and CD–ROMs (Discovery Channel) have won awards on both sides of the Atlantic.

This dazzling spread of labels presents just a hint of the diversity of Belgian beer. It is from a poster published by the proprietor of the Hopduvel beer tavern, in Ghent, and displayed in cafés all over Belgium.

I would like to thank all of the countless beer-lovers in Belgium who have helped me over the years in my researches into their country's beer. Among them are many brewers, the Confederation of Belgian Breweries, the beer-writer Peter Crombecq, many journalists in Belgium, and several café owners, especially Antoine Denooze.

Michael Jackson

THE GREAT BEERS OF BELGIUM

© *1991, 1992 Michael Jackson*

© *1994 revised and expanded edition Michael Jackson*

© *1995 reprinted Michael Jackson*

First published in Belgium MMC/Coda

This edition Duncan Baird Publishers
6th Floor, Castle House
75–76, Wells Street
London
W1P 3RE

Imported and distributed exclusively by Vanberg and DeWulf, Cooperstown, NY 607-547-8184

ISBN 1 900131 35 8

Printed by Imago, Singapore

MICHAEL JACKSON

THE GREAT BEERS
OF BELGIUM

Vanberg and DeWulf
in association with
The Frances Kelly Agency

PREFACE TO THE SECOND EDITION

In every country, and especially in the great brewing nations, particular beers rise and fall in popularity, make their entrances and exits. What seems at a glance like an unchanging scene behind the bar is, in fact, an unfolding story.

St Arnold is the patron of Belgian brewers... but can he ensure that the traditions are maintained? That depends upon the observances of consumers, too.

That is one reason why I have dipped my pen in Belgian beer again only a couple of years after the first edition of this book. Another reason is that, in the intervening years, I have visited more brewers and have learned more about their beers.

In the unfolding story, there are both sad and happy moments, but the latter are in ascendancy. Speciality beers once had scarcely more than 20 per cent of the Belgian market, and now enjoy closer to 30. A price that has been paid is that some beers have become blander, sweeter, and less characterful.

The Belgians are people of great individuality. I urge them to the bar, to demand the most individualistic of beers.

Michael Jackson

CONTENTS

Reverent moment... in the church of Madeleine, in Brussels, the Prelate of Grimbergen Abbey blesses the beer, at anual mass on behalf of the Chevalrie du Fourquet.

To be served with reverence

The respect reserved for wine in most countries is in Belgium accorded also to beer. No country can match Belgium in the gastronomic interest of its beers. No country has so many

The basket, bottle and Burgundian glass are more than display. A "Méthode Champenoise" beer requires a strong bottle, and the sedimentation demands gentle handling. The glass highlights colour and aroma.

distinct styles of beer (though several have more breweries). No country has beers that are so complex in character as the finest in Belgium. No country has so many individualistic brews. Nor does any country have such a sophisticated beer cuisine (extending far beyond the dishes that are commonly associated with beer).

The spontaneously-fermenting, "wild", Lambic beers of the Zenne Valley represent a tradition unique to Belgium. So do the tart, acidic, "sour" beers of Flanders. In the production of top-fermenting brews and wheat beers, Belgium is one of the world leaders. No country has as many "Méthode Champenoise" beers, in which a second or even third fermentation is induced in the bottle either by a dosage of yeast or a blending of young and mature brews. No other country has so persisted with the use of fruits, herbs and spices in beer. Germany and Belgium are the only two countries to have kept alive on any scale the practice of brewing in monasteries; only Belgium and The Netherlands have Trappist beers.

The "King of Beer" was most probably a Belgian, though he can be spotted all over Europe.

In all traditional brewing nations, the legendary "King of Beer" is a character called Gambrinus. This name (sometimes spelled with a "C") is widely considered to be a corruption of "Jan Primus", or Duke Jean I (1251-95), ruler of Brabant, Louvain and Antwerp: regions and cities of what is today Belgium. Jean was born in Burgundy, today better known to the world for its Pinot Noir wines and a hearty cuisine starring Charollais beef and Dijon mustard. In the late Middle Ages, Burgundy was a kingdom embracing much of present-day Belgium. The term "Burgundian" is used in Belgium even today to indicate a man who enjoys his food and drink, in both quantity and quality. "Burgundian" is a usefully approving word, which I would like to draft into English to replace "gourmand". It is said that, during a single feast, Gambrinus could drink 144 mugs of beer; perhaps the feast lasted as long as some Belgian lunches I have enjoyed. Gambrinus is also credited with having invented the toast, though it surely dates beyond him, to superstitions intended to ward off evil spirits.

A less widely-held theory concerning the name Gambrinus associates it with the once-famous brewing town of Cambrai, in French Flanders, and there are several even more tenuous notions.

12

The conservatively Roman Catholic Belgians also remember Burgundy for the most powerful of Benedictine monasteries, Cluny, and for Cîteaux, which later began the Cistercian order. St Arnold, an 11th-century monk from the abbey of St Médard, at Soissons (near the Champagne town of Rheims), and later bishop, is the patron saint of brewing in Belgium. St Arnold founded the abbey of Oudenburg, between Ostend and Bruges (he has also been linked with Oudenaarde). At a time of plague, St Arnold is said to have immersed his crucifix in a brew-kettle, thus encouraging the populace to drink beer, rather than water. Miraculously, the plague ended. The water had probably been communicating the infection, while beer - being boiled during production - remains a much safer drink. Another story has St Arnold miraculously producing beer after the destruction of an abbey brewery.

The abbey of Oudenburg was itself largely destroyed during the French Revolution and a new monastery to replace it, called Steenbrugge, was established in Bruges. Every year, Belgium's brewers pay homage to St Arnold at a church service in Brussels.

LE GOUT DU TERROIR

Warm countries grow fruits (especially grapes) to make into wine. Cool places cultivate grain (most often barley) to turn into beer. Their lands of origin are what devide wine and beer. It is the weather, and not the people or their apparent tastes, that makes the difference.

In many parts of the world, wine is regarded as more worthy of study, and is in consequence better understood. Beer is more widely consumed, and is often taken for granted.

People with a fundamental appreciation of food and drink are the least likely to fall into this misunderstanding. In wine-making regions like Franconia, Bordeaux and California, beer is widely enjoyed. In the cafe that faces the main square of Bordeaux, I have been pressed to sample a Belgian brew by a solicitous waiter, and not been alone in accepting the suggestion. Anyone who can appreciate a fine red wine can enjoy a good copper-coloured ale; the two are counterparts, in more than colour, in the worlds of wine and beer.

Examples from the world of wine are useful in the understanding of beer. The similarities are greater than the differences. The two

St Arnold watches over the brew-kettle at Jumet where Cuvée de l'Ermitage and other renowned beers are produced. He is to be found in several Belgian breweries.

products are equally noble, complex and varied. They came to maturity as neighbours, in the civilisations of Europe. Even their territories, instead of being cleanly separated by the Alps, interlock like pieces of a jigsaw puzzle. It happens between Moravia and Bohemia, again in Franconia, and once again on the Rhine, with the Jigsaw then slicing south of the Ardennes, Picardy and Artois. In the New World, the jigsaw continues its journey in California and the Pacific northwest. These wine-and-beer frontiers are some of the most interesting brewing regions in the world. One of them is spectacular.

Close to the region where the Champagne grapes grow, the land is also golden with barley; France begins to sound Flemish, and blends into Belgium; the wine nations yield to the beer lands. With fine wine so close, and rule by the Burgundians not so many centuries distant, the Belgians seem instinctivily to feel the nuances of both drinks. Not only the respect, but also the

France's northwest is where wine gives way to beer. The nine provinces of Belgium are all brewing lands. So, of course, are Germany and The Netherlands.

15

ceremony, that other nations reserve for wine, the Belgians also accord, with a special flourish, to beer. They enjoy wine but make none; beer is their national drink.

Like all countries, Belgium has a head of state; like most, it has a national soccer team; like many, it has a predominant religion (Roman Catholicism, though more pervasive and conservative in the north than the south); but nothing unites this land like its

Beer, an unifying element in Belgium's social culture, was enjoyed by King Baudouin, who is remembered as a unifying monarch.

love of beer. Such a unifying toast is much needed. Belgium is a small country, but it has more than one culture. Its most difficult division is between its own mini-states of Wallonia, in the south, and Flanders, in the north. They may be small, but each is as much a nation as England, Scotland or Quebec.

Culturally, Flanders stretches from Northern France to the Netherlands, and the Flemish language is much the same as Dutch. Wallonia prefers French. Within these two mini-states are provinces with histories that cross national borders. There is a Belgian province called Luxembourg, next to the sovereign state with the same name. Belgium has Flemish and Walloon Brabant, while the Netherlands has North Brabant. Limburg is the name of provinces in both Belgium and the Netherlands and a city in Germany. Two Belgian towns Eupen and Malmédy (and the surrounding cantons) speak German. Belgium has three languages, ten million people, and 35,000 places in which beer is served. That is twice the density of pubs in Britain.

THE BURGUNDIES OF BELGIUM

The winiest-tasting beers are made in Belgium. Many of them look like wines, as they emerge in their rich ambers, pinks, deep reds and Madeira browns from Champagne bottles into flutes, goblets or Burgundy samplers. Several have names like Grand Cru, Cuvée, or Grande Reserve, often with justification. I even know of one brewer who pours a bottle of white wine into each fermenting vessel when he is making a particular beer. It is hard to say what result this might have, but the beer has always been made in this way.

In a café, or at a family dinner, a rare bottle, perhaps vintage-dated, is borne from the cellar slowly, cradled horizontally, so

Some Belgian classics disport themselves on the capital's magnificent main square. One of the most elegant buildings on the square is the brewers' guild house, with a small beer museum open to the public.

that the yeast will not be aroused from its dreams. There may be a wrap of tissue paper to remove. The seal is opened, or the cage unhooked, as if it were a seduction, and the cork gently drawn. To most of the world's drinkers, many Belgian brews are scarcely recognisable as beers, but that is what they are: fermented from grain (even if fruit is added later), and seasoned with the hop (even if that magic cone is sometimes helped along with herbs and spices).

18

Some styles of Belgian beer are specific to a province, others to a district, valley, or town. No country has so many idiosyncratic brews as Belgium.

This individualism is intentional. While other countries have more enthusiastically moved toward universal systems in the production of beer, a great many Belgian brewers have preferred to retain the methods of their district and refine those. In no other country are as many different techniques used. Belgium has produced some great brewing scientists, most famously Jean De Clerck (1902-78), but even they have shown a notable appreciation that the making of beer is also an art. Anyone who loves food and drink, and its quality and diversity, must thank Belgium for this contribution, and take pleasure in it.

Never simply ask for "a beer" in Belgium. For that matter, never do it anywhere. Would you go into a restaurant and request "some wine, please"? Or, "a plate of food"? Ask for "a beer" in Belgium and you will get a modestly hoppy Pilsener-style lager, but think what you will miss. Inquire instead what beers are available. Even in the humblest establishment, there will be an interesting selection. A railway station bar may offer a dozen or fifteen different styles of beer.

If you have a thirst, cut it with a tart, refreshing, Gueuze (from the wild-fermented Lambic family), or a Rodenbach (aged in oak); if you want to arouse the appetite, try a dry-hopped Orval, or a Duvel (fermented and matured warm and cold, twice over); if something rich and satisfying is your heart's desire, opt for a Trappist or abbey beer, perhaps rounded out with a rummy dash of candy sugar.

WHERE IS BELGIUM?

To explore beer in Belgium is a journey of discovery. My own journeys began with a weekend in Belgium in the mid 1960s. On that trip, I discovered Gueuze, an ale called De Koninck, and an abbey beer of uncertain origin. They were intense and fascinating potions. In the early 1970s, I began to plan my first book on beer. It was to be about the beers of the whole world, but I found myself heading for Belgium to research a pilot chapter. In the late 1980s, I started to develop a series of documentary films for television, again on the beers of the world. Again, I began with Belgium.

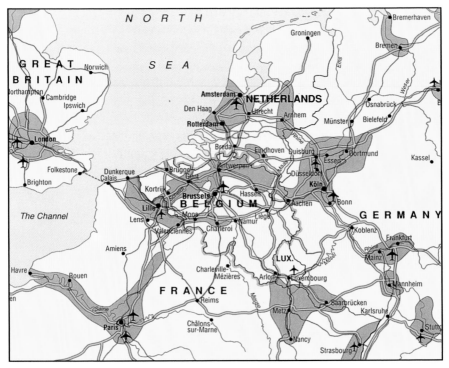

Britain, Belgium and Germany are three of the great beer-making nations. To Germany's immediate east lies Czechoslovakia, a fourth great brewing country.

When I first visited Belgium with serious research in mind, almost 20 years ago, a senior member of the brewing industry said to me: "Don't bother mentioning our country; it is small, and no one knows where it is."

Perhaps he was worried that, if Belgian beers reached a wider market, their quality would have to be compromised. That

20

would have been a reasonable fear, but I doubt he was being so rational.

When Caesar came to this part of the world, he found the Belgae a stubborn lot. Later, in the livery of Flanders, they were for centuries a great trading nation, but that may have been an aberration. Which Belgian would miss lunch in order to conquer the world? Even a journey a couple of hundred miles north to Protestant Holland is fraught with the threat that there may be nothing for lunch but a meatball, and the likelihood that the selection of beer will be less interesting.

Drinking and eating are lingering pleasures in Belgium, as organic, vivid and robust a part of its national life as the paintings of Rubens and Bruegel, the tapestries of Oudenaarde, the gilded gables of Brussels and Bruges. At the table, the quality of the food and drink matches that in France; the quantity would satisfy a German.

Every European nation has ruled others, or been ruled, been divided and joined, throughout its history. The Austrian, Burgundian, Spanish and Dutch Empires have all at one time or another absorbed Belgium. It has had more rulers than Louisiana or Texas. Today, its greatest city, Brussels, is Europe's "Federal Capital" and its French and Dutch-speaking halves sometimes seem to outsiders to merge with their linguistic neighbours. From the inside, this is clearly not the case.

While far larger nations have marched across its territory, Belgium has taken from them but less often given to them. Faced with rule by others, the Belgians have set their face against all authority, and become a nation of individualists. This may be one reason why there are so many distinct styles of beer. Belgium has been compacted, and hugged its greatest assets to itself. Belgium's beers have been its best-kept secrets. The knowing say, airily, "ah, yes, the Belgians have good beer", but who has really explored them?

Water: a Good Beginning

Devotees of spring water, whose numbers have increased of late, will know that the word "spa" originates from the name of a town in the Belgian Ardennes. The springs there were known to Pliny and rediscovered in the Middle Ages, and the word "spa" was introduced to the English language by two British doctors in the 1700s. The term has been suffixed to many towns, but there is only one called simply Spa, with a capital "s", and that is the original, in Belgium. The town of Spa still offers baths where the cure can be taken, pavilions and fountains (as well as the traditional casino), and a spectacularly deep valley setting, with skiing in a snowy winter. Having restored their health, visitors can indulge themselves in a gentle cup of bouillon (named after another town in the region) and perhaps a snack of local trout or oak-smoked Ardennes ham. Spa has at least 25 springs. Several bring forth water that is rich in iron and carbonic acid, and this has over the years been taken, both as a bath and a drink, by people suffering from anaemia, gout

The queen of spas... taking the water in the town of Spa. It tastes better when malt and hops are added.

and rheumatism. Other springs in the town pour water that is unusually pure. The mineral water that has been for 100 years sold commercially in bottles with the label Spa has a far lower level of dissolved solids that any of its principal competitors.

Several Belgian breweries use spring water from the Ardennes, the rolling hills and forests that rise to the east of the river Meuse. There is another famous source at Chaudfontaine, near Liège, and its waters are also available commercially bottled. Anyone wishing to produce beer - especially on a commercial scale - would be pleased to have his own, reliable, pure source of water. That asset helped determine the location of many breweries in the early days of the trade. Budweis and Pilsen, in Bohemia, and Burton, in England, are typical examples. A great many breweries in Belgium have their own wells, and are proud to say so.

The character of the water available also helped determine the style of beers in the 1700s and 1800s. Lager beers like those produced in Budweis, Pilsen and Munich require soft water. Pale ales like those from Burton gain their characteristic firmness from hard water. Today, brewers can remove or add the appropriate natural salts to produce the character of water they seek.

A source of good water will not in itself ensure a wonderful beer, but it is a valuable beginning.

THE STAFF OF LIFE

Civilisation may have begun with beer. There is an academically respected theory on these lines. On the basis of that theory, it might be argued that the Belgians have their priorities right. In pursuing their enthusiasm for beer, they are simply seeking to be a civilised people.

The proposal is that, when humans stopped being hunters and gatherers, and settled in organised societies in order to grow grain, their purpose was not to bake bread, but to brew beer. Research in this field has been based on excavations stretching from Ancient Egypt to what is now Israel, Syria, Iraq and Turkey.

Archaeological finds from Egypt and the Fertile Crescent are rich in evidence of brewing.

Wild barley was being gathered at least 33,000 years ago, in what is now northern Israel and Syria, according to recent studies. It was apparently roasted, and may have been used to make beer, though no one knows. It is now thought that barley and wheat may have been planted in the same area as early as 13,000 years ago. These conclusions are based on examination of flint tools. The segment of Iraq that formed Mesopotamia, with its region of Babylonia and its district of Sumer, provides the earliest evidence of beer being consumed, as depicted in a decorative seal of 6,000 years ago.

A series of Sumerian tablets 5,000 years old, which has been described as the world's oldest recipe, explains the making of beer from barley. A Sumerian text 4,000 years old mentions both beer and wine. Excavations in Egypt, and work on Sumerian pictograms, are still yielding new evidence of early brewing in the Middle East.

LIQUID BREAD

The thought that beer may have preceded bread could have been inspired by an expression common to the brewing monasteries of Austria and Germany, Belgium and The Netherlands. In the strictest regimes, the monks were always allowed to drink beer during Lent, and called it "liquid bread". The academic theory had its origins in a German-language paper published in the 1920s, and excavations in Iraq in the 1930s, and was further developed by Professor Solomon Katz, of the University of Philadelphia, in the late 1980s.

Beer may have preceded wine, too, but snobbism soon developed. During the early Roman Empire, Tacitus noted of the Germanic peoples: "Their beverage they prepare from barley or wheat, a brew which slightly resembles an inferior quality of wine." By then, it seems, the warmer countries were concentrating on the grape and the cooler ones on the grain (though some made mead, from honey; or cider, from apples).

Perhaps the snobbism derives from the fact that wine was the drink of the governing classes, and beer of the colonies, when the Romans held sway over Europe, when the Normans conquered England, and in the various periods when the

Climate divides Europe into wine, beer and spirit "belts". This map was devised by Interbrew, who make beer in Leuven and Jupille, among other Belgian communities.

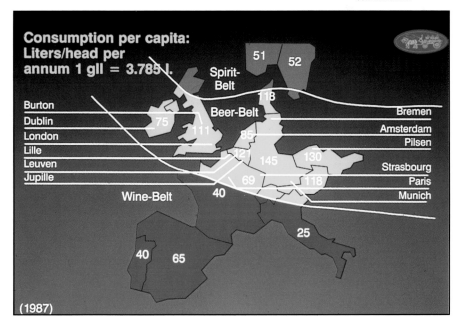

Consumption per capita:
Liters/head per
annum 1 gll = 3.785 l.

Spirit-Belt

Beer-Belt

Wine-Belt

Burton
Dublin
London
Lille
Leuven
Jupille

Bremen
Amsterdam
Pilsen
Strasbourg
Paris
Munich

51 52
118
75 111 85
121 145 130
69 118
40
25
40 65

(1987)

25

Anyone passing by a vineyard understands that wine (or brandy) may be in cultivation. These fields of barley are growing beer (or perhaps whisky).

Burgundians and the Napoleonic French ruled Belgium. Perhaps the Romance tongues have imparted a greater sensuousness to their native drinks than the Germanic languages have to theirs. Perhaps the warm south, and the fleshy grape, are themselves more sensuous than the cool north and the less yielding grain. Barley is the grain that can most easily be turned into beer, and it is one of the least satisfactory in the baking of bread. Wheat and rye are more suited to the baker. It is thus that barley has always been the principal grain in brewing, though wheat is an ingredient in several classic styles of beer, and is especially widely used in Bavaria and Belgium. Rye is occasionally used. Oats are used in some Belgian beers, and very occasionally in the English-speaking world. Barley imparts a firm, clean sweetness; wheat has a tart, quenching quality in beer; rye is spicy, almost minty; oats add a silky smoothness. Rice is sometimes used to lighten the body of beers, and maize as a cheaper ingredient, though one that can impart an unpleasant stickiness.

Varieties of barley

Two varieties of grape may produce dramatically different wines; the distinctions between barleys are less obvious, but the brewer is still interested in the selection of variety, the region of cultivation, and the season.

Two races of barley, distinguished by the number of rows of grains in each ear, are used in the making of beer. Many brewers prefer two-row barley, and feel that the six-row varieties have too much husk character. Some brewers feel that the influence of the husk adds to the flavour of their beer. As farmers seek better yields, new varieties of both races are constantly being

A classic farmhouse brewery in Brabant... this is Lindemans, making Lambic beer, and especially known for its fruit variations.

bred. Many brewers prefer spring barley (sown in March and harvested in July and August), feeling that the winter varieties (whose season is from October-November to June) are too harsh. Again, some take a different view. The requirement of the brewer may also be influenced by the style and character of the particular beer to be made.

Farmers were once commonly also brewers. Grain is perishable, and was hard to transport in the days of horse and cart. There

On this canal, barges bring barley to fill the towering silos of Interbrew, at Leuven. The barley is turned into malt, and that is brewed into beer. The finished product, Stella Artois, can be exported by the canal.

was much work on the farm in summer, but less in winter. During the cold months, the grain could be fermented into beer (and then perhaps distilled into spirits). There are still farmhouse breweries in Belgium. Girardin is the best example. Others are recognisable as having been farms, even if they are today exclusively breweries. There are also monasteries that have both farms and breweries. The rhythms of farming, harvesting, brewing, maturing and drinking are also remembered in the

tradition of seasonal beers. Agricultural and religious seasons tend to coincide, of course.

In those days, Belgium grew enough barley to quench its thirst. Today, the cultivation of barley for the brewer is having a minor revival: around Gembloux (between Brussels and Namur); in the province of Liège; and in the area between the city of Antwerp and the border with The Netherlands.

Far more barley is imported. Belgium is surrounded by barley-growing countries: France (with cultivation in the region between Orléans and Paris, and in Champagne); Germany (especially Lower Franconia); The Netherlands (Dutch Zeeland); Denmark; and England (East Anglia).

While the grape is delicate, and disinclined to travel, barley is much more robust. Indeed, it will not give up its sugars, or the enzymes needed in their fermentation, until it has gone through the process of malting. This may be done in the country of cultivation, or closer to the brewing of the beer. It takes place in an establishment known as a maltings. Wherever barley is grown for malting, they can be seen, though many of the smaller ones have been turned to other uses (in Britain, one is a celebrated concert hall). The older maltings are very distinctive buildings. They usually have at least two or three storeys, with vents on the roof, pulleys to hoist the grain, and shutters to control the temperature.

Belgium still has seven or eight maltings, well known throughout the world of brewing for the quality of their products. Today, maltings are usually free-standing, though in the past many shared a site and ownership with a brewery. In the Belgian city of Leuven (Louvain, in French), a maltings is still a part of the Interbrew complex, where Stella Artois is made.

MALT

Barley is steeped in water, allowed partially to germinate, then dried, in the process of malting. The end product is known as barley malt. Or simply as malt. It is the raw material not only of beer (a fermented drink) but also whisky (its distilled counterpart).

The procedures of malting take about ten days in total. The steeping, in tanks - with several changes of water, and aereation to allow the barley embryo to breathe - is much the same in all maltings. The steeped grains may then be spread on a stone floor, and turned by rakes to ensure that they remain aerated and separated while they begin to germinate. Or they may be

placed in shallow, ventilated boxes, or in rotating drums. The floor system is the most traditional, and some maltsters feel it produces the best results. Its disadvantages are that it is very demanding in space and labour, and the method is most commonly found in rural Bohemia or the whisky country of Scotland.

Maltsters, brewers and beer-lovers who visit Belgium are astonished when they see the site at Leuven. This is a floor maltings... but on six storeys. Each floor is 200 metres long, and divided into five lanes, about 12 cm deep in germinating grains. They look like running tracks on golden grass.

Stella returned wholly to this traditional system in the 1960s, after having used a variety of other techniques. The maltsters and brewers feel that the traditional method produces a clean

They look like some kind of running track, but these are malting "streets", paved with barley that has been steeped and is now germinating. Inside the six-storey maltings building at Interbrew, in Leuven.

Maltsters still check the progress of the grains by the unscientific eye. A maltster uses science, but he is still an artist, too.

dryness in the finished beer that is not matched by any other technique. In floor malting, the germinating grain forms only a shallow layer, and this has an influence on its moisture and temperature. That could explain the method's contribution to flavour, but no one is totally sure. Although malting and brewing are now highly developed sciences, every practitioner has his own views and instincts, just as a chef-de-cuisine would. "We cannot explain everything by science - and we are still learning," a maltster at Stella told me. He had been in the job for 36 years.

COLOUR AND FLAVOUR

Just as the length of contact with the grapes' skins influences both colour and flavour in wine, the drying of the malt does the same in beer. A very gently kilned malt will be pale in colour and delicate in flavour, and make a golden, beer. A malt that has been "stewed" will provide a more reddish colour and a sweeter, slightly biscuity, or even toffee-ish, flavour. A malt that has been roasted will be dark brown or black, and may have a flavour reminiscent of dark chocolate or espresso coffee. The kilns at a traditional maltings are not dissimilar in outward appearance from those at a pottery. Where very dark malts are made, there will also be drums like those used by coffee roasters. Even the smell is similar to that of coffee being roasted.

A maltings may make just the very pale type, or as many as a dozen variations, each with its own regime of moistures and temperatures. Some are known by the name of the beer-style they produce: Pilsener Malt, Pale Ale, Vienna, Munich (in ascending order of kilning). Others are described by their characteristics: Aromatic Malt, Biscuit, Chocolate, Roasted. There are several variations on the aromatic malts, and these are notably favoured in Belgium.

Some beers are made with just one style of malt, many with two

Some breweries take delivery of all their malt by the sack. Others receive only their darker malt this way, and have the basic, pale, type delivered in bulk to a silo.

or three. Speciality beers may employ as many as eight, though that is unusual. A bèer made from several malts may have an especially complex, subtle, colour. In the scale used by brewers, a golden beer using only pale malts might have 6.5 International Units of Colour. A stout could have 150-200.

INFUSION AND DECOCTION

Grapes will yield their juices simply by being crushed; malt is tougher. At the brewery, the malt is cracked in a mill, then soaked in hot water for an hour or more to release its fermentable sugars. The duration and temperatures of this mashing procedure vary according to the brewery and the style of beer being made. It may be a simple infusion, at just one temperature, or there may be series of steps. There may even be a decoction, involving

The mashing fork, known in old French as fourquet, was used to stir the grains. The technique can be seen at the museum at the Brewers' House, in Brussels.

transfer between two vessels at different temperatures. When the sugars have been released, the liquid - the "juice" of the barley - is strained into the brew-kettle. This "juice" is known by brewers as wort. The term has its origin in the Germanic word for "root". This "juice" is the root of the beer.

The "juice" is very sweet, and that is why it needs the subsequent seasoning of hops. It would not be a very refreshing drink "straight", though I have been served it hot, laced with whisky, as an alternative to coffee, and found it most sustaining.

The instantly-recognisable brew-house is the type with the copper vessels shaped like bathy-spheres. This one is at the Westmalle Trappist brewery.

THE BREWHOUSE

The simplest brewhouse has just two principal vessels: the mash-tun, where the infusion takes place, and the kettle. In an artisanal

brewery, perhaps one that had its beginnings as a farm, the mash-tun may be an open, circular vessel, made from cast-iron, and looking like a spare part from a steam locomotive. Inside may be a stirring device that would look equally happy on an early harvesting machine. The kettle may be nothing more than a copper tub, heated underneath by gas flames, or by internal steam coils, and sometimes bricked-in.

This type of brewhouse is still common in Belgium, but there are few elsewhere in the world. Belgium and the adjoining areas of Northern France are one of the last homes of truly artisanal brewing. Franconia is another, and there are a hand-

The brick-clad kettle at De Troch is typical of those found in several artisanal breweries. The brick insulation retains the heat.

ful of such breweries in England and Scotland.

Very old brewhouses, and the techniques of beer-making that they demand, will often resemble one another within a particular area. There was probably in the past a local engineer who did the design work for all the breweries in his district, as though they were railway stations on a country branch line. This was no doubt an influence on regional styles of beer.

The more instantly recognisable brewhouse is the one where both the principal vessels are of a similar, dome-shaped design, in copper. These are reminiscent of one of Jacques Cousteau's bathyspheres (or a creation of Jules Verne?). This style of brew-

37

house is still being built today, though often in stainless steel, and in more angular designs. There are also modern brewhouses where the vessels are walled-in, perhaps behind tiles, with hatches and sight-glasses that make the whole thing resemble a huge launderette. Others mimic a food-processing plant, and some would not look out of place on the Starship Enterprise.

Whichever design is used, the procedures are the same in principle. The actual act of brewing is the boiling in the kettle of the juices of the barley and the seasoning of hops.

SPICES AND HOPS

The first wine-makers added herbs, spices, flowers, berries, fruits or tree-barks to their products. Wines spiced with camomile, quinine bark and rhubarb are still made today, but we know them as vermouths. Today's wine-makers prefer to give the grape a balancing, dryish, aromatic, character from the oak of the cask. In ancient times, clay amphorae did not have that effect. Some brandies are still spiced with essences of nuts or fruits. Gin is a spirit aromatised with juniper berries, coriander, orange peels and other "botanicals". Liqueurs are spirits with spices, herbs, nuts or fruits added. Only in Belgium are herbs, spices and fruits still widely used in beers.

Even in Belgium, the custom was diminishing until recently, but it is now enjoying a revival. I once visited the very old-established wholesale herbalist Robert Meyskens, in Quévrain, near Mons.

Segments of orange peel, of the type originally grown on the island of Curaçao, are an important ingredient in some of today's Belgian beers. So are coriander seeds, hops (shown here in pelletized form) and malted barley and wheat.

He showed me faded, handwritten ledgers detailing orders for a wide variety of herbs from a dozen or 20 brewers. Mr. Meyskens said that the numbers of brewers among his customers had dwindled to two at the beginning of the 1970s, but had risen again to about 10 by the time of my visit, in 1986. Three years later, he wrote to tell me that his business with brewers was "good".

Many current Belgian beers contain herbs and spices, especially coriander, licorice, the peppery paradise seed, ginger and Curaçao orange peels. This is especially typical of "white" wheat beers in the style of Hoegaarden, though it also applies to other brews. A few of these are specifically categorised as Kruidenbieren. A Kruid is a herb. In old Germanic languages, the addition of herbs to beer was known as a Gruit. In modern English, the term grouts is used semi-colloquially for the residue of leaves at the bottom of a cup of tea.

As a result of Belgian influence, one or two brewers in France, The Netherlands and North America have in recent years begun to make beers with herbs, spices or fruits. Traditional home-brewers in Norway and Sweden use juniper twigs, with berries, as a filter, a flavoring agent and a preservative. Finland has a traditional home-brew called Sahti that is often aromatised with juniper.

At least one commercial brewer in Denmark employs bog-myrtle. None of these countries, nor any other, remotely approaches Belgium in its production of spiced beers.

Once, all beers were spiced. There is some reason to believe that the ancients used honey and dates. As brewing spread west and north, coriander, juniper, bog myrtle and alder twigs were among the flavourings that came into use.

JETS D'HOUBLON

It has not been established beyond doubt quite when the hop was pressed into service. Hops were known to the Ancients, but it is not certain how they were used. Pliny knew them as a garden plant, whose young shoots were eaten as a salad. In Europe, this custom is still known in Bohemia, Germany, and elsewhere, but thrives only in Belgium. In his book "Food", the late Waverley Root, the Paris-based, American essayist put his finger on it in characteristic style: "The most fervent admirers of the hop are the Belgians." He was speaking gastronomically, but "admire" is the right verb.

The eating of hop shoots, jets d'houblon, is enjoying a revival. The natural season for this succulent, nutty, delicacy is short: for

Hop shoots are the central delicacy of this lobster treat. Pliny would recognize them... and now a farmer's snack has become a gastronomic event.

41

about three weeks, from mid March to the beginning of April, during which time the shoots are normally being thinned. In the hope of extending this season, there have been experiments with cultivation under glass, but the shoots grown this way are on the woody side.

Like many classic dishes (the pizza of Naples, the eggs and spinach of Florence, the quiche of Lorraine), jets d'houblon had humble beginnings in the desire to utilise every last scrap. The shoots had to be thinned, so why not eat those that were picked? The thinning is done when the shoots are just peeping a couple of inches above the ground. Today, it can be done partly by spraying: thinning by hand has become very expensive, and that is another reason for cultivation under glass. Hop shoots have become a rare and expensive luxury.

The most basic way of serving them is to blanch or poach them in salty water with a seasoning of lemon juice and present them in a soup plate, with one or two softly poached eggs on top, and butter, cream or a simple sauce - velouté, béchamel or a mousseline. Modern-day refinements might include the addition of slivers of smoked salmon. Escoffier recommended croutons of fried bread, and insisted that they be cockscomb-shaped. Like eggs Florentine, jets d'houblon is a simple but delicious snack - or entrée. Like asparagus with scrambled eggs (another dish that is often served with beer), it has the ritual and fun of a short season. Like both of those dishes, it has appetising contrasts of texture between the eggs and the vegetable or salad ingredients.

FROM BABYLON TO BELGIUM

While it is the shoot of the hop that is eaten, it is the leafy cone, sometimes known as the blossom, that is valued for its oils, resins, tannin, acids and aromatic qualities. The hop, which is a member of the Cannabis family, has been used through the ages as a sedative (in herbal pillows), a preservative (where there are isolated reports of its use in embalming and tanning) and a medicine or beauty aid (as in beer shampoos).

Accounts of the Jews' captivity in Babylon refer to hops being used in a sicera ("strong drink"; the word may be the root for "cider") that prevented leprosy. The Romans recorded that the hop grew wild among willows, and this was the origin of its botanical name, Humulus lupulus.

Humulus lupulus

More persistent references to the cultivation of hops do not appear until the eighth and ninth centuries A.D., when gardens are mentioned in Bohemia, Bavaria, and other parts of Germany. King Pepin of the Franks (the father

The vine and its cones (above) will soon climb the strings stretched between hop poles at the abbey of Affligem (below). Some historians say the monks at this abbey introduced hops to Flanders.

43

of Charlemagne), who was enthroned at Soissons, in Northern France, is recorded as having given a hop farm to the Abbey of St Denis. There is also a significant mention of hops being required by monks in Picardy prior to 822.

The early references do not say why the hops were grown, though there are also plentiful records of beer having been brewed in the same areas at the time. There are vague allusions connecting hops, grain and beer from the beginning of this millennium. The abbey of Affligem, founded in 1086, is credited by one writer with having introduced hops to Flanders. Another account has hops being introduced to the region by monks in the French-Flemish town of St Omer some time prior to 1322, at which point cultivation began east of Dunkirk, in Poperinge, near Ypres. In 1364, the Bishop of Liège and Utrecht referred to the use of hops in beer as having been in vogue for 30 or 40 years. The Flemish exported hopped beer to England in the 1400s. It is a short sea crossing from Flanders to the East of England, and the two regions already had a history of trading in wool. Engineers from Flanders and Holland had also worked on draining the lowlands of East Anglia. At the time, the English were still making beer without hops. Initially, there were protectionist measures against hopped beer, but these were swept away by Henry VI. Hopped beer had given the Flemish fat faces and bellies, and could cause death, said an English writer of the time (curiously, he had a Flemish-sounding name: Boorde). It became popular nonetheless. In the 1500s, Flemish immigrants started growing hops in England.

On the borders of the hop-growing counties of Kent and Sussex, in a church at Playden, near Rye, there is in the floor a stone slab dating from about 1530, with an inscription showing a crossed staff and fork (used in mashing, and a symbol of brewing) and two casks. A Flemish-language engraving says that this is the tomb of Cornelis Roetmans. No doubt he was a brewer. By the 1700s, the Flemish hop-growing industry was suffering severely from English competition.

Hops had by then also been introduced to the New Netherlands, in North America. Hops followed the development of the United States, beginning in what is now New York State, migrating to Wisconsin, in the Midwest, and thence to California. Today, they are mainly grown in Oregon and Washington state, and across the Canadian border in British Columbia.

Varieties of hop

Today, different varieties of hops are used according to the style of beer being made. The variety native to Bohemia, and grown around the town of Zatec (Saaz hops) are prized for the their delicacy, and used in the finest Pilsener-style lager beers. Several similar varieties, most notably the Hallertau Mittelfrüh, are grown in Bavaria.

While the Saaz and Hallertau-Mittelfrüh are used principally to impart aroma to the beer, other varieties contribute dryness, or bitterness. One of Bavaria's favourite bittering hops is Northern Brewer, which is also grown in Belgium, and originated from Britain (hence the English name). Germany grows, mainly in Bavaria, between a quarter and a third of the world's hop crop.

At harvest time, the vines are heavy with the cone-like, pale green blossoms, or flowers, rich in aromatic resins, oils and acids.

Flanders contributes less than one per cent of the world's crop, but has a rich hop lore. I have even tasted a Flemish gin called Hopjenever, made by a firm called Verhofstede, in Nieuwenkerken-Waas, near Sint-Niklaas. I found it hard to detect the hop aroma and flavour, but loved the eclecticism of the idea.

Although varieties of hop are internationally recognized, they still emerge with a different character depending upon the country in which they are grown. Hallertaus cultivated in Belgium are, for the example, the "secret" ingredient in one well-known speciality beer made in the United States. The Bohemian Saaz and the Northern Brewer were the parents of Record, a variety that was first grown in Belgium. This has some of the aroma of a Saaz or Hallertau, but a more assertive bitterness and fullness of flavour. Although the Record might be regarded as the principal Belgian variety, Brewers' Gold is also grown. This hop, which has a sweetish perfume, originates from Britain. Belgian ale-brewers often use British varieties of hop,

45

The vines grow to their full height of 15 to 20 ft in four or five months. Pickers used stilts or mobile platforms before mechanical methods were devised.

notably the earthy, powerfully aromatic Golding of East Kent. Belgium grows fewer hops than Britain, but the latter is small in world terms. Britain is, though, noted for hops that perform well in ales. British hops have also been used to parent varieties in North America, Australasia, and Styrian Slovenia.

Hops like shelter, a temperate climate, with light rain and moist soil. They tend to thrive at fairly similar, and corresponding, latitudes in the Northern and Southern hemispheres, and they are grown in several other countries, including Japan and the Soviet Union.

The principal growing region in Belgium is still around Poperinge, and there is a smaller district around Asse and Aalst, between Ghent and Brussels.

FLANDERS' HOP FIELDS

Just off the Roman road from Boulogne to Cologne, and part of the lands of the abbey of St Omer until the French Revolution, the country town of Poperinge is keenly aware of its history. It has three Gothic churches, a British military cemetery, and the house where the philanthropic organisation Toc-H began, but most of all it is a hop town.

There are only 12,000 inhabitants, with another 8,000 in the adjoining five villages, but its population was doubled in the days when seasonal hop-pickers would arrive each September. Local engineers were active in pioneering mechanical methods of hop-picking, which were shown at the 1958 World Fair in Brussels. After more than 100 years as a weighhouse and pressing room for hops, a sturdy building in the town centre was assigned in 1975 to become a national museum of the industry (71 Gasthuisstraat). It is open during the holiday season (check hours with the local tourist board: tel. 057-33.40.81; fax 057-33.75.81). The floors are still stained with the green resins of the hop cones, and the collection of equipment and photographs provides a vivid peep into the past.

The Palace Hotel, its dining room decorated with hop blossoms, has a hearty kitchen featuring local dishes. In season, I once ate delicious jets d'houblon there. They were served as an intermediate course - an entrée in the European, rather than the American, sense. "Would you like the Beef Poperinge to fol-

Young Belgians soon develop the national passion for cycling... and Poperinge offers a route through the hop gardens, seat of another national devotion.

Poperinge, close to the border with France and the Channel ports, proudly maps its tourist attractions. Note the hop poles and beer glasses.

low?" I was asked. "Of course..." This turned out to be beef garnished with hop shoots. Perhaps I should have gone for another local favourite, Hennepot, a casserole of rabbit, chicken and veal. The dessert was a further Poperinge speciality, Tarte Mazarine, a very sweet, syrupy, cinnamon-flavoured cake similar to a rhum baba.

Perhaps this confection was named after Cardinal Mazarin (1643-61), successor to Richelieu, at a time of French influence in the region.

For Poperinge's local crop, the Flemish language uses the word hop, which has Germanic origins, but the term Hommel (deriving from the Latin Humulus) is also employed locally, especially to describe the cone or blossom. This confuses visitors, as Hommel is also Flemish for bumble-bee. D'n Hommelzak is a tea-room at 10bis Paardenmarkt, in the centre of Poperinge, and d'Hommelkeete a stylish restaurant at 3 Hoge Noenweg, on the outskirts of the small town.

In a former brewery building on the main square of the nearby small town of Watou, an establishment called 't Hommelhof gained a national reputation in the late 1980s as a pubby restaurant specialising in cuisine à la bière. In the early 1990s, chef-patron Stefaan Couttenye and his wife An turned the original premises into a brasserie, while extending their efforts to include a more formal restaurant, called Het Land van Amen, in a former bakery next door. (The address and phone number for both is 17 Watou Plein; tel. 057-38.80.24).

Stefaan strongly features local beers and, among many delights, I especially recall his interpretation of the classic Flemish fish soup Waterzooi, prepared with the coriander-tasting Watou's Witbier.

This beer is made by one of the town's three breweries, Van Eecke, which is just round the corner from the main square. Van Eecke's real speciality is a hoppy, golden-bronze, ale called Poperings Hommelbier. This beer is made from a blend of winter, summer and aromatic pale malts, at a starting density of 16 Plato; soft water, from the brewery's own well; Brewers' Gold and Hallertau hops, both grown in Poperinge; and top-fermented with a very attenuative yeast that precipitates quickly. It is primed with white sugar, and re-yeasted for a fermentation in the bottle. The finished beer has 7.5 per cent alcohol by volume and 40 units of bitterness, though it tastes lighter on both counts. Some drinkers feel, and I am inclined to agree, that it has a faintly honeyish yeast character - or is this thought deposited by the bumble bee? The beer certainly has a great deal of hop aroma and flavour, and is very refreshing and cleansing when served lightly chilled.

There also seems to be a honeyish yeast note, and some wineyness, in the brewery's complex abbey-style beers,

Every hop-growing region should have its own speciality beer... Poperinge's stands proudly, offering a flavour of Flanders.

under the name Het Kapittel (the name means a "chapter" of monks). These beers are said originally to have been created to a recipe supplied by the Trappist monastery of Mont des Cats, just across the French border, though it is not known when this abbey last had a brewery. It did make cheese, and had a farm in Watou.

The Van Eecke family has owned its brewery since the 1840s. It was founded as the estate brewery of a local chateau, and dates from 1642. A former brewery of a similar period stands opposite, now functioning as an art gallery.

The town also has the St Bernardus brewery, noted for a very fruity, orangey, spicy, Tripel of 7.0 per cent alcohol by volume. St Bernardus also has a fruity range of abbey-style beers called Sixtus. These were made under licence for the nearby St Sixtus abbey of Westvleteren until it expanded its own brewhouse. Watou additionally has a new micro-brewery, called De Bie, making a dry, orangey, strong ale known as Helleketel (after a local woods) and a sweeter, pruney, chocolatey one called Zatte ("Drunk" - a Dutch brewery uses the same name).

On Watou's second square, De Kleine Markt, is a statue of a brewer, erected in the early 1980s, at a time when the whole Poperinge area seemed to be awakening to public interest in its heritage.

Every three years, on the third weekend in September, a hop pageant is held in the town. On the other years, there is a beer festival weekend at the same time, with a wide selection of brews, and regional cheeses. Once again, information is available from the tourist board. The area does not have a great deal of accommodation, so arrangements should be made early.

Farmers also have their own private celebrations to mark the conclusion of a successful harvest. Wherever it is grown, the hop

The Hop Devil (below, left) is in the famous café of the same name in Ghent, in East Flanders. The statue of the brewer (right) is in the hop-growing area, at Watou, West Flanders.

is very susceptible to blights and pests, and the farmers feel they have a permanent struggle against the Devil. At the end of the harvest, the devil somehow metamorphoses into a lovable rogue (rather like England's Guy Fawkes). Some farmers burn a straw figure called the "Hop Devil", and serve their harvest workers a ceremonial meal called a Hommelpap. The word Pap derives from a typical meal for small children, though this is not served. A statue of the Hopduvel stands in the town centre of Asse, in the more easterly growing region. The Hopduvel also gives his name to one of Belgium's best beer cafés, in Ghent (10 Rokerelstraat; tel. 091-24.33.92).

Hops in the brewery

Only the cones of the hop are used by the brewer. They may be supplied in their natural form (pressed and dried, in sacks known as "pockets"), or compacted into pellets (vacuum-packed in foil, like coffee), or as an extract (a jam-like liquid, in cans). The cone is the simplest form, and some brewers feel that it is the best. In pelletized form, the cones are less exposed to air, and therefore to staleness through oxidation, and are easier to handle, but some brewers feel that the compacting diminishes the qualities of the leaves. Extract is even easier to handle, but is farthest away from the original cone.

Brewers like to cup their hands, full of hops, rub the cones in their palms, and inhale the aromes. These blossoms, of the Styrian Golding variety, were being tested "by hand" before being passed as suitable for Palm ale.

When the hops are added to the boiling brew in the kettle, their flavours and aromas are taken up, and their additional qualities as a natural anti-infectant and clarifying agent come into play. Some brewers boil for only an hour, most for 90 minutes. Speciality beers may take a much longer boil.

Hops added at the beginning of the boil will confer the greatest dryness or bitterness. Those put in later will impart more aroma.

Hops may be added in the kettle only once, or two or three times. If whole cones are used, the boiled brew will be run through a strainer to remove the leaves. Some brewers add further hops in the strainer. As the hot brew drains through them, it picks up further aromatics. When the brew has spent some days in fermentation vessels, and been moved on to maturation vessels, more hops may be added. This technique is known as "dry-hopping", and is intended further to enhance aroma. One or two brewers in Belgium use this method, though it is more common in Britain.

Some brewers use the same hops at every stage, but most will choose different varieties for bittering and aroma. These are sometimes known as "kettle" hops and "finishing" hops. All of these variations in procedure will be based not only on the preferences of the brewer but also on the type of beer to be made. By using a formula based on the quantity of hops used, and their acid content, brewers can measure the bitterness of their beers according to an international scale. A very bland beer might have only 10 or 15 International Units of Bitterness. An assertively dry and full-flavoured beer could have 40, 50, 60 or even 70. Working brewers often choose a hoppy beer for their own consumption, but believe - perhaps because they have been told as much by their marketing colleagues - that the public prefers something blander. By making propaganda for bland beers, the brewers thus persuade the consumer that he or she should really be buying mineral water.

YEAST: THE LIFE-FORCE

When grapes are crushed, they issue simply juice. Wild yeasts that reside on the skin were the first agents of the fermentation that turns juice into wine, with all its complexities of flavour. As the juice metamorphoses into wine, it also naturally becomes

The foamy "head" on a vessel of fermenting beer. If this foam is scooped off, it can be used to start fermentation in the next batch. Brewers did that empirically, in the days before yeast had been isolated and cultured.

alcoholic. Some wines are still made in this way, others by the addition of a yeast that has been cultured for the purpose.

For much of the history of wine-making and brewing, the practitioners were unaware of the existence of yeast. Wine-makers knew that a transformation took place, but were not aware that it was caused by a scarcely-visible micro-organism on the skin of the grape. Neither did brewers realise that the more resilient grain, once its sugars had been liberated by malting and mashing, was receptive to visits from yeasts that were airborne, or resident, in the brewery.

Excess yeast is still skimmed by hand, or pumped off, especially in the making of ales. Even the most modern brewery sees moments when its beer is handmade.

LAMBIC: SPONTANEOUS FERMENTATION

The distinctively winey acidity of Belgium's unique Lambic beers derives from their continued use of this method: spontaneous fermentation. These products are sometimes labelled in Flemish Bier van Spontane Gisting and in French De Fermentation Spontanée. (The Flemish Gist means yeast, in English, and the two words share the same root).

In the developed world, the makers of Lambic are the only brewers still to pursue this technique, which they have taken to a high level of craftsmanship. Lambic is the most traditional brew anywhere in the world that is recognisable as beer. The only other brews made by spontaneous fermentation are the turbid, porridgy, "native beers" of many Third World Countries. Lambics are immensely complex beers, whose production can last for three years or more; the nearest process is the production of fino sherry, with its reliance on the wild yeast called flor. Even the smells in a Lambic brewery and a sherry bodega are similar. It is no insult to the cultures of Africa and Asia to say that their native beers, fermented in a matter of hours, are far less refined products. Nor, despite the name, are they recognisable as beer. When beer ferments, its surface develops a foam. The first step into a more methodical system came when brewers observed that it helped to scoop the foam off the fermenting vessels used for the last batch, and add them to the next one. Brewing is an uncertain, vulnerable process. Several of the great brewing regions are deeply religious, and beer-makers have often felt that their success was in the hands of The Lord. As they became aware that the foam was an agent - that it ensured further fermentations - they gave it names. One was Godisgood.

Yeast is cultured in flasks of unfermented beer. This yeasty liquid is then added to the next batch, to start the fermentation.

ALE: TOP-FERMENTING

In any environment, there are many wild yeasts and other micro-organisms. By re-pitching their foamy "Godisgood", the brewers were empirically selecting the strains that thrived on their beer. The wild strains that were thus "domesticated" naturally rose to the top of the brew during fermentation. They were what we would today call "top-fermenting", or "ale", yeasts. In cultured form, they are used today to ferment wheat beers, almost all Belgian speciality brews, as well as ales, porters and stouts.

The characteristically fruity palate of top-fermenting brews is a product of that family of yeasts, known as Saccharomyces cerevisiae. While these yeasts can produce beers that are very complex in flavour, they were - before the days of refrigeration - very vulnerable to infection from airborne micro-organisms. This could turn the beer sour.

The traditional response to this problem was to brew only in the winter, and to store stocks for consumption during the summer. The last beer of a brewing year was produced in March, and the stored stocks would be ceremonially exhausted in late September and early October before work re-started.

Traditional Lambic breweries still operate in this way. The summer lay-off would also allow farmer-brewers to attend to their agricultural work. This custom probably gave rise to production of certain beers that benefit from long periods of storage (Flemish "sour" beers like Rodenbach and brown brews of the Oudenaarde type being examples).

LAGER: BOTTOM-FERMENTING

When the Munich brewers stored their beer for the summer, some did so in nearby caves in the foothills of the Alps. In time, they noticed that the caves not only kept the beer in good condition, but also seemed to impart a stability to it. This was because, in the cold, the yeast sank to the bottom, out of harm's way. This method came to be known as lagering, after the German word for storage. It is first mentioned in 1420, in the minutes of Munich town council, but it was not understood until much later. Yeast was first viewed under a microscope by the Dutch scientist Anton van Leeuwenhoek, in 1680. In the 1700s and 1800s, the work of the French chemists Lavoisier and Gay-Lussac and the German Liebig furthered knowledge in this area. In the 1830s, the Bavarian brewer Sedlmayr began to develop a methodical technique to make bottom-fermenting beer. Those early Bavarian-style lagers were dark brown and they were quickly followed by an amber Vienna-type and, in 1842, the golden product of the town of Pilsen. Brewers' growing ability to precipitate their yeasts - and for the first time make a clear, bright, beer - meant that a translucent, golden, product was an attractive novelty, especially at a time when opaque metal or stoneware drinking vessels were being replaced by mass-produced glass. It could be argued that darker beers often have more flavour than golden brews, but the appreciation of that has taken a long time to emerge.

It was still not until 1857 that a real understanding of yeasts was resolved, by Pasteur, and in 1883 the first single-cell, bottom-fermenting culture was isolated, by Emil Hansen, at the Carlsberg brewery in Copenhagen. Bottom-fermenting yeasts became known as Saccharomyces carlsbergensis.

In this period, the brewing of lager beers, and especially those with a golden colour, began to spread to the western extremities of Europe, but there were still pockets of resistance to this new style. The cities of Cologne and Düsseldorf still largely drink top-fermented brews. Most Belgian specialities are top-fermented, and so are the classic ales and stouts of Britain and Ireland. In Belgium, a beer that is top-fermented will often be labelled in Flemish as Hoge Gisting and in French as Haute Fermentation.

TIME AND TEMPERATURE

In theory, and at its most basic, the production of top-fermenting beers is quicker and easier than the making of a true lager. In practice, many Belgian brewers take a great deal of trouble over their top-fermenting specialities, and not every lager gets the time it really needs in which to mature.

At its simplest, top-fermentation takes place at a temperature rising naturally to 24-28 °C, lasting for three or four days. In practice, some brewers like their top-fermenting beer to spend two sabbaths in the vessel. Most top-fermenting beers have some form of further maturation. This may range from a few days' "warm conditioning" at 13-16 °C to a full-scale cold lagering, to a secondary fermentation in the cask or bottle, and perhaps even a chilly stabilisation after that. Some top-fermenting beers have several such stages. Some have a total of three

The Urquell ("Original Source") brewery in Pilsen makes the world's most famous bottom-fermenting beer. The beer is matured in huge wooden casks or stainless steel vessels before being filled into the kegs shown here.

fermentations. Among the brewers of top-fermented beers throughout the world, some Belgians are notable for the elaborate nature and duration of these regimes. The brewers of Duvel and Orval are good examples.

While both the Germans and the British have some beers that enjoy a secondary fermentation in the bottle, this technique is unusually widespread in Belgium. It is used only in respect of top-fermenting beers, and in their case might be considered a typically Belgian method. The Belgians refer to it as "Re-fermentation in the bottle" (Hergist in de fles / Refermentée en bouteille).

While bottle-fermented wheat beers are usually poured with the yeast in suspension, other styles are served more gently, as though they were being decanted, so that the sediment is left behind.

Bottom-fermentation classically rises to only 9 °C, and is followed by anything from one to three months' lagering at, or

around, 0 °C. There are fewer variations on this method, and those that do exist are more likely to be found in Franconia than in Belgium.

A beer made only with the higher cycles of temperature will express its flavour most fully at around 13 °C. A strong, rich, example like Chimay Grande Réserve might even benefit from being served warmer, at around 19 °C. The palate of such a beer is destroyed if it is served heavily chilled. Once beer has been lagered, it seems to express its flavour best at cooler temperatures, ideally around 8-9 °C.

STRENGTH AND FERMENTATION

The strength of beer is an equation between its original content of natural sugars and the extent to which these have been fermented into alcohol. Just as wine-makers have the Brix scale to express sugar content, so brewers have a number of measuring systems. In some countries, these systems, rather than alcohol content, have traditionaly been used in labelling. Even alcohol content can be expressed in two different ways: by weight or volume. Because alcohol is lighter than water, the weight system produces lower figures; volume is easier to understand.

The same sample of an internationally-known brand of Pilsener beer, for example, could be described as having 12 degrees Balling (Czech Republic), a similar rating in the German Plato scale, 4.6-4.8 degrees in a Belgian system, 1048 original gravity (British), 4.0 per cent alcohol by weight (the American means of expression) and 5.0 by volume (the European Community, Canada, Australia...).

While the measures of sugar content (otherwise known as "original gravity" or "density") are of interest to knowledgeable beer-lovers, the consumer is probably happy simply to know the product's alcohol content.

"Table beers", of low strength, are a tradition in Belgium but there will be a more potent brew to precede or accompany a fine meal or celebration.

No topic is more subject to myth and legend. Drinkers swear that one country's beers are stronger than other's, but that is not true. Every brewing nation has beers at a wide variety of strengths. The most that can be said is that an imaginary average beer, based on total consumption, would have 4.7 per cent alcohol by volume in Germany and Belgium, 3.7 in Britain and 4.5 in the U.S.

Belgium's average is derived from a pattern of consumption that is more varied than in any other country.

Belgium has many weak beers and an unusually wide readily-available, and well-patronised selection of strong ones. Whether they do so consciously or not, Belgians seem to pick the beer that suits the moment.

One of Belgium's many civilised habits is its production of table beers. Long before "no-" and "low"-alcohol brews, Belgium had light beers that could be served to the family, including the children, at the dinner table. Although this category has declined, there are still about 80 of these beers. These are usually lagers, both pale and dark, and they range in alcohol content from 0.8 to 3.2 by volume. A child accustomed to the choice of such brews at table is less likely to be excited into irresponsibility in his or her teens, when beers of a more conventional level become available. Beer is a part of civilised life in Belgium; it is not a rite of passage into an adult garden of temptation and sin. Belgians would do well to retain this understanding, and perhaps even teach it to others.

Most everyday beers in Belgium are a little under, or occasionally just over, a 5.0 per cent mark. These include well-known Pilsener-style beers like Stella Artois, Maes and Jupiler; ales such as Palm, Ginder and Vieux Temps; and the "white" wheat beers like Hoegaarden.

Belgium has scores of stronger beers, in a broad range from 6.0 to 10.0 and plenty more potent than that, with brews like the Trappist Westvleteren Abt (11.5) and Bush (12.2, and similar to a British barley wine) at the top end. The British, Germans and Swiss have all produced individual beers that are more potent, but none of those countries has anything like the Belgian variety of styles among its strong beers.

Potency is not a measure of quality. On a hot day, a beer that is quenching but light in body and low in alcohol might be just what is needed. With dinner, a brew that is moderate in both

An appetizing, sociable ale for a reflective moment... being appraised here by the owner of the renowned Kulminator beer café, in Antwerp.

alcohol and body might be perfect. Before or after dinner, something slighty more assertive may be preferred. Nor do body and strength always coincide. It is easy to make a low-strength beer that is full in body, though it is more difficult to produce a very potent one that is light. Most very strong beers are heavy, and therefore hard to drink in any quantity.

All the same, a Bush Beer with a book at bedtime is another civilised habit. Nowhere to drive. Nowhere to go but to sleep.

L'ÉBLOUISSANT

Bières spéciales

Divine	95
Alexander (2 ans d'âge)	95
Arabier	105
Bonne Espérance	95
Bos Keun	105
Bourgogne des Flandres	95
Brigand	95
Bush	95
Carolus	95
Charles Quint	95
Corsendonck blonde	95
Corsendonck brune	95
Grimbergen optimo	105
Duvel	95
Faro Lindemans	95
Fruit défendu	95
Hoegaard Grand Cru	95
Hommelbier	95
Judas	95
Julius	95
Leffe Triple Blonde	95
Leffe Radieuse	95
Livinus blonde	95
Lucifer	95
Maredsous 10°	95
Oerbier	105
Rodenbach Grand Cru	95
Saint Feuillien blonde	95
Saint Feuillien brune	95
Scotch Gordon blonde	95
Triple Brugges	95
Toison d'Or	95
Watou Prior	95
Witkap stimulo	95
Witkap triple	95
Scotch de Silly	95

Bières 75 cl

(minimum 2 personnes)

Bière de table de Silly 1,5°	100
Bonne Espérance	200
Chimay G^{de} réserve	200
Chouffe	200
Fakir	200
Faro Lindemans	200
Hommelbier	200
Moinette blonde ou brune	200
Marie de Hongrie	200
Caracole brune	200
Caracole ambrée	200
Troublette	200
Montagnarde	200
Abbaye des rocs	200
Blanche de Honnelles	200
Le Pavé de l'Ours	250

Gueuze

Cantillon 1/2	120

Gueuzes aux fruits

Pêcheresse	95

Kriek

Liefmans 1/2	120
Cantillon 1/2	120

Framboise

Liefman's 1/2	120

66

THE STYLES...
AND THE BREWERIES

Grape-growing nations like Italy, France and Spain each have not just one distinct and native style of wine but many. Great brewing countries like Germany, Belgium and Britain each have their own populations of beer styles (as distinct from brands or breweries). Just as French wines differ dramatically from Burgundian reds to Champagnes to Sauternes, Belgian beers extend from the Lambic family to wheat beers like Hoegaarden to a whole brotherhood of Trappists (the five monasteries in Belgium make between a dozen and 20 beers, of at least three distinctly different types).

A brewer who makes the original, or finest, example of a particular type of beer does not like the notion of style. For example, the Czech brewery that made the original Pilsener gains no comfort from the 5,000 or 10,000 imitators all over the world. The name Pilsener was legally protected too late. Belgian beers like Duvel and Rodenbach have imitators, but none that is remotely their equal. If their names were not proprietary, Duvel and Rodenbach would be types. We have to settle, instead, for calling Duvel a strong golden ale, and Rodenbach a sour red

The selection on the facing page is featured at L'Eblouissant, an outstanding beer café in the city of Namur. Even super-markets (below) offer a choice many countries should envy.

Kobbegem
De Keersmaeker

Breendonk
Moortgat (Duvel)
Liezele
Vieille Villers
Buggenhout
Bosteels

Steenhuffel
Palm
Merchtem
De Block
Opwijk
De Smedt
Wolvertem
Brabrux
Brussegem
Belgor

Meer
Sterkens

Ettelgem
Steedje

St-Lievens-Esse
Van Den Bossche

Laarne
Walrave

Malle
Trappists of Westmall

Brugge
Gouden Boom
Straffe Hendrik

Eeklo
Kruger

Ertvelde
Bios

ANTWERP
De Koninck

Ichtegem
Strubbe

Temse
Piessens

Waarloos
Alken-Maes

Esen-Diksmuide
De Dolle Brouwers

Evergem
Neyt

Kortemark
Louwaege

Dentergem
Riva
Olsene
Damy

Melle
Huyghe

Mechelen
Het Anker
Lamot

Boortmeerbeek
Haacht
Kampenhout
Biertoren

St Truiden
Kerkom

Boezinge
Leroy

Bavikhove
Bavik

Gavere
Contreras

Herzele
De Ryck

Wieze
Van Roy

BRUSSELS
Belle Vue
Cantillon

Leuven
Artois (Interbrew)
Domus

Vichte
Verhaeghe

Zottegem
Crombé

Flobecq
Voisin

Ninove
Slaghmuylder

Neerijse
De Kroon

Hoegaarde
De Kluis

Halle
Vander Linden
Lembeek
Frank Boon
Dworp
De Koninck
Hanssens

Silly
Silly

Pipaix
Brass. à Vapeur
Dubuisson
Tourpes
Dupont

Mont St Guibert
St Guibert

Poperinge
St Bernardus
Van Eecke

Ghlin
Brassico

Namur
La Caracole

Westvleteren
Trappists of St Sixtus

Bellegem
Bockor
Facon

Le Roeulx
Friart

Jumet
Union

Roeselare
Rodenbach

Binche
La Binchoise

Ingelmunster
Van Honsebrouck

Montignies-sur-Roc
Abbaye des Rocs

Philippeville
Devaux

Purnode
Du Bocq

Oudenaarde
Liefmans
Roman
Clarysse
Cnudde

Chimay
Trappists of
Chimay

Gedinne
Poncelet

Blaugies
Blaugies

Beersel
Vandervelden
Drie Fonteinen
St Pieters Leeuw
Moriau

Quenast
Lefèbvre

Momignies
Février

Schepdaal
De Neve
Eylenbosdch
Wambeek
De Troch
St Ulriks Kapelle
Girardin
Itterbeek
Timmermans
Vlezenbeek
Lindemans

St Genesius Rode
Wets

Belgium has more than 100 breweries. The towns and villages are shown in bold, the breweries in lighter type.

Bocholt
Martens

Opitter
St Jozef

Neerpelt
De Teut

Alken
Alken-Maes

Chalkhoven
De Es

Jupille-sur-Meuse
Jupiler

Eupen
Eupener
Bierbrauerei

Durbuy
La Ferme au Chêne

Soy
Fantôme

Achouffe
Achouffe

Rochefort
Trappists of Rochefort

Orval
Trappists of Orval

Gerouville
Brass. Gigi

Meix-devant-Virton
Maire

69

beer in the style of Flanders. In many styles, there is no identifiable original; those beers seem just to have emerged from local practice.

Some brewers argue, too, that every beer is different, and therefore they should not be shepherded into styles. It is true that beers differ, styles overlap, and terms used on labels sometimes vary in interpretation, and the same follows for wines. A particularly oaky red Burgundy may resemble a wine from Bordeaux, and vice-versa, but an indication of style is still useful to the consumer. All wines do not suit the same moment, nor do all beers.

Confronted by a shelf full of bottles and labels, the consumer needs some guidance as to the right choice for the moment. An understanding of the different styles of beer, and the meanings of the designation on the label, is a help. Some beer-lovers understand all the labels but, even in Belgium, many more do not. The principal native Belgian families of styles are Lambic (which also includes Gueuze, Faro, most Kriek, Framboise, and some other fruit beers); the type of wheat beer originally made in Hoegaarden (that, too, is a proprietary name); the red and brown sour beers of Flanders; the Saisons of Wallonia; the Belgian interpretation of conventional amber-red ales; a handful of golden ales of conventional strength; the strong type of golden ale; strong dark ales; the distinct styles of ales pioneered by the Trappist monasteries and emulated by Abbey brews; and a good many district brews that really do defy classification. Many of the latter contain spices. Belgium also has its own distinctive interpretations of some British and German styles, and a wide selection of golden lagers, many of the Pilsener type. Based on several of these styles, there are also a good many seasonal variations, especially for Christmas. That season in particular is associated in Belgium with extra-strong versions of Scottish-style ales. That is curious; the Scots traditionally did not take a holiday at Christmas, preferring to do so at New Year.

That breakdown of ten or a dozen styles is the simplest way of categorising the beers of Belgium, and is used in this book.

They can be further divided, into more specific categories. Sixty-odd principal classifications, and a further 16 "other sorts" are set out in the highly-analytical Beer Yearbook compiled by Peter Crombecq, of the consumer organisation The Objective Beer-Tasters. Crombecq, being a precise person, has his doubts about trying to categorise such individualistic products, but users of his books insist that he should.

The analytical Crombecq, with a specially-chosen tasting glass, documents the products of every brewery in Belgium.

Whether styles are divided into ten or a dozen, or 60, 70 or 80, Belgium has about 90 brewing companies, owning more than 100 breweries. The industry produces at any one time about 400 beers, under more than 800 labels.

The production of the same beer under more than one name is not unique to Belgium.

In some instances, one of a brewery's principal products may appear under a different local name in a particular region; or "label beers" may be produced for cafés or supermarkets.

Because this practice can be confusing, or misleading, to the consumer, The Objective Beer-Tasters campaigns vigorously against it.

71

LAMBIC

People who would appreciate
the stony, grassy flavours of a
true, Burgundian, Chablis or
the refreshing life-force of a
yeasty fino sherry, even the
appetisingly rhubarby fruitiness of a fine dry vermouth,
often fail to recognise the
comparable complex of qualities in a Lambic beer.

"Hard but not harsh," says
the wine-writer Hugh John-
son, describing the ideal
Chablis. He could have been
discussing a Lambic. Hard but
not harsh; bone-dry, but not
astringent. Drinkers who find
Lambics too assertive may
simply be suffering from the

*A classically simple
Lambic café...
Jacques Van Cutsem,
of the Timmermans'
brewery, samples his
own product with
Jean Meert, patron of
Café 't Verdiep, in
Vlezenbeek.*

shock of a taste that they did not expect in a beer. Or they may
be drinking a Lambic that is excessively acidic. Occasionally, a
Lambic is too tart, but more examples have been blunted by
sweetening. The best start soft, but harden toward an extra-
ordinarily long finish.

Both fino sherry and Lambic are the products of fermentation by
their own distinct cultures of wild yeasts. Like a fino sherry, a
Lambic is a product that has been aged for some years yet is
notable for its freshness of flavour. The Andalusians drink a
small bottle of fino with fishy tapas, and knowing Belgians
snack on a Lambic with sharp, soft, local cheeses and radishes.
I once shared a fino with a member of the Domecq family, at
their headquarters in Jerez, and the conversation turned to my
interest in beer. No sooner had beer been mentioned than Señor
Domecq asked me if I was familiar with Lambic.

Not only are there similarities in the fermentation process
between fino sherry and Lambic, and in colour perhaps between
the palo cortado and the beer (when it is fully matured), but also
in aroma and taste. In the Belgian magazine "Revue", in 1986,
I found myself comparing the pinkish tinge of some Lambics
with the Arbois wine of the Jura, described by A.J. Liebling in his
classic "Between Meals" as, "the colour not of the rose but of an

*Photo p. 72
The cobwebs must not
be disturbed, if the
very special
environment is to be
preserved for the
development of
Lambic... but brewers
of other styles would
be horrified.*

onion-peel, with russet and purple glints." I later learned that the grape of the Arbois, the Savaguin, collects a great deal of yeast, and is also used in the region's Vin Jaune, which is fermented with a "flor" yeast, like sherry.

Jean-Xavier Guinard, a North American brewing scientist and devotee of Lambic, finds similarities in taste and texture between the mature brew and the classic Jura wines. He takes up the theme a couple of times in his book "Lambic" (1990), one of a series on classic beer styles published by Brewers' Publications, of Boulder, Colorado. In his book, Guinard also quotes from an article I wrote in the American magazine "Zymurgy" in 1982. What I felt then, I still believe: "The Lambic family are not everybody's glass of beer, but no one with a keen interest in alcoholic drink would find them anything less than fascinating. In their 'wildness' and unpredictability, these are exciting brews. At their best, they are the meeting point between beer and wine; at their worst, they offer a taste of history."

It is a family based on one type of brew, Lambic, but also including a blended version, called Gueuze; the sweetened Faro and Mars; and styles like Kriek and Framboise, in which cherries and raspberries are added. Between Belgium's two main languages, and the various dialects of Flemish, these names appear in a variety of spelling.

The Lambic at Old Beersel in the village of the same name is made in the adjoining brewery Vandervelden.

THE NAME

Much mystery surrounds the name of this most mysterious among beers. The most likely explanation is that the name derives from that of Lembeek, a small town in the area of production. The town itself may be named after limey soil (Leem) and a beck (stream or creek) flowing into the river Zenne (in French, Senne). The "Lime Creek" theory has recently been challenged by a suggestion the first syllable was corrupted from Leen, a word referring to loans (English also has the word lien) and rights to property: the Lien on the Beck.

Lembeek was a Neolithic settlement on a piece of land almost encircled by a sharp bend in the river Zenne. The Celts protected this peninsular town by walling it off, and later it was an

A samplers' route through Lambic-brewing country might roughly correspond with the signposted tourist trail of Bruegel landscapes.

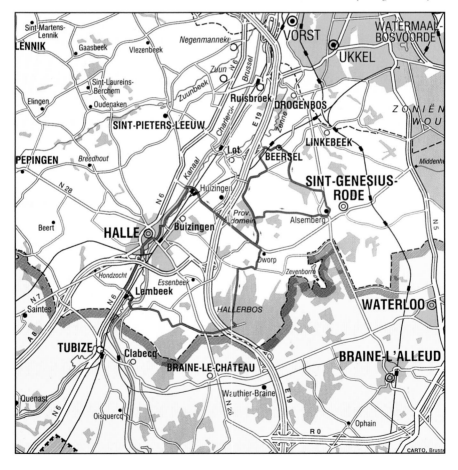

independent "city state" between the duchies of Brabant and
Hainaut. During this period, Lembeek granted its farmers the
unusual right to combine the brewing of beer with the distilling
of genever gin. A farmer would have used the same part of his
premises for both activities. Did the Spanish rulers in the 1500s
and 1600s simply call such a premises a distillery - an alembic?
Was that corrupted to Lambic?

*The army of Lembeek
patrols its frontiers. It
is a matter of pride for
a soldier to possess a
horse... and these
Brabant beauties look
fit to pull a dray.*

There is an appealing thread to this notion. Distilling is said to
have been developed by the Arabs and introduced by the Moors
into Europe, and to have spread north from Spain to the Low
Countries, where grain and juniper were first turned into gin. It
is a tenuous thread, though. Yet another theory is that the name
derives from Lambere, the Latin verb to sip, but that notion is
even farther fetched.

Lembeek had a Guild of Brewers 500 years ago, and became an
important centre in the region of production of Lambic beers -
the Zenne Valley and the countryside to the west, known as
Payottenland. The Zenne, which rises in Hainaut, sneaks under
Brussels, eventually joining the river Dijle, which flows into the
Schelde.

Along the river, and in the country districts to either side of
Brussels, farmers grew barley and wheat, and provided beer for
the growing metropolis. Like all brewers in medieval times,
they used spontaneous fermentation, and they never abandoned
that method. This part of Brabant is perhaps the most conservative

corner of the brewing world, even more traditionalist than Bavaria (with yeasts that make phenolic wheat beers), Berlin (with lactic fermentations) or Burton (with its technique of linked wooden barrels like a sherry solera).

The beer did not all come from Lembeek, but neither was the first Kentucky whisky made in Bourbon County, or the greatest blue cheese of England produced in Stilton itself.

Lembeek's brewer-distillers were gradually driven out of business by restrictions on spirits, culminating in tough laws in the early 1900s, at a time when the whole of the developed world was going through a temperance phase.

The restrictions on gin did not benefit Lambic. Spontaneous fermentation produces beers of modest alcohol content, and the disenfranchised spirit-drinkers turned to stronger styles like Trappists and Scotch Ales.

Today, Lembeek, little more than a town-square perched on top of a hill, has 4,000 people and, down by the river, one brewery, run by the revivalist Frank Boon.

As a city-state, Lembeek had its own army, and four "regiments" have been maintained, the distinction passing from father to son. These men are paid a small stipend by the municipality to lead a ritual on the Monday after Easter. At 3.0 in the morning, they blow bugles to alert the citizens, who must assemble at 8.0 to walk the bounds of the town. The religious start from the church, the less devoted from the town hall, and the walk rambles for 20 kilometres, stopping at each café in the town. Where cafés once stood, the householders man tables loaded with Lambic and genever gin, purchased communally and dispensed free. The consumption of these precious fluids was held to ward off bubonic plague and rabies, though the pilgrims also kiss a shrine to St Veronus to make doubly sure.

This being Belgium, the walk stops for lunch.

THE DISTRICT

The tradition has died on the Eastern side of Brussels, though the beers in blended form are still served in the cafés of Jezus-Eik to strollers in the forest of Soignes on a Sunday afternoon. Today's production area is on the Western side of the city, from Anderlecht to Schepdaal, Beersel, Lembeek and beyond.

Bruegel lived on this side of Brussels, in its Flemish Old Town, and wandered in the villages of Payottenland. The church in "The Parable of the Blind" is clearly Sint-Anna-Pede, between Itterbeek and Schepdaal. Nor, 400 years later, could anyone fail to recognize the Flemings of "The Peasant Dance" or "The Wedding Feast" enjoying a beer in one of the many cafés of the valley, probably within sight of Brussels' skyline.

In "The Wedding Feast", beer of a strawy-russet colour is shown being decanted from the type of stoneware crock still often used for Lambic today. The same crocks feature in "The Peasant Dance". There are similar images in the paintings of the aptly-named artist Brouwer, who came along in the next century, and no style of beer features more pervasively in Flemish popular art, literature and folklore than the Lambic family. (Nor, arguably, is any theme more central in Flemish

At "The Wedding Feast", the man on the left decants beer that is surely Lambic... The guests drink it from stoneware crocks. Even the faces are familiar in modern Flanders.

culture than the brewing and consuming of beer of any kind). The signposted Bruegel Route passes through several Lambic-brewing villages. None of them is more than 10 or 12 miles from Brussels, yet Payottenland switches from the urban to the suburban to flat farmlands and wooded folds in sudden hills. Every now and then, a Lambic brewery, some-times disused and a miniature item of industrial archeology, makes its distinct mark on the landscape. Over the years, many of the valley's breweries have closed, and some work only occasionally, but there are still about a dozen in the district, making Lambics or related beers to varying degrees of au-thenticity.

Suggestions that the district be given an appellation contrôlée have been rebuffed on the basis that it would be hard to de-lineate. Surely it would not be difficult. Existing breweries in the traditional region form a semi-circle around the West-side of Brussels. Their beers could be styled as Original Lambic.

A couple of companies who have long established the precedent of using the name Lambic to describe Gueuze-type products made in West Flanders should be allowed to continue to do so, but to hyphenate the designation with their town or province, like German "Pilsener" brewers. No one else should be permit-ted to use the term.

Bruegel and Brouwer painted vivid moral tales, but with an earthy sympathy for their subjects. Their down-to-earth view of life is recognized, and celebrated, by today's Belgians.

Traditionally, Lambic breweries also mashed the wort for establishments that carried out only the fermentation. This is rather like a press crushing the grapes for several wine-makers. The breweries also sell wort or beer to the odd blender. This is more like a Cognac distiller selling his output to a shipper for blending into a "house" style. Or a malt whisky distiller supplying a blender.

Neither of these practices is common in the production of other styles of beer, but Lambic is especially shaped by its fermentation, and the related style Gueuze by blending. Sadly, there seems now to be only one free-standing blender, Hanssens, of Dworp. One café, Drie Fonteinen, of Beersel, does its own blending, and several buy young Lambic to age.

In the days when the people of Brussels knew no other beers, the Lambic family did not seem eccentric. Now, it does. These are products that do not conform to today's conception of beer, and for that reason, they are at risk of death through incomprehension. The complex, tart, examples made by the traditional method are the most threatened in an age when children are weaned on sugary soft-drinks. If the world of beer were to discard its Lambics, that would be as great a loss as if the universe of wine were denied any more sherry.

The valley of the Zenne is clear enough, even in a flat, Lowland, country... and its rusticity survives on the edge of a European metropolis.

THE NATURE OF THE PRODUCT

Lambic is a type of wheat beer, and that distinction already places it among a group of speciality styles. It is unique in that the wheat used is not malted. No one seems sure why. Perhaps the farmer-brewers simply found they could make beer without this step. That is possible because, as in all wheat beers, a proportion of malted barley is also used. The local, small-grained, Brabant wheat is sometimes used, and often the coarser winter barleys.

The ratio of wheat to barley has varied over the years, but was eventually formalised in law. The most recent regulation, of 1965, says that at least 30 per cent unmalted wheat must be used. Most Lambic breweries use 30-35 per cent wheat and the remainder malted barley. Some also add proportions of corn, rice, or even rye.

Lambic beers are made from an original density of 1047-1054 (11.75-13.5 Plato, 12.7 is the classic level), and in their unblended form usually emerge with an alcohol content of around 5.0-6.5 by volume.

A variety of mashing regimes, some very long, are used to extract the fermentable sugars from the grains. What they all have in common is the production of a milky-white wort rather than the clear type that is expected by conventional brewers.

This "turbid mash" results from the use of the unmalted grains. There are further peculiarities at the boiling stage. Far more hops are added than in a conventional brew, perhaps six times as many. Perversely, these are hops that have been aged for up to three years. The object of aging the hops is to diminish their aroma, flavour and bitterness: the very attributes for which they are valued by conventional brewers. In this instance, the hops are being used for their secondary purpose, to protect the beer against unwanted infections and excessive oxidation. In this role, the choice of variety is not especially important. I have seen Belgian-grown Brewers' Gold, British Fuggles and Bohemian Saaz, among other varities, in Lambic breweries.

The brew is run into the upper vessel, which is a sieve to strain out the leafy hop cones. The lower vessel is where the brew cools overnight, and is "impregnated" by its first wild yeast.

While conventional brewers typically boil for an hour and a half, the makers of Lambic have a much more exhaustive process. In their case, the boil lasts for more than three hours, and sometimes as many as six.

Then comes the most critical procedure. The boiled wort is cooled in a shallow, open vessel in the loft of the brewery. This vessel, made of copper or steel, will take up most of the floor space in the loft. It will be perhaps seven or eight meters long, five or six wide, but only 30-50 cm deep, so that a large volume of the brew is exposed to the atmosphere. Nor is the vessel filled to its full depth. The room will have windows that can be opened, and louvred vents. Once, all brewers cooled their wort in this way, and the louvred vents can often be seen on the apex of their pitched roofs. In time, brewers learned that this was a perilous method. If the wort remained in the vessel until it was really cool, there was the danger of intrusion by wild yeasts. Conventional brewers sealed their cooling areas, shortened the period in which the wort remained in the vessel, or augmented or replaced this system with heat-exchangers. Today, most use heat-exchangers: enclosed systems, in which the wort is run through pipes jacketed with cold water or a cooling fluid.

The Lambic brewers took the opposite view: they worked with nature, rather than fighting it. They welcomed the wild yeasts, and let them help determine the character of the beer.

In a Lambic brewery, windows and vents are left open, and even the odd tile may be allowed to go missing, in order to allow in the wild yeasts. If he is worried that there is too little activity, the brewer might adjust the vents. As one brewer put it to me: "We can play with the wind." The wort spends the night there, and the yeasts enter and have their way with it.

Lambic brewers also hesitate to replace their roofs, or any part of their fabric, in case they disturb resident wild yeasts or other microflora that give a house character to their beers. Every beer, of any type, has a "house" character, but none more than the Lambics.

Once the wort has cooled, it will begin to ferment. The simplest way for the brewer to handle this is to fill the wort into casks and let nature get on with the job. Once, all brewers proceeded in more or less this fashion. As brewers learned to pitch their own yeasts, more controlled systems were developed, like the linked

Architecture has gained its own features from the procedures of brewing. Many breweries are examples of industrial archaeology. The tower at Bockor was built to cool the brew before fermentation. Today, the brewery is known less for its Pils than its "red" Vander Ghinste's Ouden Tripel and its "Lambic"-style Jacobins.

casks of the "Union" system in Burton or the larger stone troughs of Tadcaster (those two towns being brewing centres in England). Today, most brewers use stainless steel vessels, with cooling systems that will control the progress of the fermentation. Very few breweries anywhere in the world still ferment in wood, and only the Lambic-makers in free-standing casks. Here again, the situation developed naturally. In no major city do the Romance and Germanic cultures meet quite as they do in Brussels. It is a city that imports and consumes a great deal of wine. In the days when the wine came in casks, these were snapped up by the local brewers for use as fermentation vessels. There is a parallel in importation of sherry to the English city of Bristol, and the selling-on of empty casks for the maturation of Scotch whisky. Just as a whisky warehouse in Scotland will contain casks bearing the legends Domecq, Gonzalez Byass or Osborne, so the evidence of Port, Rioja or Muscat may be stencilled on the barrel-ends in a Lambic brewery.

Today, less wine is shipped in the barrel, but Lambic-makers can still buy casks that have been used in vinification. As wine-makers begin to use more stainless steel, that releases wood to the Lambic-brewers. Regrettably, the closure of Lambic breweries has also released wood for the survivors. There are also coopers in the industry to repair vintage casks.

I have seen casks more than 100 years old in Lambic breweries, but even those acquired recently soon have their own population

Belle Vue has more than 10,000 casks of Lambic and Kriek, each stencilled with the density of the beer, the number of the brew, and the year.

of resident microflora. These, too, play an essential part in fermentation. In a brewery that began life as a farm, I have seen more than two thousand casks, divided between 15 cellars and attics. The favoured size is 250 litres (the "Brussels tun"), but much bigger sizes are also used. Like the makers of Port, the Lambic brewers like casks called pipes, which hold 600-700 litres. Some breweries have "foudres" of 3,000-10,000 litres, but these can mature the beer too slowly. One way round that is to keep tapping and topping up as though it were part of a sherry solera.

The casks lie in long galleries, often cloaked with moulds and cobwebs. Once again, the brewers are hesitant to clean up too much in case they disturb an essential guest. Although the Lambic-makers differ widely on the extent of cleaning up that is desirable, they agree in regarding as their best friends what other brewers would view as the creatures of nightmare. One Lambic brewer told me that white moulds on the casks had a favourable influence, but black ones on the walls were insalubrious.

When I showed galleries full of cobwebs at Lindemans in a television documentary, many brewers were astonished at the sight. Although I was well acquainted with such scenes at Lambic breweries, I also remembered the whisky writer Philip Morrice saying that the Linkwood distillery, in Scotland, had once forbidden the removal of spiders' webs. In his book,

The cooperage shop of Belle Vue is fully employed in maintaining the casks. Most are the usual oak, but some are chesnut. Most once held Port, but others contained Sherry or Bordeaux wines.

85

Guinard talks of Lambic brewers who consider the killing of a spider to be a crime. Why? Because spiders are predators of flies. Fruit-flies are attracted to yeasty wort, and often bring to it unwanted micro-flora. I once noticed fruit flies in a brewery in an apple-growing region of the United States. The brewer said they were a dreadful nuisance, but gave me an odd look when I suggested he install some spiders.

Traditional Lambic-makers do not brew in summer, because the wild inoculation of the wort at that time would be just too unpredictable, and the beer would be sour.

They stop sometime between March and May, and re-start in September or October. In the traditional manner, they regard the summer as the time of storage, continuing fermentation and maturation. As the only brewers who still observe this seasonal regime, they measure their fermentations in "summers". Some Lambics stay in the cask for just one summer, at which stage they are still regarded as "young". A Lambic of two or three summers is regarded as mature. Some breweries have far older Lambics among their stocks.

Cobwebbed galleries like these at Timmermans can occupy several floors of barn-like buildings in a farmhouse brewery. There are no breweries like these anywhere else in the world.

It is not unknown for Lambic to be served when it is less than three months old, but that is not ideal. Beer brewed at the end of the winter brewing season, in March, will make good young Lambic in July or August, the leisurely months when people like

to stroll in the villages around Brussels and stop for a drink. Young Lambic for blending might be older, perhaps six months. While most beer (and wine) has a primary and a secondary fermentation, Lambic has five or six phases, forming a chain reaction. This helps explain why it is so complex in bouquet, palate and finish. Many brewers elsewhere have traditionally regarded the choice of grains, malts and hops as the dominant factor in the character of their beer, but the influence of yeast and fermentation behaviour on aromas and background flavours is increasingly being appreciated. No beer is as complex in this respect as Lambic.

While most beer-makers would regard strains of only the carlsbergensis or cerevisiae types as permissible brewing yeasts, at least five major groups of wild yeasts and other microflora are found in Lambic breweries. In one beer, these major groups may manifest themselves in 15 or 20 forms. So far, 86 strains of wild yeast or other microflora have been identified in Lambic beers. These notably include four oxidative yeasts that form a film on the fermenting beer, similar to the flor on sherry. There are also wild yeasts of the Brettanomyces family, which was originally associated with British styles such as Stock Ale, Barley Wine and strong Porter, traditionally aged for long periods in wood. Brettanomyces impart aromas that have been described as

The Cantillon brewery, in Anderlecht, Brussels, is famous for its authentic Lambic beers. It is a working brewery that is also a museum.

"horsey", "leathery" and "blanket-like". About a dozen strains of Brettanomyces have been identified in the Zenne Valley, and two are taxonomically identified with the district: bruxellensis and lambicus.

"Brettanomyces bruxellensis is the richest niche in the micro-biological spectrum of Lambic fermentation," I was once told by Professor Hubert Verachtert, who has done much work on the subject with colleagues at the University of Leuven. Their work is densely argued, yet Professor Verachtert still had a wry smile for many of my questions: "That is a factor we don't quite understand yet... that might necessitate another Phd study..." The Zenne Valley still holds its mysteries.

Can a valley so close to a large and partly industrial city retain its own ecology of micro-life? Perhaps only in the sense that everywhere has its own unique eco-system. Certainly every brewery creates its own habitat, and nowhere more obviously than in Lambic country. As casks change hands, and wort is sold to fermenters or blenders, even as brewers visit one another, perhaps the industry has developed its own ecology.

It is possible to make spontaneously-fermenting beer elsewhere, and this has been done on an experimental basis, but the results have recognisably not been the Lambic of the region. While the Lambic-makers struggle in the market at large, there is a growing connoisseur interest in their beers. One or two brewers outside Belgium have announced the intention to make "Lambic", but such ambitions pose two questions:

Even on the label for its Gueuze, the Timmermans brewery hints at fruity variations. St Louis, outside the traditional region, prefers the Duke of Flanders.

Why, without the heritage, would any brewer wish to practice such a difficult and unpredictable art? For the challenge, perhaps?

And would anyone really risk developing a household of wild yeasts in a brewery where he also intended to produce more conventional beers?

When Lambic is made, it is very dry, with very little carbonation. Traditionally, brewers sold it in this form, in wooden casks, directly to cafés. They cellared it, and sometimes aged it further. In the cellar, the cask would be tapped into a stoneware jug, which would be fetched up to the bar to serve the customers. Some brewers no longer supply Lambic in this form, saying there is no demand for it. These brewers may continue (or not?) to produce genuine Lambic, but exclusively as a component for Gueuze: blended to create a secondary fermentation and sparkle. The classic form of Gueuze or its related fruit beers is not sweetened or pasteurised, and has a continuing development in the bottle. The more widely-available examples are often sweetened, and always pasteurised.

The "juices" of the wheat and barley-malt are stirred and infused in the mash-tun at Lindemans.

PRODUCERS OF LAMBIC

In Brussels itself, a wonderfully austere, dry, acidic, Lambic can be sampled at Cantillon, a working brewery and museum (56 Rue Gheude, Anderlecht; tel. 02-521.49.28). The Cantillon family were originally brewers in Lembeek, and came to Brussels in 1900. Their descendant Jean-Pierre Van Roy is a famously outspoken advocate for dry Lambics.

On the same side of town (where Brussels meets Molenbeek-St Jean), but at the opposite end of the size scale, the largest traditional Lambic brewery, built around the time of the First World War, was for many years owned by the firm of Vanden Stock, producers of the sweetened and blended Belle-Vue products (marketed under the name Bécasse in some countries). Since the company was taken over by Interbrew at the beginning of the 1990s, this canalside brewery has opened its doors to the public (43 Quai du Hainaut; tel. 02-410.19.35).

Art Nouveau is as Belgian as it is French... Lindemans evoke the spirit of a bygone age in the label for their innovative peach Lambic.

In its guest bar, in its former stables, it offers a draught beer, with a low carbonation, described as Lambic. This is actually a blend of four or five Lambics, most of them young but some up to five years old, sweetened with candy sugar and served without a great deal of further fermentation. It starts sweet, but has some good Lambic flavours. A bottled product called Sélection Lambic is in fact a Gueuze (it has been given a secondary fermentation, to create a more evident carbonation), with an older average age and no sweetening. It has much more attack, and a very drying finish. Belle-Vue's younger Lambics are produced at a 1970s brewery not far away in Zuun (where Brussels meets St-Pieters-Leeuw). Interbrew now uses a third former Vanden Stock brewery, De Neve, at Schepdaal, purely for fermentation and maturation. The various locations do produce beers of differing characters. Beers fermented and matured in Molenbeek's many thousands of tuns, pipes and foudres (some made of chestnut, rather than the more usual oak) are quite hard, with a touch of oakiness, some evocatively musty cellar notes and an aromatic hint of mandarin-skin; those from Schepdaal are more lemony, "fresher" and more crisp.

In Lembeek, René De Vits blended Lambics on a site that had accommodated a farmhouse brewery and distillery as far back as 1680. In 1977, he retired and sold his business to Frank Boon, then a blender. With Frank Boon, I met Mr De Vits in 1986, and he was still wearing the leather apron of a brewer, and living in his former café. Boon moved to a more spacious building, a former iron foundry closer to the river Zenne, and began to brew. He owns the brewery in partnership with the ale-producers Palm.

Although, like almost all Belgians, Boon has family connections in the brewing industry, he came in as an outsider, having developed a great interest in beer during his student days. While many Lambic brewers are elderly and contemplating retirement without a successor, Boon has brought new life to the craft, for which he has become a knowledgeable spokesman. His Lambic has an excellent complexity and a winey, Chardonnay, note. A good outlet is the Café Triangle, in Basiliekstraat, Halle.

The Vieux Château d'Or (26 Rue Ste Cathérine), is the Brussels outlet for the Lambic of Girardin. This brewery produces the most widely-available pure Lambic, with lots of wheat character, well-rounded and dry. Girardin is a remarkable enterprise, set like a tiny chateau farm among fields of wheat just outside the village of St-Ulriks-Kapelle.

The brewery began in 1845, as a part of an aristocrat's estate. The Girardins have owned it since 1882, through four generations. When I visited, in 1993, Louis Girardin was a robust 69, running the brewery with his wife Jacqueline and sons Paul and Jan, with no employees. They grow their own wheat, brew Lambic in winter and produce a Pils in summer.

The Girardins use 40 per cent wheat in their Lambic, and still have a mill that grinds the grain between stones, as well as a more modern one with metal cylinders. "We continue to use the stones for some of the grist," Louis told me, "in case it contributes to the character of the beer."

They still have a cast-iron, open, mash-tun and bricked-in kettle, though they had just installed a more modern (1950s or 60s?) copper brewhouse, bought second-hand in Germany. They had spent a month in Germany dismantling it themselves, then fitted it back home in Belgium. Their advance calculations of the space required had proven correct down to a notch of a couple of centimetres made in a ceiling support.

"If you damage or dirty anything in our brewery, you must pay for it," said Louis. He was only half joking. When I made to lean on a kettle to take a photograph, a cloth was quickly placed beneath my elbows.

The fastidious Girardins even have two open-coolers, one in the attic and another at brewhouse level. Why? "The temperatures are d ifferent in the two places. Depending upon the weather outside, we can juggle to get the best possible inoculation of wild yeasts." This is truly craft brewing... hand-made beer.

The Lindemans brewery, at Vlezenbeek, used to juggle the fire under its kettle to get the right kind of boil, but now has a more modern brewhouse. It still makes Lambic in the traditional way, but the product is almost impossible to find unblended. Lindemans has been very successful with its Gueuze and fruit beers.

At Café 't Verdiep, in Vlezenbeek, in 1993, I tasted the delicate, complex, Lambic from Timmermans, of Itterbeek. The brewery told me this was the last café to seek its Lambic au naturel, though a sweetened version was on sale at Café Bécasse, at 11 Rue Tabora, just off Brussels' Grand' Place.

There is believed to have been a brewery on the site in Itterbeek since 1650, though the present buildings date from 1888. When Germaine Timmermans married Paul Van Cutsem in 1935, her wedding gift from her father was a new open cooler for the brewery. It is still there. A device in the cooler rings a bell in the concierge's office when the wort reaches the temperature at which it should be run-off. Paul Van Cutsem's son Jacques told me of the times he had been awakened by this bell. He still has a share in the brewery, but control is in the hands of John Martin's, a company better known for its pale ale.

Lines of control can be long, even in such small, rustic, breweries. France's Kronenbourg controls Belgium's second-largest brewer, Alken-Maes, which has a majority stake in the De Keersmaeker Lambic brewery, of Kobbegem. This brewery supplies a famous café in Brussels. The café, built in about 1880 but re-fitted in 1926, was once favoured by journalists from "La Libre Belgique", who played a dice game there. If one was called back to the office urgently, the game would be terminated by "Sudden Death". The café came to be known as Mort Subite (French for "Sudden

Death"), and that is today its official name. It is at 7 Rue Montagne aux Herbes Potagères, and still serves the brewery's beers, but not its unblended Lambic. The Mort Subite was the favourite café of Maurice Béjart, who used it as the setting for a ballet.

The brewery in Kobbegem produces a herbal-tasting (hyssop, said one devotee) Lambic that is still sold, under the confusing designation De Keersmaeker Faro, in some cafés in the area. The brewery is better known for Gueuze and Kriek under the Mort Subite name. The Gueuze can be found unfiltered, in which case the bottle either has no label, or one saying that the beer has a re-fermentation.

Wort is also brewed at Kobbegem for shipping to the old Eylenbosch brewery, in Schepdaal, where it is cooled and fermented in the traditional way. The Eylenbosch Lambic has a nuttier character, but cannot be found unblended. Eylenbosch Gueuze and fruit beers, all filtered and pasteurised despite their Cuvée Special label, historically have a particular following in Limburg and West Flanders. In Beersel, the beer-lover can find the flowery, piney, ale-like Lambic of Vandervelden. In Halle, Vander Linden has a tart product, very ale-like, but robust and full of flavour.

Young Lambic can be straw-like in colour and sometimes has a reddish haze (described as Vos, indicating "foxy"). It is often very assertive, perhaps lactic (like a sharp soft cheese), acidic, cidery and apple-like. It is sharply refreshing, though also drying, and arouses the appetite.

I have experienced its aperitif powers several times at the café In De Rare Vos (22 Marktplaats, Schepdaal; tel. 02-569.20.86; closed Tuesday and Wednesday). This hearty café has a fine cellar of Lambic and Gueuze, cooks with the beers, and specialises in mussels, pigeon and blanquette of horse.

The publican at In De Rare Vos, photographed as Bruegel painted his forbears more than 400 years earlier. His speciality is home-matured Lambic, and blanquette of horse.

Either young or old, real Lambic is very dry, because it is so exhaustively fermented. Paul de Neve, of the brewing family, once described it to me as "the world's first low-carbohydrate beer". This is just as well, since a glass can make you want to eat a horse.

Mature Lambic has much more subtle colours, sometimes including the onion-like, pinkish-purple tones. It is mellower, more rounded and complex, with fruity (sometimes rhubarby), notes, that hint of Chablis, and its characteristically sherryish flavours. There is no more enigmatic drink.

GUEUZE

The soubriquet "The Champagnes of the Beer World" is often applied in general to the tart, refreshing styles of beer that can be made from wheat. The term Méthode Champenoise is sometimes informally borrowed by brewers whose beer has a further fermentation in the bottle. Just as the wine-makers in the Champagne region have made that style of fermentation their speciality, so have Belgian brewers. Comparisons with Champagne can be applied on one or both counts to many Belgian beers, but none more than the Lambic family's sparkling Gueuze. Being Lambic in origin, this is a wheat beer. It is made by the blending of two or more Lambics to create a secondary fermentation and a Champagne-like sparkle. Sometimes the words Lambic and Gueuze are hyphenated, especially if the product is

Brussels' lusty answer to Rheims and Epernayl, the subversive, surging, Gueuze, in ten of its manifestations. Love it or hate it, you cannot deny its swash-buckling charm.

being served from the cask. This may have been an early form, made with the intention of turning the rather flat Lambics into a sparkling drink. (The British add sugar primings to their cask ales for the same reason, and the Germans Kraüsen with wort). It was when they bottled the result that the Belgians truly discovered what an elegant drink a blend of Lambics can be, and today that is the classic manifestation of Gueuze. Because the fermentation builds up considerable pressure, Gueuze is put into the same bottles as are used for Champagne.

The name

Gueuze is pronounced almost like cursor, though for such an artisanal product that seems an inappropriately high-tech mnemonic. The word Gueuze may derive from the same root as gas and geyser, and simply refer to the possible consequences of tapping a cask or opening a sparkling bottle, and thus releasing a great amount of carbon dioxide. (In the United States, there is a similar story about Steam Beer).

Another suggestion is that the name derives from political pressure and uprisings in Payottenland against Spanish, or in favour of Dutch, rule. One account specifically pins the name on a Mayor of Lembeek who was political a Liberal (a "Geus") and who is said to have pioneered the adaptation of the Méthode Champenoise to Lambic beer. This is recorded as having happened in 1870, at which point Belgium had for some decades been an independent country. Coincidentally, Kir (originally white Burgundy and today often, royally, Champagne, with crème de cassis or framboise) is named after a resistance hero who was the Mayor of Dijon.

A much earlier reference, in the 1600s, indicates that Lambic brewers already had some means of naturally carbonating their beers. There is also a suggestion that beer was the drink of the peasants, who were likely to be Gueux in their political sympathies, while the ruling class drank wines from France or Spain.

The blending of wines to make Champagne pre-dated Dom Pérignon, in the late 1600s, and by the early 1800s, the Widow Cliquot had already developed the means of remuage and dégorgement, which have yet to come to Gueuze, though there have been experiments along these lines in Belgium.

THE BLENDING

The characteristics of the Lambics will be carried over to the Gueuze, but the further fermentation will have created a greater complexity and finesse - as well, of course, as the sparkle. A naturally-carbonated drink can be matured for some time in a cask, but it will be better contained in glass, and Gueuze is usually given some bottle age before it is served. A true Gueuze is dry, tart and fruity, and several have a toasty aroma reminiscent of some Champagnes. Because of the fermentation in the bottle, its alcohol content by volume should be marginally higher than that of the original Lambics, usually around the 5.5 mark.

The foam around the bung indicates that the first fermentation has begun. This cask of Lambic was beginning its career of fermentations at De Neve. Eventually, it would marry, and a Gueuze would be born.

The choice of Lambics is critical to the palate of the finished product, but also to the functioning of the fermentation in the bottle. The young Lambic in the blend will have more residual sugar, while the old will have developed some interesting yeasts during its chain of fermentations. Having undergone five or six stages of fermentation in the cask, the Lambics when blended will proceed through a further three phases, in which

perhaps five of the original yeasts and microflora will again play an important part. Small wonder that these beers are so complex. While blending is normal in the production of Champagne (and other drinks like Cognac and Scotch Whisky), it is unusual in the making of beer. A big brewer may blend batches to achieve consistency, but not to impart character. One or two British products, including Newcastle Brown Ale, and several Flemish specialities, are made by blending different beers, but not for the purpose of creating a further fermentation.

The Lambic brewer is not only unique in trying to work with spontaneous fermentation but also in his variation on the Méthode Champenoise. Even the Champagne-maker adds yeast and priming sugar. Not every Gueuze is made wholly according to the classical manner, but several still are.

Unlike any other brewer, the Lambic-maker has to consider what purpose he should put each cask. Should it be sold as unblended Lambic and, if so, young or old? Or should it be a component of a Gueuze - and, again, at what age? In general, the casks that seem to be developing best will be kept longest.

Some brewers feel strongly that the beers which start out best are those brewed in the cool weather of January and February, when the wild yeasts are at their most restrained. How those beers perform subsequently will be in part determined by the weather over the next year or so. There are good and bad years for Lambic: the "vintages" of grain may not vary critically, but the temperatures in maturation do.

Other factors will include the origin and size of the casks into which a beer has been filled, and even their location within the cellars and attics of the brewery. These are factors that also concern, for example, producers of Single Malt Scotch. There are many analogies in the crafts that produce very traditional, artisanal and individualistic drinks. None of these crafts is more esoteric than the making of Lambic and Gueuze beers.

Beyond all the considerations of temperature and wood lies the unpredictable: yeast is a living organism, a life-force, and its behaviour can never be relied upon even in the most conventional of breweries. The proportion of young Lambic to old varies. About 70-30 is quite common, though such a high proportion can produce an excessively lactic Gueuze. The more old Lambic that is used, the greater aroma and, depth and length. A classic Gueuze might have only 15 per cent young Lambic.

The Lambic may be centrifuged or filtered to remove cask sediment, and dead and excess yeast, but sufficient live cells will be left for the further fermentation. How many casks go to make one blend may depend upon the style of Gueuze to be made, and the equipment at the brewery. One brewer told me he always had a coupage of between 40 and 50 casks - coincidentally, the same number of Single Malts goes into some blended whiskies. The blending will take place in a large wooden tun or metal tank, and the melange will then be bottled for anything from five or six to 18 months' maturation at the brewery.

After cask fermentation comes a further phase of development, this time in the bottle. Breweries that make Gueuze have not only galleries of casks but also cellars full of bottles containing beer that is maturing.

The bottles are racked exactly as in wine cellars. Not only does a Lambic brewery have many rooms full of casks stacked on their side, it also has cellars full of bottles.

Because the breweries are allowed to retain mould and damp, makers of Gueuze prefer not to label their bottles. The labels are inclined to become grubby, or peel. Traditionally, the brewers have simply dabbed a little whitewash on the bottle to indicate which side has been uppermost during maturation. Whenever

100

the bottle has been handled, it has been kept the same way up, so that the natural sediment, mainly yeast, will remain undisturbed.

A sign of a good Gueuze is the way in which the yeast has settled against the side of the bottle during maturation. If the yeast has been working well, it will have formed a shape resembling a fish-bone. A good secondary fermentation will create small, persistent, bubbles, like the bead in Champagne, and a character that is brisk but not aggressive. In a good café or restaurant, the bottle will be carefully cradled on its side, and brought gently to the table.

There are still whitewashed, unlabelled, bottles in use, though they are being phased out to meet new regulations. In the past, the daub of whitewash indicated a "real" Gueuze, made in the classical way by secondary fermentation in the bottle. A labelled one suggested a product that had been made by secondary fermentation and/or carbonation in a tank, filtered, then bottled. Some producers amend their labels to indicate whether the beer has been filtered. The tank-conditioned type is often also sweetened.

The De Troch Lambic brewery... the hoist is there to raise the sacks of malt, but the horse was taking part in a film.

Cafés and restaurants often cellar "real" Gueuze for a further two or three years. At that extreme, some of the beer in the bottle could be seven or eight years old.

Some private individuals like to keep their bottles for 18 months before opening them. I have sampled a Gueuze of 45 years. It was surprisingly soft and well-balanced, but with an intense fino character and remorseless dryness in the finish. It was totally flat.

101

The tank-conditioned, filtered, type does not develop in the bottle, and is not cellared for any length of time.

Girardin's kettle overlooks the wheat that it boils. There is a pane of glass between the two, though it is scarcely perceptible in this photograph.

THE PRODUCERS

A Lambic-brewer will normally also produce Gueuze, and the house character will carry through from the one to the other. The influence of weather means that, even with blending, batches will vary over the years. For one reason or another, producers may occasionally create what they consider to be a "vintage" blend or a Cuvée. Cantillon is keen on these special editions, and they offer a valuable opportunity to experience beer as the naturally variable product that it is. "Consistency" is imposed by brewers; makers of fine wines are not so foolish. Belle-Vue uses the soubriquet Sélection Lambic, and a vintage date, to distinguish its unfiltered, unsweetened, unpasteurised Gueuze from the more widely-available version that undergoes those processes. De Neve, and some other producers, label their unfiltered version "with re-fermentation in the bottle". Frank Boon produces exclusively re-fermented Gueuze for his own national market, though a filtered and sweetened version of his beer is sold as Belgian Ale by the British supermarket

The Belle Vue brewery is on the Molenbeek side of the canal. The other side is Brussels. The brewery's Sélection Lambic is actually Gueuze.

Sainsbury's. Belgian purists have criticised Boon for making concessions to the British, but he should be praised for his efforts to popularise the style there. Like all traditional Lambic-brewers, Boon continually monitors casks to see how they are developing. His favourite old Lambics are set aside for blending into Gueuze and bottling in March as Mariage Parfait. "March is the best time to bottle," he says. "All nature is waking up. The warmer evenings wake up the yeast." He likes the Lambic to be two years old when he blends it for Mariage Parfait, and he matures it in the bottle at the brewery for another year or two. Many devotees then cellar it at home for the same period again.

The dice were thrown to achieve "sudden death" (Mort Subite) in a café game. Now the name is given to a life-enhancing range of beers.

Girardin does not filter any of its Gueuze, but some is centrifuged, in which case it is given a white label. The style with re-fermentation has a black label. I have greatly enjoyed the black label version many times over the years but, like all beers, it tastes best at the brewery. Louis Girardin first gave a bottle that had been in his cellar for five months. I thought it had a remarkable combination of intense dryness and smoothness. "No!" said Mr Girardin. "This is too young!!" A three-year-old was fetched, and I found it one of the most complex beers I have ever tasted. The unfolding aromas and flavours reminded me of talcum powder, freshly-cut cedar sawdust, hay, apples, cider and dry oloroso sherry.

Lindemans comes back with its sherryish taste in his unfiltered, unsweetened Gueuze Grand Cru. This version is being marketed in the United States as Cuvée René, after the owner of the brewery. Timmermans' unfiltered version, called Caveau, has a faint touch of malty sweetness and a refreshing fruitiness.

Any brewer's unfiltered Gueuze will have more character than any processed version, simply because the development in the

104

bottle add complexity. The unblended version of Mort Subite Gueuze illustrates this very well.

In Wambeek, the brewery De Troch has come to be better known for some outlandish fruit beers, but it still produces a traditional, unfiltered Gueuze. This beer has lots of wheaty, apple-like notes in its aroma and palate, becoming drier in the middle and finishing light and clean. The brewery itself is very traditional, and still uses a coal-fired kettle.

Excellent unfiltered examples come from the two surviving blenders. Hanssens, in Dworp, blends a fruity, rhubarby, Gueuze. The Café Drie Fonteinen, in Beersel, blends an excellent dry, firm, flavourful, style of Gueuze, as well as having a sweet Kriek on draught. This café (3 Herman Teirlinck Plein; tel. 02-331.06.52) also functions as a brasserie-restaurant, and uses beer in the preparation of some dishes. There are also good Gueuzes to be found at Café Drie Bronnen and Oude Pruim. In the Oude Pruim some years ago, I had a Sunday lunch comprising simply a glass of fruity, apple-like Gueuze with a hearty plate of blood sausage. It was a Proustian moment. Champagne has never been so good.

Presumably regional sensibilities stopped the production of Gueuze spreading across Brabant's border into East Flanders. That being the case, how does the style come to reappear in farther-flung West Flanders? Though textiles and trade have

The classic snack foods of the region, and a house-matured brew or two, are available at the Drie Fonteinen, in Beersel. This is the last café to blend its own Gueuze.

105

been historically important in both provinces, perhaps the East is slightly more oriented to manufacture, and the maritime West to commercial buccaneering. Even in such a small country, there are local differences of character.

In the late 1960s and early 1970s, when in several countries the post-war urge to be "modern" and uniform gave way to some rediscovery of cultural heritage, there was in Belgium a new flurry of interest in the Brussels' area's traditional Gueuze beers, and this style was taken up by two brewers in West Flanders.

This showpiece café, in the former stables of the Belle Vue brewery, features several variations on the Gueuze theme.

Originally, the Van Haelen brewery of Ukkel, Brussels, supplied Lambic as an addition to the range of the family firm of Van Honsebrouck, in the historic town of Ingelmunster, West Flanders. When Van Halen closed, in 1968, Van Honsebrouck fermented some of the brewery's wort in wood as a starter for its own "Lambic", and created its own micro-climate. From this beginning, Van Honsebrouck became well known for a sweetened Gueuze under the brand-name St Louis. Now, the company has added a product more traditional in style. Beers brewed in December, 1991, and September, 1992, were blended to make an unsweetened, unfiltered, product called Gueuze Fond Tradition, which was launched in 1993. This has a light body; a clean, very refreshing acidity; and a tart, spritzy, finish, with a touch of cellar character. Van Honsebrouck is otherwise known for a "red" ale in the local style of West Flanders; a strong brew called Brigand, in loosely the Triple style; and a "Castle Beer" that the British or Americans might call a barley wine.

The other brewery in West Flanders to make a Gueuze is that of the family Vander Ghinste, in the village of Bellegem, near

KRIEK LAMBIC **FRAMBOISE** St Louis **GUEUZE** LAMBIC **PECH**

another historic town, Kortrijk (in French, Courtrai). This brewery, originally part of a farm, has been in the same family since the 1890s. In the 1930s, it had as its speciality a "German-style" lager which it called Bock. The beer was golden, and the brewery eventually became known as Bockor (the "or" meaning gold, in French). Bockor started to produce Gueuze in 1970, originally using in its blend a proportion of Lambic bought from Heyvaert, in Asse, in the traditional region. That brewery closed in 1981, and Bockor now produces its own beers for blending. All breweries used open coolers before the invention of heat-

St Louis Grande Réserve is part of Van Honsebrouck's range of sweetish Lambic-style beers, but the brewery also has the much drier "Fond Tradition". (Photo p. 108)

107

Whitewashed markings are given way to labels, but Van Honsebrouck graphically marries the two.

Gueuze à La Mort Subite... patron Théophile Vossen made the name official in 1910. Previously, it was La Cour Royale.

exchangers, and Bockor still has one, in an elegant tower characteristically curved to run-off the condensed steam. It uses the cooling vessel only for its "Lambic". It also has 16 fixed wooden tuns, which are used for both "Lambic" and a beer in the sour-and-sweet brown-red ale tradition of West Flanders.

Bockor's Gueuze is called Jacobins, a name with both ecclesiastical and democratic connotations. The term derives from a Dominican friary near the church of St Jacques, in Paris. The building housed a club for radical democrats at the time of the French Revolution.

The youngest beer in Jacobins Gueuze has been fermented and matured for a couple of months. The oldest has 14-20 months. The finished beer begins tart, and retains some of this character throughout, staying fairly dry and developing a nuttiness toward the finish. It is filtered, but not pasteurised.

While Gueuze is a wonderful aperitif, it is also a refreshing drink. The people of Brussels like to go out for Sunday lunch, then have a stroll, and finish with a glass of Gueuze. One favourite spot, on the South-Eastern fringe of the city, is the Foret de Soignes, with footpaths through the oaks, chestnuts and beeches. On the edge of the forest is the one-street vil-

108

*Aux Armes de Tirle-
mont is a delightful
surprise in Antwerp.*

lage of Jezus-Eik, in the grape-growing community of Overijse-
Hoeilaart, off the Brussels-Namur route. Dessert grapes are
grown there under glass. Along the single street of Jezus-Eik are
a dozen cafés and restaurants, and even a trailer selling seafood
and escargots. Several of the cafés make a point of promoting
Gueuze, albeit the better-known names.

A further use of Gueuze is to "calm the nerves". This use was
suggested to me when I fell into conversation in Aux Armes
de Tirlemont, a tiny, 400-year-old, café on Eiermarkt, a main
shopping street in Antwerp. Beneath a statue of the Virgin
Mary, this café dispenses Gueuze from a well-filled cellar.
Enjoying my drink there, I began to think that it did have
magical properties.

Perhaps it is the beer of the seducer, as Champagne is the wine
of the romantic... a brush with Bruegel rather than a stroke of
Art Deco.

KRIEK & FRAMBOISE

The pink Champagnes of the beer world are, of course, Kriek and Framboise. These are Lambic beers in which a further fermentation has been brought about by the addition of cherries or raspberries.

In a Champagne flute, which is how they are often served, no beers look prettier. In palate, no beer is more elegant. They are the perfect beers with which to greet guests at a summer party. An authentically dry Kriek makes a wonderful aperitif. It has the acidity of a Champagne, the bouquet and delicate flavour of cherries, and a balance of almondy dryness from the stones, as well as the sherryish background of the base beers. A traditional Framboise fills the air with its bouquet, and is even more delicate in palate and finish. A seducer would be tempted to engage it, and a sexist to deem it the most feminine of beers.

The essence of a true Kriek is whole fruit, not just syrup. The sprig of beech twigs loosely pushed into the cask is the evidence. They prevent the cherries inside from floating up and blocking the bung.

The less traditional, sweetened, examples may be less distinguished (not so much a Champagne as a Lambrusco), but they go perfectly with a sweetly fruity dessert. I have American friends who love them with Cherry Jubilee, the flambeed dish of hot fruit in its own syrup, and ice-cream.

Though they may look it, Kriek and Framboise are not novelties. The traditional use of small, dark, cherries probably has its origins in the days when juniper and other berries were also employed, as a seasoning, before the universal acceptance of the hop. Even today, the hop in Lambic beer that provides the base is a preservative rather than a seasoning. If the cherries turned out not only to add flavour but also to cause a further fermentation, all the better. Take a beer that is immensely complex in the first place, then add a fruit that provides both a seasoning and a further fermentation, and you have a product of astonishing depth and length. No other country has a beer to compare with an authentic Kriek or Framboise.

No doubt other countries have made beers with fruit in the past, but these traditions are lost in the mists of time. Belgium has

The flavour of whole cherries is more evident in Belle Vue's Primeur than in its year-round Kriek.

persisted, and in recent years its Kriek and Framboise have in-spired more conventional fruit beers in France, Britain, Canada, the United States and probably elsewhere.

In the world of beer, the nearest tradition is most certainly the Northern Germans' habit of adding a dash of raspberry juice to Berliner Weisse, their sharply lactic style of wheat brew. This, however, is not a part of the production process; the addition is made by the bartender. In a springtime ritual, some German taverns make a whole-fruit syrup to add to beer or wine as a "May Bowl". The Southern Germans sometimes add a slice of lemon to their spicier Weisse or Weizenbier, but that is hardly the same thing. Nonetheless, these are both interesting drinks. These customs in Germany and Belgium start with a beer that has an intense character, and complement it. Some other countries use a strong flavour to "enhance" a relatively neutral-tasting beer. The French have been known to add the patent aperitif Amer Picon to lager from Alsace. British women used to add sweet lime cordial to lager beers, and it has become the custom among inexperienced drinkers in the English-speaking world to add a segment of the fresh fruit to some of Mexico's lightest-tasting beers. In Canada is not unknown to add toma-to juice to beer, to make a Calgary Red-Eye. This approaches cocktail country, though a Bloody Mary is a much more sat-isfactory drink.

Among wines, the raspberry vermouths of Chambéry are well-known and delicious. Among liqueurs, cherry "brandies" like that made by Peter Heering in Denmark are nodding acquaintances of Kriek. Among spirits, flavoured gins, vodkas and aquavits are distant relations.

THE NAME

While cherry beer is always identified in Belgium by the Flemish name Kriek, its raspberry counterpart is known either as Frambozen or, very often, Framboise, the French-language name. (Framboise is also used to indicate an Alsatian brandy made with raspberries).

Kriek is the Flemish word specifically for a black cherry. It is the name of the fruit itself, and the beer is usually labelled in full as Krieken-Lambic. No doubt the cherry was originally used because it was local. The tradition is to use the Schaarbeek variety, which takes its name from a community in the North-East of Greater Brussels. Although

The fine fruits of the Belgian brewers' craft. A Kriek or Frambozen made with whole fruit may have a sediment that reveals its origins. Once again, gentle handling is required.

Timmermans' fruit beers are less sweet than some. Cantillon's very dry Gueuze Vigneronne is made with Muscat grapes. Cassis (blackcurrant) is one of the more "commercial" flavours.

the area has become a suburb, there are still cherries grown there, and also around the Northern fringes of Brussels in general and in a Westerly direction, toward Ninove. Makers of the beer have even been known to contract to pick the fruit from domestic gardens.

Some producers of Kriek say they use only Schaarbeek cherries, while others augment or replace that variety with another called Northern, grown mainly in Belgian Limburg, Germany and Denmark. The Northern Cherry is larger, and has a less complex flavour. Some producers use only whole cherries, while others also employ a proportion of pulp, or a syrup made from the fruit.

In the traditional method, the Schaarbeek cherries are allowed to dry, like prunes on the tree. Cherries in this condition are doubly scarce, because the birds enjoy them so much. A café-owner blending his own Kriek, or a home-brewer, is best-placed to be so choosy about the cherries he picks. The drying intensifies the fruity flavours (as, for example, in sun-dried tomatoes) and concentrates the fermentable sugars (as in the production of "Noble Rot" dessert wines.

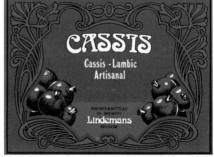

THE MACERATION

Soon after the harvest, at the end of July or beginning of August, the cherries are introduced to the beer in the cask. The Lambic used may be as young as three months or, more traditionally, 18 months. More likely still is a blend of both. Some producers print on the label or cork two dates: when the old beer was brewed, and when the cherries were harvested.

The most cherryish flavours emerge if the brew stays on the fruit for about six weeks, but some beers will remain much longer. From the viewpoint of fruit character, October is a good time to bottle, but the yeast activity in the beer will be better in March,

Similar scenes at Belle-Vue (left) and Liefmans (below). Belle-Vue specify in their promotional material that they use one pound of cherries for every three litres of beer.
The industry has been moving to the mixing of whole fruit with syrups.

April or May. The yeast character is important to the further fermentation in the bottle. This is one reason why not only the base Lambics but also finished Kriek may well be blended to

include different ages. A small, artisanal, brewery cannot bottle all of its Kriek in a single optimum month, or even one season. If the cherry harvest is good, the brewer will probably make more Kriek than he can sell in a single season, and keep it for future years.

Kriek that has spent long periods in the cask picks up more dryness and bitterness from the stones of the cherries. This can add balance and complexity, especially if a young and older Kriek are blended. After six months or a year, this pleasant bitterness can turn to astringency, but much depends upon the condition of the cask, and the temperature (as always, the brewer likes cool weather). It is unusual, but not unknown, for beer to stay on the fruit for more than one summer.

In winter, a pile of cherry stones outside a Lambic brewery will indicate that genuine Kriek has been made. Some breweries use a pound of cherries for every two or three litres of beer, others are less generous. Some also use a proportion of elderberries, for colour and added complexity. Some, having drained the cask but left the fruit inside, will then add a second charge of beer. They will then blend the first and second "extracts". Some will add young Lambic before the bottling. The traditional producer will then mature his Kriek in the bottle for one summer before releasing it. The beer will have had a further fermentation in the cask, caused by the sugars from the fruit, and will then have a period of maturation in the bottle.

In a traditionally-made Kriek, the further fermentation caused by the blendings and the addition of fruit will add to the strength. The strength of the original Lambics will, of course, influence the potency of the final product, which may vary from around, or a little over, 5.0 per cent to more than 7.0.

THE PRODUCERS

Almost all producers of Lambic, and many brewers who make other styles, use a proportion of their output as the basis for a Kriek, a Framboise and perhaps other less-traditional fruit styles. These beers have enjoyed a great growth in sales in recent years, though the authentically tart examples are less popular than the sweeter interpetations.

Cantillon is noted for very dry-tasting fruit beers. The outstanding example, called Rose de Gambrinus, is made from a ratio of 25-to-75 per cent cherries and raspberries, and a dash of vanilla. This estimable brewery has also pioneered the production of grape (Druiven) Lambics, with the Muscat variety. This brings beer and wine even closer, though the characteristics of Lambic seem to me to overpower the muscat.

Belle-Vue launches a Kriek Primeur each April, using younger Lambics and sweeter cherries than are employed in

Gambrinus in characteristically lusty mood. Rosé is fruited with both raspberries and cherries. Cantillon makes authentically tart beers.

its year-round product. The Primeur - which has a fresher, fruitier, character - is intended to signal the new season for the style, and remains on the market for about a month. It is not intended to be laid down, and is filtered and flash- pasteurised like the year- round version. The regular Belle Vue Kriek is less overtly sweet than it once was. Lambics of four months are given cherries for a year, then blended with younger beers, "smoothened" with a small proportion of cherry juice, and sweetened with fructose (fruit sugars).

Boon, with its Mariage Parfait, and Hanssens, make excellent traditional Krieks. Café Drie Fonteinen has a well-matured, dry, Kriek in the bottle but a very sweet one on tap. Several Lambic brewers have both a filtered (or centrifuged) and a sedimented version, with some form of legend on the label to distinguish them. Lindemans have bottled a tart version under the name

Krieklambiek and a sweet one without the reference to the base beer. Lindemans have also used the term Foudroyante for sweet styles in Francophone markets.

There is a market for both dry and sweet Krieks, but some brewers have taken the myopic view that demand can only be for one or the other. These brewers have dropped their dry examples in favour of the sweet. De Troch produces both styles, but its pleasantly tar t dry version is less easy to find in Belgium than in Britain.

Lindemans and De Troch have been the breweries most active in less traditional flavours, using concentrated juices or syrups rather than fresh fruits. The flavours have included blackcurrant, mirabelle plum, peach and even banana. Some argue that Lambic breweries are being kept alive by such hard-headed, commercial, ideas; others that the original product is being lost in the rush to gimmicry. Outside the Lambic region, the production of Kriek and Lambic is especially long-established around the town of Oudenaarde, in East Flanders. There, the Liefmans brewery is well known for its Kriek and Framboise.

Among the fruit beers, those from De Troch are given to the most exotic flights of fancy.

In West Flanders, Rodenbach has a cherry-flavoured dessert beer called Alexander, though this is not a Kriek, and is not presented as one. In Limburg, the St Jozef brewery, better known for its Pax Pils, uses that as the basis for a soft, fruity Bosbier. This is made from Bosbessen (bilberries, or blueberries), which are also used locally in flavoured genever gin, and in fruit pies. In the province of Luxembourg, I have tasted a beer made by Fantôme with a dash of raspberry juice. Other examples come and go.

Belgian fruit beers have inspired similar products in adjoining countries, and in Britain and the United States, though none is based on Lambic. A mis-named "Cranberry Lambic" made

118

in Boston uses real fruit but it is not based on a sponta-neously-fermenting beer.

As a devotee of authentic products, I acknowledge a prejudice against the use of juices and syrups. I was prepared to dislike all beers made in this way, especially the peach products, so obviously inspired by similar "schnapps" (actually, liqueurs) that enjoyed a short vogue in the United States. To my dismay, I found the peach Lambics quite pleasant, if lacking in depth. Perhaps not the stuff of seduction, but a flirtatious beer.

Cherry orchards like this one are part of the landscape of Brussels' northern suburbs, but they are disappearing, to a Chekhovian sigh.

Faro & mars

Just as France, Italy and Spain have their rough, rustic, wines, so all brewing nations once had traditions of beers that were inexpensively made, relatively low in alcohol, and intended for everyday refreshment. These beers could be consumed in large quantities, and were suited to times when manual work was more widespread than it is today. Some were specially associated with harvest times.

Like some rough-and-ready wines (or comparable dishes, such as the pizza of Naples, or the quiche of Lorraine), the traditionally inexpensive beers can often be most enjoyable.

The hearty poster for the Lambic family featured in a joint campaign by the Senne Valley Brewers in the 1920s. Each brewer overprinted its own name in this remarkably early example of generic advertising. Faro was obviously popular at the time.

In the early and mid 1800s, the Lambic family of beers were emphatically the local brews of Brussels, and the most common manifestation was Faro. It is greatly celebrated in Belgian folklore, and was obviously much appreciated, even if Baudelaire was famously scatological about it.

Between the late 1800s and the two World Wars, Faro lost its dominance to more conventional (and stable) ales of what might broadly be regarded as a Belgian-British type, and lagers of a

BRASSERIE DE LA TAUPE

Fr. Timmermans-Walravens

Téléphone 656,18   ITTERBEEK

LAMBIC
ET
FARO

SONT LES MEILLEURES
BIÈRES DU MONDE

ATTESTATION :

1 Lit. de LAMBIC équivaut en valeur nutritive à : 200 grammes de PAIN, 180 Id. VIANDE, 72 centilitres de LAIT.

VERELST.   DENAMUR.

Bohemian and Bavarian style. There were also later fashions for the Dortmund and Danish types of lagers.

The newer styles were no doubt seen as being more sophisticated but, fortunately, the Belgians remain eclectic beer-drinkers. Most of these styles are still readily available, and Faro still exists, in a small way.

The older type of low-alcohol beers were often made by a procedure that is basic to brewing. When a brewer extracts the "juice" from his grain, he does so by running warm water through it. The first time he runs the water through, he obtains a rich extract. Some speciality beers are made only from these "first runnings". Weaker beers may be made from second and third runnings. (Some Italian espresso bars do the same: offering a choice of "first pull" or second). That is how Faro and the related style Mars were originally made.

Faro was stronger than Mars. No doubt these two styles sometimes represented simply beers made from the second and third runnings respectively. On other occasions, the various runnings were blended to achieve finished beers of different strengths. Or Faro was simply watered to produce Mars. Cafés also made their own blends from these variations, typically half of one and half of another.

Boon has only one Faro, but it has about 6.0% alcohol, and he calls it a double. The small print promises that it has aged in oak for two years. It totals up to an odd brand-name.

Such traditions were widespread in other brewing countries, notably England, and still exist vestigially there today. "A pint of mixed" will indicate two differing gravities of Bitter, or perhaps the second half will be Mild (another example of a rough-and-ready beer, originally for harvest time). In the world of wine, several regions blend brandy and fresh grape juice to make what is variously known as a Pineau, a Ratafia or a Mistelle.

THE NAME

Faro is the name of a town in Portugal. Troops from that region of Iberia were a part of Spanish rule in Belgium. Did they bring with them the dark, sherryish, wine of Faro? Or did they remember it when they saw the dark, sherryish, beer of Brussels? Perhaps the occupying elite drank the Iberian wine, while "The Faro of the People" was the local beer. Such a self-deprecating soubriquet would be typical of those people.

That is the most recent theory on the origins of the beer's name. Or was the designation perhaps derived in the same period from the Latin farina, meaning flour, to describe a "wine" produced from grain? In the same way, the British have the term "Barley Wine", though for a very strong beer. In modern Spanish, faro means a light or, colloquially, a bright idea. The British have an expression for becoming drunk: "Getting lit-up". Perhaps that is a clue.

In the early days, when the tart, acidic, beers from the Zenne Valley were delivered to the caf, the bar-keeper would hang into it strings of candy sugar. This agent of sweetening, and secondary fermentation, came in a very convenient form. String had earlier been suspended in extract of sugar-beet so that the crystals would form. This is how candy-sugar is traditionally made.

Today, the odd caf still provides candy sugar and a small tool with which to crush it (like the muddler used in a cocktail bar). More often, the Faro will already have been sweetened at the brewery, with candy sugar, caramel or molasses, and perhaps further flavoured with herbs and spices.

In the days when Faro was an everyday beer, it would have been served as an unpasteurised draught, but its turnover would have bee n sufficiently fast to prevent the sugar fermenting out, or the beer returning to sourness. The cask would have been exhausted within a day. With its Lambic origins, the "locked-in" sugar, and perhaps some spicing, a good modern Faro has some of the characteristics of a sweet sherry.

Some examples are a blend of a sweetened, possibly spiced, Lambic and a top-fermenting beer. There have even been beers labelled as Faro that were simply sweet dark lagers. In general, they are soft-tasting beers.

In the traditional Lambic district, examples have in recent years been made by Cantillon, Boon, Lindemans, and Vander Linden. The last has even made a regular Faro at 4.0 per cent alcohol by volume and a "double" at 6.0.

Mars took its name from the month of March. Why a weak brew instead of the medium-strong style more commonly associated with this month? Perhaps it was the final runnings from a strong brew being laid down for summer's maturation. If the weather was beginning

A new type of beer, with no designation of style, but Lembeek's 2% is a delightful refresher from the enterprising Frank Boon brewery.

to warm, a lighter beer would, of course, have been welcomed. While all beer-making countries have products set around the past difficulties of brewing in summer, the descriptions used are a tangle. In another example, the term "Bock" is used in Belgium and France to mean a relatively weak beer, while most countries reserve it for something strong. Such confusions bedevil the names applied to many drinks and foods in different countries (for example, what the Belgians call the endive, the French regard as chicory, and vice-versa).

Mars is no longer made. Boon's product Lembeek's 2% (the figure represents alcohol by volume) is not intended to be a Mars, but is loosely based on the idea. It is made from a mash of 9.5-10.0 Plato, containing 15 per cent unmalted wheat and 85 per cent malted barley. Three strains of yeast cultured up from the Lambic menagerie are used, but the fermentation is not in wood; conventional stainless-steel vessels are used. The beer is spiced.

Lembeek's 2% is a golden beer, with a refreshing, fruity, bouquet and palate. It is somewhat reminiscent of a ginger ale in palate. Sensibly from its own viewpoint, the brewery has registered its brand-name. That is shame, though, from the viewpoint of the beer-lover. A new type of beer has been created, but there is no name for the style.

'WHITE' BEERS

The term "white" has in several European countries traditionally been applied to wheat beers, and especially those presented with a sediment. These beers are not really white, of course, but they are very pale, and may to varying degrees have an intentional cloudiness.

The most distinguished examples are the Weissbier of Southern Germany (and especially from the Eastern part of Bavaria), which sometimes has a phenolic character, deriving from the behaviour of the yeast used; the Berliner Weisse of the North, which is made with a lactic culture; and the orangey, spiced style of Witbier, or Bière Blanche, originating from the town of Hoegaarden in the Eastern part of the Belgian province of Brabant.

Each of these styles is quite different, but they are all full of character, and all very refreshing, especially in summer. As very traditional brews, they were at one stage threatened with extinction on the grounds of being "old-fashioned", but in recent years the South German (though not yet the Berliner) and Belgian types have both enjoyed huge revivals of popularity. In their native countries, both are especially favoured among young people.

The Belgian examples are all very closely modelled on one beer. In the English-speaking world, this product is labelled as Hoegaarden White (English-speakers tend, understandably, to pronounce it as in Hoe Garden; in Flemish, it sounds like Who Garden). In Belgium, the beer has been labelled Oud

Village or town? Either way, Hoegaarden (below) is back on the map, thanks to its famous beer.

Hoegaards, and more recently just Hoegaarden. It is identified by style as Witbier or Bière Blanche. Hoegaarden is made by the De Kluis brewery. This is in the village or town of Hoegaarden, near Tienen.

From Brussels, it is less than an hour's journey east, beyond Leuven or Louvain, to the scatter of villages around Tienen that traditionally made beers in this style.

Louvain had its own "White" beer, described in detail in a brewing manual of the late 1700s, and produced until the mid 1970s. In its last days, I was told there was still a small stock at the bar in the railway station. I went there for a valedictory glass, and asked for the beer, in Flemish, to looks of incomprehension. I tried again, in French, but with no more success. Then the lady behind the bar decided that I required something native to the British Isles. She broke into a smile and said, in heavily accented English: "Monsieur, I have a beer for you." Proudly, she gave me a bottle of Guinness. It was delicious, but not what I had been seeking.

Gemeente means municipality or community, in Flemish, but this Hoegaarden street sign honours "White" beer in an international language.

In the middle of Leuven's main market square is the church of St Pieter. The parish saint gives his name to all connected with the town. Its version of "White" beer was known as Pieterman, and occasional revivalist examples have been produced under that name. De Kluis has been known to make a darkish "White" beer with the spelling Peeterman.

In the village of Neerijse, the De Kroon brewery has intermittently produced a sweet, cidery, and very cloudy, "Double White". In Lubbeek the Verlinden brewery had its own similar example until 1985. For several decades, though, Hoegaarden has been the place associated with the style.

I have been assured locally that Hoegaarden is a village. I would call it a small town. A brochure promoting the local beer extravagantly calls Hoegaarden "a fairly large town", and points out that it has Belgium's biggest rococo church. The church is certainly impressive, and I rather like the bandstand in the middle of the village/town.

Hoegaarden is in a region of rich soil and château farms growing wheat and sugar beet. Although it surely had breweries earlier, they begin to be mentioned in its history in the early 1300s, and

A white mountain is growing in the beer-shops of Belgium... testimony to the refreshing nature of a cool Bière Blanche.

126

in the 1400s a monastery that made both beer and wine was established. By the 1500s, Hoegaarden had a Guild of Brewers. Many of its members were farmers, who brewed from their own wheat and oats. In the 1700s, the town had become a brewing centre, sending much of its beer to adjoining Principality of Liège. In the 1800s, there were more than 30 breweries in and around the town, at the confluence of the Grote Gete and Nermbeek rivers. (Despite the "Grote", neither river is large).

In this century, the growth of Leuven as a brewing centre, and the increasing popularity of Pilsener-style beers (not to mention two World Wars and the advent of national marketing) helped wash away much of Hoegaarden's brewing tradition. By the 1950s, only two breweries remained. One of them had switched to Pilsener-style beer, and would eventually close. In the mid 1950s, the last remaining brewer of "White" beer ceased production.

A few years later, several locals were having a chat when one observed, sadly, that he missed the "White" beer they used to enjoy. In the gathering was Pieter Celis, who had lived next door to the old brewery. Celis had often helped out at the brewery, been fascinated by the place, and had come to know something of the production procedures. He was even involved in the

Revivalist Pieter Celis (second from right) gets an early taste of brewing. In 1991, he started to build a "White Beer" brewery in Austin, Texas.

127

selling of a white drink, though a somewhat different beverage: he was a milkman.

The enterprising Celis, then in his early 40s, felt that the tradition could be revived. With some financial help from his father, a cattle-dealer, he bought equipment from another extinct brewery, and started making "White" beer once more, in 1966. He called his brewery De Kluis - meaning "cloister", "hermitage" or "monastery" - in honour of the town's 15th-century brewers.

"I thought the older generation of beer-drinkers would support me," he once told me, "but I was concerned about the younger consumers, who would not know what White beer was." In fact, it was the young who supported him, from the start. "The movement to natural products helped. People liked the natural look of a beer with a sediment. I did not make any publicity. It was all word-of-mouth. People started coming to the brewery from Cologne and Paris. Sometimes I had no beer for them. I could not meet demand. One day, a local man said to me: "Do you know, our Hoegaarden beer is being sold on the Champs-Elysées...?"

De Kluis expanded quickly, but put a strain on the financial resources of Pieter Celis, especially after a fire in 1985. Soon afterwards, Celis sought additional investment, and now De Kluis is part of Interbrew.

The De Kluis brewery is on an old farm site, and buildings have been acquired and restored as the enterprise has grown. One battlemented wall dates from the 1500s, another from the mid 1750s, and more of the structure from the 1830s. An arched courtyard leads to pantiled former farm buildings. Over the centuries, parts of the site have been used, like many farms in Northern Europe, for malting, brewing and distilling. Today, there is also a bar and restaurant, specialising in dishes prepared and served with the De Kluis beers (tel. 016-76.74.33, open every day).

The early "White" beers of Hoegaarden seem to have been made with not only wheat but also a small proportion of local oats, and this tradition has been continued by some producers. While the wheat contributes its own fruity tartness, the oats perhaps add a pleasantly oily smoothness. Certainly this particular blend of raw materials has its influence on the complexity of flavour of the "White" beers.

There was a tradition in eastern Brabant of spreading green malt on the roof to dry. This very simple method would probably have produced very pale beers. I have also heard of brewers in the past using figs as an adjunct, again to produce notably pale beers. A pale hue was perhaps seen as being attractive and "pure" in the days before brewers knew how to make clear beers.

The original "White" beers were produced by spontaneous fermentation, in wood, and some brewers continued with this method. Old people remember the beer being very sour - and needing to be sweetened. Brewers used herbs and fruits for that purpose - coriander seeds and Curaçao orange peels have become the recognised seasoning in this style of beer. These, again, make their own contribution to complexity.

When some brewers began to pitch yeast, they would have used top-fermenting strains, as the lager method was not known. Both in Germany and

The Kouterhof bar offers the full range of beers from De Kluis, and meals prepared and served with them.

129

Belgium, "White" beers are made with top-fermenting yeasts, and in each case a living culture may be left (or added) in the cask or bottle. There are particular top-fermenting yeasts that work well with wheat, or mixtures of grains, or have adapted to do so - and each of those will add its own element of complexity. Often, one yeast is used in primary fermentation and another in the bottle for the secondary stage - adding yet another dimension. In both Berlin and Hoegaarden, people remember burying bottles in the earth to keep them cool while the beer "ripened". The German types of "White" beer do not employ oats, or spices. Hoegaarden is brewed from roughly equal parts of raw wheat and malted barley. The gravity is a conventional 12 Plato (1048), and the beer has an alcohol content of 3.8 by weight, 4.8 by volume.

It is not intended to be a hoppy beer, but it does have some Kent Goldings for dryness and Saaz for aroma. The spices are milled before being added. The brewery is very secretive about this aspect of production. There is also talk of a third, "mystery", spice. If it exists at all, I wonder whether it is cumin seeds.

The brewhouse is of a relatively traditional design, in a mix of copper and stainless steel, set in a very compact arrangement in an attractively blue-tiled room.

The brewery has a very advanced yeast-propagation system, and in the Hoegaarden it uses different cultures for

A proportion of wheat makes for a tarter, sharper, more refreshing, summery beer than pure barley malt can achieve.

primary and secondary stages. Primary fermentation is in stainless steel. The beer has a week's primary fermentation, at 18 °C (64.4 °F)-26 °C (78.8 °F). It then has three to four weeks' warm conditioning in cellar tanks at 12 °C (53.6 °F) to 15 °C (59 °F) before being bottled with a priming of sugar (glucose) and a dosage of new yeast. Once bottled, the beer has a secondary fermentation of about ten days at 25 °C (77 °F), in a temperature-controlled room.

The beer has a very pale, whitish-yellow colour, and is very hazy. It has a dense, white head. In aroma, it has wheaty, apple-like, tartness; herbal-spicy notes, with lots of coriander; orangey fruitiness; and honeyish sweetness. When the beer is young, the palate is refreshingly tart and dry, with some lactic-tasting sourness and herbal astringency.

If it is to be consumed in this way, as a refreshing drink, it should be kept refrigerated. If it is stored (in a dark place, at no less than 7.0 °C, 45 °F, and no more than 12 °C, 53 °F), within a couple of months, the orangey and honeyish notes become more evident, in a "demi-sec" sweetness. It is intended to retain some of its "White" cloudiness,

The chunky glass, filled with beer that is a cloudy yellow-white, resembles those used in France for Pernod and pastis. The brewhouse (below) at Hoegaarden looks conventional enough.

though this clears within a matter of months to a shimmering quality that the brewers call a "double shine".

It is doubtful whether the beer will improve significantly beyond six months, and it is likely to be damaged if it is exposed to light, heat, or extreme changes in temperature. In a dark, well-cooled, place, it should keep for one year, possibly two or three, and may continue slightly to round-out, but it is not really intended for such long storage. While it is most refreshing chilled, it most fully expresses its flavours if it is served at 11-12 °C (51-53 °F). With the growth in popularity of "White" beers, they are increasingly served fresh, on draught, as a summer quencher. In my view, today's examples are not hopped and spiced with such care, or matured quite as gently, as those of five or six years ago. I believe that in those days they were softer, more suited to being stored for a few months, or even years, and served with a dessert, as the beer world's answer to an Orange Muscat. A really good bottle of a Belgian "White" beer is delicious with an orange sorbet, lemon meringue, or apple pie (especially the very sweet, treacly, spicy, American type).

The Grand Cru is the Hoegaarden beer most reminiscent of an Orange Muscat wine. This beer is a classic in its own right.

"Laying down" (though not on its side) is better reserved for Hoegaarden Grand Cru. This is also identified as the brewery's "Triple". It is also a spiced beer, but made solely from barley malt and to a higher gravity (18.4; 1076; about 7.0 per cent alcohol by weight, 8.7 by volume). It has a hazy, peachy, colour and a notably fragrant aroma. Its palate is peachy, too, and sweetish - though never excessively so. Its fruity notes - not just suggestions of peach, but also of mango and honeydew melon - and its warming finish, make it a fine, liqueur-like, digestif. Some devotees prefer this beer at six months old, and it will evolve to some degree for three to four years, though it can become excessively Maderised.

Although the Hoegaarden brewery principally produces "White" beer, it does have several other specialities. An attempt to create a drier and more Champagne-like beer led in 1987 to Julius (again, 8.7 by volume). This has a golden, lightly hazy, colour; a very white head; an astonishingly perfumy aroma; a firm body; and a palate that starts sweet and emphatically sherryish (palo cortado?) but moves through a great deal of flavour development to a dry, very hoppy, finish.

Taking the brewery name as its cue, de Kluis also produces an abbey-style beer, called St Benedict (6.3 by volume). This has a rich, reddish-amber, colour; a faintly smoky, fruity, earthy, aroma; a fruity, slightly tart, palate; and a smooth finish. On one occasion, the brewery was asked to produce a beer for the town festival of nearby Diest.

Forbidden Fruit shocked the American alcohol authorities, and in consequence got a half-page in Playboy. How long before it is banned in Boston?

The town was once famous for sweet dark ales, so De Kluis made something in this style. Taking its monastic name in a more Rabelaisian spirit, De Kluis called this beer Verboden Vrucht/Fruit Défendu (meaning, of course, "Forbidden Fruit"). This beer, which has 9.0 per cent by volume, has a claret colour, a very dense head; a spicy aroma; a full, soft, body; and a beautifully balanced palate, with rich, sweet suggestions of chocolate and vanilla giving way to drier coriander notes in the finish. Very assertive at first, then soothing.

The label is based on Rubens' painting of Adam and Eve. When the beer was first exported to the United States, the Bureau of Alcohol, Tobacco and Firearms (a curious conjunction, surely?) sought to ban it on the grounds that the label was indecent. The importer protested: "How dare you say such a thing? That is a Rubens, a great work of art given to the world by the Flemish people!" The bureaucrat pondered this point, then replied: "Did Adam really tempt Eve with a glass of beer? I thought he used an apple..."

No brewery in Belgium produces such a diverse range of specialities, but it is De Kluis' house beer, its Oud Hoegaards, that has inspired so many newer rivals.

THE WHITE BEERS OF BELGIUM

These are some examples that I have tasted.

Blanche de Bruxelles: Produced in Brabant, at Quenast, near the river Zenne, by the Lefebvre brewery, better known for a Saison and an abbey-style beer. The brewery is only about 15 miles from Brussels. The white beer named after the city is one of the fuller examples in body as well as flavour, with a good malt character and plenty of orange-peel tangy dryness.

Blanche des Honnelles: A stronger-than-average (6.0 per cent), very orangey, interpretation from the family micro-brewery that produces Abbaye des Rocs, in Montingies, Hainaut.

As interest in "White" beers spread to Wallonia, the Brasserie Silly launched a fruity, quenching, entrant called Titje... another of those robust Belgian names (below, left).

Blanche de Namur: Appetizingly herbal and dry, especially in the finish. From Du Bocq, of Purnode, in the province of Namur. This brewery produces a wide variety of beers, including Saison Régal.

Blanche des Neiges: Full-coloured, fruity, sweet, smooth white beer from Huyghe, of Melle, near Ghent. This snow-white innocence of this contrasts with the threatening name of the brewery's strong ale Delirium Tremens.

Vlaamsch Wit, also labelled as Blanche des Flandres and Flemish White (right), comes from Van Honsebrouck, in West Flanders. This beer has an orangey aroma, with its sweetness turning to dryness as the palate develops herbal notes; very light and refreshing.

Brugs Tarwebier: A 1930s advertisement for August Vanneste's "Three Monks" brewery, in Bruges, mentions "Spécialités de Bière Brune et Blanche". In 1983, Paul Vanneste's "Golden Tree" brewery became an early revivalist. His "Bruges Wheat Beer" is

very soft and notably aromatic, with dryish notes of apple, orange and honey. The brewery is also well known for its Bruges Triple and abbey-style beers.

Dentergems Witbier: Another early revivalist, from the Riva brewery, established in 1857 by the family De Splenter, and still in their hands. The brewery is in Dentergem, West Flanders. This spritzy, refreshing, beer has lots of sweet apple character and a touch of honey. The names Wittekop and Riva Blanche have also been used.

Haecht Tarwebier: An older spelling is used by the Haacht brewery, near the village of the same name in Brabant, to describe its wheat beer. This dry example emphasises wheat-beer characteristics and is only lightly spiced.

Lambic Timmermans Blanche: The first Lambic-based white beer. This is a hazy, young (six-to-nine months), Lambic spiced with coriander, sweet orange peels and pale candy-sugar. The Lambic flavours are still detectable, including some toasty notes, but it is a very soft, easily drinkable, beer.

Limburgse Witte: Excellent newcomer that brings back the rounder flavours of the first revivalist wheat beers. Dense, creamy head; lightly spicy, fruity, nose; very soft, clean, orangey honey palate. Made by the Limburg brewery St Jozef (known for its Pax Pils), and marketed in partnership with neighbours Martens (renowned for its Sezoens).

White pioneers: Timmermans made the first "White" Lambic... Pieter Celis, founder of De Kluis, now produces a wonderfully fruity, refreshing White Beer in Austin, Texas. He has taken to wearing a bolo tie.

German-looking glasses, but Steendonk is definitely Belgian. Its name merges two villages.

Miroir Blanche: Lightly fruity and dry, smooth, house beer at the brewpub le Miroir, in Jette, Brussels. The café specifies on its menu that this beer has among its ingredients red wheat from Brabant, oats, and Aalst-grown Hallertau hops.

Oudenaards Wit Tarwebier: Very pale, lightly perfumy, white beer from Clarysse, better known for its hometown style of brown ale.

Steendonk: Herbal dryness is balanced with tart, lemony, notes and softer, sweeter flavours reminiscent of melon. A joint venture between Steenhuffel's respected Palm brewery and Breendonk's Moortgat, the latter famous for Duvel.

Titje: Fruit and herbal notes in the bouquet; tart, dry and thirst-cutting in the palate and finish. The name is an intentional double-entendre. A Titje is, in the local patois, a citizen of Enghien, a town near Silly, in Hainaut. This beer is made by Brasserie de Silly, better known for its Saison.

Troublette: Extremely perfumy aroma, and very soft palate. The haze in beer is sometimes referred to as "trouble", and that word has the same root as "turbulent" or "turbid". A white beer can justifiably celebrate its turbidity. This one is made by the micro-brewery La Caracole, whose own name celebrates the snail symbol of languid Namur.

Vlaamsch Wit: Also labelled as Blanche des Flandres and Flemish White. This beer has an orangey aroma, with its sweetness turning to dryness as the palate develops herbal notes. Very light and refreshing. Produced by Van Honsebrouck, of Ingelmunster, West Flanders. This eclectic brewery appears in several chapters of "The Great Beers of Belgium".

136

Watou's Wit: Definite coriander emphasis in this slightly darker (a pink tinge?), foamy, white beer from the West Flanders brewery Van Eecke, famous for its Poperings Hommelbier.

Wheat is called Tarwe in Flemish and Froment in French... the Bokrijk example is from the small brewery De Block.

BROWN BEERS

No corner of the brewing world is as strongly associated with truly dark brown ales as Flanders. At their best, ales in this distinctive regional style have a teasingly smooth, almost feathery, fluffy, body (deriving, I think, from the local water); a dry maltiness; a note of Montilla (from long periods of maturation); a light balance of sweetness and sourness; and a spritzy finish.

To my palate, this is the perfect style of beer with which to make the classic beef carbonade. The beer is as typically Flemish as the dish. In his Carbonade Flamande, Escoffier suggests either an old Lambic or a Stout. These are extremely different styles, and a Flemish Old Brown falls between them at equal distances. It is not as tart as the one or as burnt-tasting as the other in its dark malt character. Its lactic acidity seems perfectly to tenderize the beef, and that Montilla character adds piquancy to the cooking liquid. While preparing this dish, I enjoy a glass of the beer, which serves as a perfect pick-me-up in the late afternoon. Then I put my Carbonade in the oven and let my appetite become

The selection below includes some classics. No other country has such a range of brown ales, ranging from the ultra-sweet to the sour, with all combinations between.

aroused while the dish cooks slowly for three hours, in time for a wonderful dinner.

Like Lambic in the making of Gueuze, the Old Browns traditionally are blended. This is also true of several similar beers with a redder colour that are made in Flanders.

This blending of old and young beers can be a means of creating a secondary fermentation, but it is also a way of combining and balancing flavours. In the days before refrigeration, when no one brewed in summer, a stock would be laid down for those months. By the autumn, the last of this beer would have become winey and acidic, and might be blended with lighter, fresher,

new beer. Eventually, "old" beers were produced purely as an ingredient for blending. The sum is greater than the parts, and it is to be hoped that Belgium retains its hold on this aspect of the brewing art. Today, it is scarcely practised in any other brewing nation.

The sweet-and-sour nature of the style leans heavily on the action of the yeast during fermentation. Liefmans still has open fermenters.

By far the best known Old Brown is today brewed by Riva, at Dentergem, in West Flanders, but fermented, matured, blended and bottle-conditioned at its original home, Liefmans, at Oudenaarde, in East Flanders. The two sites are only a few miles apart, but the style belongs to the town of Oudenaarde and the province of East Flanders.

Riva, which was founded by its present proprietors' family in 1896, now owns Liefmans, which has tax documents showing

that it existed in 1679. The Liefmans family owned the brewery from around 1770 to 1905.

There are a couple of oblique links between the brewery and the performing arts. One was Leon van Geluwe, manager of the Royal Conservatory of Bruges; his son Pierre bought the brewery in 1905 after hearing at a dinner party that it was for sale. In typically Belgian fashion, the company history still recalls the restaurant where the dinner took place, the Pomme d'Or.

Some of the equipment from the period of the van Geluwe family was retained when the brewery moved to its present site by the river Schelde in the 1930s. In the 1970s and 1980s, former ballet-dancer Rose Blancquaert-Merckx provided the second link with the performing arts. She managed the brewery for some years, fought hard to maintain the character of its beers, and gave them a certain cult status.

If a brewery takes trouble over its beer, the presentation should suggest that. The tissue-wrapped bottle is dressed for dinner.

Traditionally, the Liefmans beers have been made from an elaborate blend of malts. Recently, two pale malts, Vienna and Munich styles, and roasted barley, have been used, and the water in Dentergem has been treated to achieve the Oudenaarde character: low in calcium, but high in sodium bicarbonate. The principal bittering hops have been English Whitbread Goldings, along with German and Czech varieties.

Though the brewing is not at Dentergem, the name of Liefmans is cause to raise a glass.

The brewery's basic beer, its Oud Bruin, is brewed from a gravity of 12 Plato (1048) to 4.0 per cent alcohol by weight, 5.0 by volume. It has seven days' primary fermentation in open copper vessels with the house yeast (which has for decades been cultured at Liefmans, although its origins can be traced back to the famous Rodenbach brewery). I will always remember Madame Rose, the former ballet-dancer, donning a pair of clogs and climbing into one of the tanks: "You should see what cleaning they need," she told me, firmly.

The traditional procedure is to brew an additional beer of 13.2 Plato (1053), which has a further maturation of six to eight months, in steel tanks, at ambient temperatures. During maturation, the brews are fined, and afterwards they are centrifuged. The two brews are then blended, given a new dosage of yeast and priming sugar, and bottled to produce Liefmans' Goudenband. The beer is filled into not only standard and 75 cl bottles but also magnums.

The bottles should have at least three months' bottle-aging aging in the brewery cellars before being released. The finished product has 4.8 per cent alcohol by weight, 6.0 by volume, and colour of 60 EBC and 20 units of bitterness.

When the beer is young, it can taste assertively fruity and winey, with the sweetness and sourness seeming to be separate, unconnected, characteristics. When it has been properly matured, the flavours combine and the beer is rounder and more complex. Many devotees then keep the beer for several years in their own cellars. When he was brewer at Liefmans, Madame Rose's son Olav Blancquaert told me he felt the brew developed its greatest balance of fresh and winy characteristics at between three and five years, but some drinkers like to keep it for ten or fifteen. The brewery's brown is also the basis for its fruit beers: a

The "Flemish" Ardennes is the somewhat extravagant name given to the gently rolling countryside around Oudenaarde. Below: the Roman brewery.

quite cherryish Kriek and a considerably sweeter Frambozen. When Riva took over Liefmans, the new owners decided that the brewhouse at Oudenaarde was too old to remain in use. It is to be hoped that a new brewhouse will eventually be fitted there. The Liefmans brewery has now been turned into something of a living museum of beer, and can be visited on a boat trip along with Schelde.

Where an arm of the river once flowed, and a Jesuit abbey stood from the 1200s, is a second Oudenaarde brewery, tracing its origins from the 1600s. It makes another Oudenaarde brown, under the name Felix. At one stage, the brewery was owned by a man named Felix, but it has been in the hands of the Clarysse family since World War II. Although the odd abbey wall still stands, the present brewery's buildings date mainly from the 1970s. The beer is very soft and sweet, with a toffeeish tinge, though it does also have a touch of tartness. The brewery also produces a fruity, abbey-style, beer called St Hermes, a perfumy Kriek and a white beer.

The "double" brown of the Roman brewery is an excellent product. All this brewery's beers are made to a high standard.

Outside the town, but still within the community of Oudenaarde, at Mater, is the brewery Roman, which traces its history back to 1545. It has a dryish brown ale, with some chocolatey notes, called Oudenaards, and a more intense Dobbelen Bruinen. This brewery has a wide range of products, which generally have a good hop aroma. It is a well-kept brewery, with some beautiful machines kept as museum pieces.

A fourth, very small, brewery in the Oudenaarde area, Cnudde, at Eine, closed when its owner retired in 1992/3. This brewery had made a subtle old brown and occasionally an excellent Kriek.

What was once one of the world's great brewing towns is seeing its traditions erode to an alarming degree. Brewing is one of the earliest traditions of Oudenaarde, even if the town is better known to some for its tapestries (it was the birthplace of Jean Gobelin). It is to be hoped that its style of beer is maintained.

A beer of a similar style, with a more pinkish tinge and a drier palate, is made not far away by the Crombé brewery, in the little town of Zottegem, East Flanders. Behind a caf and a family home, through an arch, the brewery is a hidden antique, dating from 1798. It even has the remnants of its own hop kilns. The present brewer, Jo Crombé, also has a job as a pharmacist in a hospital.

Several other small breweries in East Flanders and Flemish Brabant make sourish brown ales, and there are dozens of dark brews of other types produced in Belgium.

An example blended with Lambic is made under the name Jack-Op by the former Vanden Stock component of Interbrew. A similar style of beer was traditionally made on the other side of Brussels, in and around the town of Aarschot. In recent years, this style has been revived by the Biertoren brewery, of Kampenhout, a small town about a dozen miles north of Brussels. The brewery, which dates from 1843, originally made spontaneously-fermenting styles. Since the 1930s, it has been owned by the family Smedts, who had previously operated a brewery in a towered castle at Rotselaar, between Aarschot and Leuven. The family had at that stage made an Aarschotse Bruine. That tower, perhaps from the 1600s, and the brewery chimney, still stand at Rotselaar.

The dramatic tower of Rotselaar still stands... and features on the label of Aarschotse Bruine.

From the 1950s, production at Kampenhout was limited to table beers. In 1988, a new generation of the Smedts family came into the business, and the brewery was upgraded, with second-hand equipment. Among the elements retained were the exciseman's office.

143

Guarding the Gilden-
bier? A brew to die for
with Belgian chocolate.

A towered maltings, used in the Second World War to kiln chicory for coffee, has now been turned into a banqueting room, which is hired out for receptions and parties. Guests can enjoy the beers in a wooded garden.

The revivalist Aarschotse Bruine (12 Plato; 1048; 3.6w; 4.5v) starts fruity and orangey and finishes with a lingering tartness. Some aged beer is used to achieve the tartness. The brewery's principal produce is a spiced strong ale called Campus. The reborn company has experienced some problems, and it is hoped that it will emerge from these difficulties.

A quite different style of brown ale, brewed to the east of Brussels, is Gildenbier. This was originally the local style of Diest, and is now a speciality of the Haacht brewery. This is a very sweet, caramel-tasting, brown ale, which seems soft and innocent for a brew of 17 Plato, 5.1w, 6.3v. This unusual beer is brewed from three malts, with dosages of candy sugar in the kettle and the maturation vessel. It may seem overpoweringly sweet, but it is wonderful with a chocolate dessert.

THE 'RED' BEERS
OF WEST FLANDERS

In colour, the most obvious "Burgundies of Belgium" are surely the highly distinctive reddish-brown specialities of West Flanders, among which the beers made by Rodenbach are the definitive examples. A famous old advertisement for Rodenbach beer said simply, if confusingly: "It's wine..." In palate, though, these beers are far from Burgundy. They are relatively light-bodied, and tart to the point of intentional sourness. That characteristic may shock the unaware, but it makes for the most refreshing beers in the world. They are sharply quenching, but without the drying acidity of their closest rival, the Berlin type of "white" wheat beer.

This West Flanders style does not employ wheat, and its use of

Burgundy in colour... but quite distinct in palate. This region's specialities are astonishingly refreshing.

reddish barley malts contributes not only to its colour but also to its complexity of palate. It is one of the most unusual types of beer anywhere, though the style has no name (Flemish Red Ale? Red-Brown Old Ale? Flemish Sour Ale?). In the early 1800s, the style of "Ghent and the two Flanders" (i.e. East and West) was known as Uytzet. This bears at least a passing resemblance to the term "Backset", used by American whiskey distillers to identify the residue of one batch, which is added to the next in the "Sour Mash" technique. Although the method is not quite the same, blending is involved in the production of these Flemish beers. Perhaps they were once produced by a Sour Mash technique? A lesser producer of the style once told me his beer was Type Rodenbach, though that brewery's name is, of course, proprietary. Rodenbach Grand Cru is in my view an undisputed world classic.

"It's wine" says the old advertisement below, but the maturation vessels look as though they belong in a brandy distillery. They stand today as they did when this picture was taken.

The Rodenbach brews are made by a most unusual method, employing a relatively conventional top-fermentation, followed by a couple of years' maturation in avenues of fixed, ceiling-high vessels made of unlined oak. The oak is not cosmetic: it has a powerful influence on the character of the beer. Outside Belgium, the only beer I know that is made in this way is just across the sea in a region of past Flemish influence, Eastern England: Strong Suffolk ale, from the renowned Greene King brewery, in the town of Bury St Edmunds. Strong Suffolk is a speciality, made

on a small scale in comparison to Greene King's best-known product, its premium bitter.

Rodenbach's beers are not small specialities. By Belgian standards, Rodenbach is a middle-sized brewery (with a capacity of 240,000 hectolitres a year), and all three of its beers are variations on the red, sour, West Flanders style. In the days when everyone drank their local type of beer, it made sense to have a brewery of this size devoted to the style of West Flanders. Today, Rodenbach survives by selling its beer as a (large) speciality not just in its home province but throughout Belgium. As the highly-individualistic brews of Belgium gradually become known to connoisseurs in countries where most beers are bland, the Rodenbach products could gain a more widespread "cult" following.

The world has only a handful of major brewing companies devoted to speciality beers - though Guinness, of Ireland, is a far bigger example (with a beer whose "burnt", bitter, taste is almost equally shocking to the novice). Rodenbach is even more unusual in that its style of production requires special equipment. No other brewery anywhere in the world has anything like so many fixed oak tuns. Not only is Rodenbach Grand Cru a classic beer, the brewery should be regarded as a national treasure.

The Rodenbach family themselves had a colourful and distinguished history. They traced their roots to Andernach, on the Rhine, near Coblenz. In 1747 or 1750, during the rule of the Austrian Empire, Ferdinand Rodenbach came to the West Flanders town of Roeselare (in French, Roulers) as a military surgeon. He wrote scientific

Alexander was a great man... but was he sweet? His name has been given to a distinctive dessert beer.

147

papers on medicine (in German), became a local physician, and married a Flemish woman. In 1820, a member of the family, Alexander Rodenbach, bought a small brewery that already existed in the present site in Roeselare, at Spanjestraat. ("Spain Street" - the whole history of Belgium seems to be wrapped up in the brewery). In 1836, the brewery was sold to another member of the family, and this date was taken as the basis for Rodenbach's 150th birthday celebrations in 1986. Although by then no one with the name Rodenbach remained in the company, four descendant families were represented on the board.

The founder, Alexander Rodenbach, was the most remarkable character of all. He had been blinded in an accident at a fairground

Rodenbach's "St George" brewery takes its water from wells beneath this ornamental lake. In the background, the director's house... a beer château.

shooting gallery when he was 11, but this did not stop him laying the foundations of a great brewery, devising a rudimentary form of braille, becoming a politician, and taking part in the movement for Belgium's independence. Alexander's brother Constantine was ambassador to Greece, and is buried in front of the Parthenon. In the 1870s, Eugene Rodenbach went to England to study brewing techniques there. What he learned there, especially about blending, helped to perfect the Rodenbach method. No one knows in which English breweries he worked, but it is interesting to note that the production of Greene King Strong Suffolk also involves blending. Like the (Graham and Sir Hugh) Greenes of that brewery, the Rodenbachs are also a literary family. Georges Rodenbach wrote in French, and Albrecht - who is remembered in a statue in the town - in Flemish.

The tower of the malting at Rodenbach has been turned into a museum... the whole site should be regarded as a national treasure.

The Rodenbach brewery itself is like a great monument to the art of beer-making. On one side of the street, set into a couple of acres of garden wooded with pines, horse-chestnuts and weeping willows, is a 19-room château built in 1891 for the director of the brewery. The garden slopes away to a lake, about 30 metres in diameter, which is fed by 70 small wells. There are trout in the lake, and their well-being is a good indication of the purity of the well-water, which also serves the brewery.

Across the street, a 150-year-old maltings, a circular structure, the height of a four or five-storey building, with a conical tower, is the centre-piece of the brewery. The maltings no longer operates, and has been turned into a small but carefully-conceived museum. That project took two years, including the complete restoration of the tower.

The town of Roeselare is an inland port on an important canal across Flanders. It has historically been an important trading centre for agricultural produce in West Flanders, and has some interesting industrial archaeology. The people of the region are considered in Belgium to be hard-working and financially prudent.

What Alexander Rodenbach bought was the St George Brewery. Englishmen know George as their national saint, but he was also the inspiration of breweries in several countries (another of

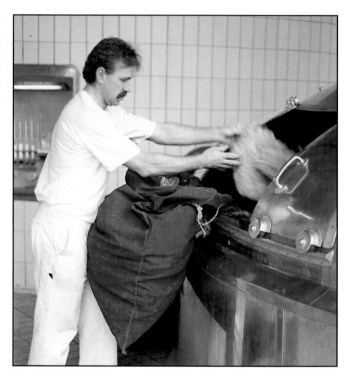

Hops being added to the brew in the kettle. The varieties are Brewers' Gold and Kent Goldings, but this is not intended to be a bitter beer.

my favourites is St Georgen-Brau, noted for its Kellerbier, in Franconia). Perhaps monks once made beer on these sites, though the convention of naming breweries after saints was itself widespread. At Rodenbach, a spectacular relief of St George slaying the dragon, dated from 1836, decorates the wall of the present-day malt silos, built in 1962. That faces across the brewery yard, to greet visitors. On one side of the yard is the brewhouse, which does not seem to have changed much since it was built and fitted in the 1920s and 1930s. The various levels are linked by three brass-railed stairways.

150

Rodenbach beers are made from four malts: one is pale malt made from summer barley; then there are two- and six-row varieties of winter barley malt; finally, there is a reddish, crystal-type malt of the style sometimes described by Continental Europeans as "Vienna". These malts comprise at least 80 per cent of the grist, and the rest is corn grits. A version of double decoction is used. The hops are mainly Brewers' Gold, with some Kent Goldings. These varieties have spicy characteristics, but are low in bitterness. Like all tart beers, the Rodenbach brews are not intended to be bitter. Tartness and bitterness do not meld well. It is, though, important that the hops help preserve and clarify the beer during its long period in wood.

The beer called simply Rodenbach is made by the classic old method of blending "young" and "old" brews. The young beer is brewed to a gravity of 11.4-11.5 Plato (1045-6). The beer intended for aging has 13.0 (1052).

When I first visited the brewery, it was using an open cooler and copper fermenting vessels, but these have now been superseded by more modern equipment. As brewing science has developed, so Rodenbach has looked more closely at its yeast, which has been in use for about 70 years. The first time I visited the brewery, I was told that the yeast, which is top-fermenting, contained three strains. By my next visit, five strains had been identified. Since then, the yeast has been more analytically examined, at the University of Leuven, and it is now considered to embrace 20 cultures.

The product may look like Burgundy, but the label could enwrap a Champagne. Rodenbach is light in hops, but the cone in the logo is perhaps a reminder that it is a beer.

Fermentation takes about a week, which is a conventional enough period for a top-fermenting brew, but it is in the subsequent maturation that Rodenbach's beers fully develop their character.

Seventy-five per cent of the blended product is young beer, though even this has five to six weeks of maturation, during which period it undergoes a secondary fermentation. This takes place in metal tanks.

After secondary fermentation, the beer intended for further maturation goes on to spend not less than 18 months, and sometimes well over two years, in wood. During this time, there is a third sequence of micro-biological activity, caused by lactobacilli and acetobacters. The lactic acid develops in the beer, and the acetobacters are resident in the wood. A degree of evaporation also has an influence on the character of the aging beer.

The wood, with its tannins and caramels, makes a direct contribution to the beer's palate and colour. I once expressed surprise that the wood would continue to impart character after constant employment, and it was explained to me that the inside of each tun was scraped after every use.

Would this not eventually result in the tuns being too thin to be safe, I asked? I was told that the walls of the tuns varied between five and ten centimetres in thickness, that each scraping would remove a fraction of a millimetre, and that even the most exhaustively used would have seen only 50 or so brews. The oldest vessel is 125 years old, and many have been in place since the earliest days of this century. When the brewery expanded at one stage, some were acquired from a competitor that was closing. They are variously made from oak from the Vosges and from Poland. The brewery has four coopers to maintain them, working with numbered staves, hoops, reeds and beeswax. The tuns make a remarkable sight: the smallest containing 120 hectolitres, and the largest fives times that size. One hall contains nearly a hundred, and there are twice that many arranged in ten smaller rooms. In the biggest hall, there are five lines of 20 tuns each, with narrow paths between them. The halls are heated if the ambient temperature falls below 15 °C (59 °F).

Although much of the matured beer is used in the blending of the regular Rodenbach, some is held back to be bottled "straight" as Grand Cru.

The regular Rodenbach is a complex, tasty, sweet-and-sour, refreshing beer, with suggestions of Madeira, passion-fruit, oakiness, and hints of iron. The Grand Cru is more assertive all round, very slightly bigger in body and darker in colour. Both beers are so tart that they are sweetened slightly with caramelised sugar before being bottled (and then stabilised by flash-pasteurisation). Neither is intended for laying-down, though they do have relatively good keeping qualities. Some of their admirers would welcome an unsweetened, unpasteurised, version, perhaps to a slightly higher gravity, with the age of the Grand Cru. Like several "old" beers, the Grand Cru has its own distinctive freshness - a paradox in brewing.

Although the whole point of these beers is their tartness, some drinkers sweeten them with a dash of Grenadine syrup. For its 150th anniversary, the brewery made a sweeter version named Alexander Rodenbach, after its founder. This blends some of the freshness of the Grand Cru with a cherry essence. The regular Rodenbach has an alcohol content of 3.7 by weight, 4.6 by volume. The Grand Cru and the Alexander have 4.1, 5.2. They are normally served in Belgium in the range of 8-12 °C (47-53 °F). Ideally, the quenching Rodenbach would be at the lower end of that scale and the winier Grand Cru and richer Alexander at the higher.

I have had some wonderful meals prepared and served with the Rodenbach range, not only in its native country but also prepared

Reeds used to repair cooperage are grown in the Lowlands of Flanders... another link with East Anglia.

153

by Belgian chefs in London and New York. In the beer's home town of Roeselare, the restaurant Den Haselt (19 Zuidstraat, tel. 22.52.40) makes a feature of using the proud local products.

At Den Haselt, I once had an elaborate Rodenbach meal that began with Aperitif Grand Cru (comprising 90 per cent beer, the rest being equal proportions of Amer Picon and Crème de Cassis). The appetisers included oysters marinated in Alexander, a cup of prawn soup made with Rodenbach, and rabbit pat in a cherry confiture flavoured with Alexander and honey. Then there was goose liver with apple, served with Rodenbach. This was followed by monkfish with celery, presented with Grand Cru. Then rabbit with langoustines, offered with Alexander. Finally came a sorbet made from Alexander, a custard flavoured with Rodenbach and a sabayon Grand Cru. On another occasion there, I was served a bread made with Grand Cru and almonds; ris de veau in a sauce made from Rodenbach, and a passion fruit meringue flavoured with Alexander.

The façade of the maltings, and the oast, at Rodenbach... captured by architect, artist and brewer Kris Herteleer. His sketches of breweries and cafés are a recurrent feature of the beer scene.

Rodenbach itself, with its light acidity, goes especially well - in my view - with shellfish dishes and salads; the heavier Grand Cru (with that hint of iron, as in a Cheval-Blanc) is a perfect accompaniment to liver, rabbit, and game birds like quail; Rodenbach Alexander is, of course, a natural dessert beer. The marriage of Rodenbach and prawns is so popular that people forget its original role as an everyday beer of its region. It survives as such in Roeselare, and the province of West Flanders is dotted with advertising signs for rival brews in the same style from other breweries. Unlike Rodenbach, none of these breweries makes only this style, but some do retain a number of wooden tuns for the purpose. Others use a lactic culture in metal vessels.

A good example of the style is Petrus, made by the De Brabandere brewery at Bavikhove, near Kortrijk. (This historic city, once known as the capital of the linen textile industry, is also the centre of a brewing region in the south-west of Flanders). The Bavik-De Brabandere brewery, which was founded in 1894,

Petrus proudly displays its wooden tuns on its label. A beer like this would stand up to the acidity of gherkins and tomatoes.

makes a point of its wooden tuns. Bavik Petrus, described as an old brown, but with a reddish colour, is made in the classic way. It is very aromatic, has a good balance of sweetness and sourness, and seems to develop complexity in the bottle. It has an alcohol content of 4.4w, 5.5v. The brewery also makes a Bavik white; an aromatic, malty, ale called Petrus Speciale; and a filtered, bronze-coloured, Petrus Triple, among other styles.

I have very much enjoyed Van-der Ghinste's Ouden Tripel, from the Bockor brewery, of Bellegem, also near Kortrijk. Again, this has been described as an old brown, but has a very good Burgundy colour. It is unusual in that 30 per cent of the grist is wheat (raw). The rest is a blend of pale and crystal malts. Otherwise, it is made in the classic way, again with maturation in oak. The beer is light and refreshing, with a good tartness and the iron-like notes that are an

The label of Bockor Ouden Tripel formerly described this beer as an Old Brown but it, too, has a Burgundy red.

essential component of this style at its best. It has an alcohol content of 4.8w, 6.0v. This beer is filtered, but not pasteurised. Other examples from the traditional region include Bacchus, from Van Honsebrouck, of Ingelmunster; Ichtegems Bruin, from Strubbe; and Paulus, from Leroy, of Boezinge. The Verhaege brewery, of Vichte, near Kortrijk, has over the years produced a number of beers in this style. These have included the very tart, acidic, Vichtenaar and a much sweeter type under the name Duchesse de Bourgogne.

At least two more of these reddish beers with names referring to Burgundy are produced outside West Flanders. Vlaamse Bourgogne is a drier type, from Bios, of Ertvelde, East Flanders. It is aged in metal tanks for two years or more, and not pasteurised. Bourgogne des Flandres, a brand-name that has existed since 1911, has its origins in Bruges. The name is owned by Michel van Houtryve, who has been in the brewing business for seven generations. Van Houtryve does not have his own brewery, and his smooth, rich, beer is a blend of elements from two sources, both in Brabant: a specially made dark ale from Palm, of Steenhuffel, and a Lambic from Timmermans, of Itterbeek.

SAISONS

The most endangered species among Belgian beers are the Saisons. These are an elusive speciality. They are produced especially in and around the western part of the province of Hainaut, and to some extent elsewhere in Wallonia. The breweries that make them are in most cases very small, old and artisanal, and several have closed in recent years. Some visibly show their origins as farms, and others speak of the small beginnings of the industrial revolution.

The breweries themselves are part of Europe's industrial archaeology, in a region of Belgium rich in such delights, especially in the nearby Borinage coalfield. Their beers are a classic style. They should be saved by the attention of the drinker - this could be a pleasurable form of conservation. One problem is that Saisons are little known outside their region, and scarcely at all in Flanders. Nor are they all as assertive in character as they were even a decade ago.

The making of Saisons was regarded as a distinctly Belgian technique by brewing scientists in the late 1800s and early 1900s.

"Wine" bottles are favoured for many Belgian speciality beers... but especially for the Saisons of Wallonia.

These beers were originally produced to a variety of strengths, including "children's", "family", "double" and "royal" (Regal), but they were especially associated with the summer season. The beer had to be strudy enough to last for the summer months, when brewing was impossible, but not too strong to be a harvest quencher.

High mashing temperatures were employed, to produce a substantial degree of un-fermentable sugars, and in some cases the wort was allowed to develop a degree of natural lactic acid before the boil. Or this may have happened afterwards, in the wort-cooling. Some breweries used the Baudelot system, in which the wort was exposed to the air, and any wild micro-organisms present, as it flowed over the outside of pipes containing cold water. Some of the beers gained acidity during maturation, usually in mild steel tanks. In some instances, the refreshing acidity was imparted by a blending of young and old beers.

Today's Saisons are often presented in corked Champagne bottles, with a secondary fermentation, and they can pour with a dense, rocky, head. They have a distinctively orangey colour and a refreshing carbonation and crispness (some are made with quite hard water, and the high mashing temperatures perhaps add to this characteristic). Their accent is toward fruitiness, often with citric notes; they are sometimes spiced, and in the past were often dry-hopped.

THE PRODUCERS

From Brussels, the main road south-west has scarcely passed Lembeek, and is still in the Zenne Valley, when there is a glimpse of the massive quarries at Quenast. The stone dug there was once used to make cobbled streets, and today provides ballast for the trans-European express railways. Its digging created a monumental thirst that could be slaked only by beer. There was a brewer called Lefèbvre in Quenast in 1797, at the time of the French Revolution. No one is sure whether he was a forbear of Jules Lefèbvre, gamekeeper, farmer, maltster, brewer and publican. When the men came to dig the stone, in the 1870s, Jules "The Keeper" built a new brewery, and established cafés at every exit to the quarries.

Dupont is a typical farmhouse brewery: Brasserie de Silly is a delightful country brewery, which exports to the U.S.

He prospered, and his son was able to build a baronial house, almost a château, next to the brewery, by the river Zenne. "At the end of the First World War, British troops were billeted here, to wait for the Peace of Versailles," I was told by a member of the family. "The officers were English and Scots; the men were Indians. They drank Scotch whisky and seemed happy, then they fell silent. There was an epidemic called Spanish Flu. They began to die. One went home for Christmas and never came back. My grandmother used to talk about this."

The house still stands, but only fragments of the brewery. After the First World War, the family bought another brewery, high on the side of the valley. It still operates, with a coal-fired kettle. Pierre Lefèbvre and his son Philippe, the fourth and fifth generations in the brewery, told me how the direction and intensity of the wind affects the fire under the kettle. If the fire is high, the hot spots on the surface of the kettle will caramelise the beer to a greater degree. The way the draughts

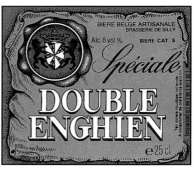

are manipulated will influence the flavour of the finished product. This truly is artisanal brewing. "We cannot put on the label a note to apologise for the lack of wind on the day this particular brew was made," Pierre observed to me wryly.

In the great days of the quarry, the brewery sold immense quantities of an ale named after the blue-grey, porphyritic stone. There are fewer workers today, the cafés have become private houses, and the men go home to watch television. A hint of the famous Porph Ale can be found in Saison 1900, the date of which recalls the height of production. This is a full-bodied Saison of 14 Plato (1056), 4.0w, 5.0v, hopped with Styrians and Saaz and very evidently spiced with ginger. The brewery also makes its white beer, and spicy products for the abbeys of Floreffe and Bonne Espérance. All of these beers have a secondary fermentation in the bottle.

Quenast is just in Brabant, but right on the border with Hainaut. Just across the border, near the town of Enghien (in Flemish, Edingen), is the village of Silly, which sounds perfectly sensible in French. This village, on the river Sille, grows sugar-beet and wheat. In the centre of the village is a café proclaiming the beers of the family Meynsbrughen (who seem to have fiddled with the spelling of their name over the years). Next door, behind a restored façade, is a cobbled yard that looks straight into the brewhouse. It is still very much an agricultural brewery.

Farmer Nicholas Meynsbrughen established the brewery in 1850, and his family still run it. All of its beers have a very soft fruitiness, reminiscent of nectarine. Its Saison de Silly (4.0w, 5.0v) also has a distinctive wineyness and tartness. This beer is made by the blending of a pale brew with a darker one that has been aged for about a year in a metal tank. Some devotees feel that Saison de Silly is the example most loyal to the tradition, though it does not have refermentation in the bottle. The brewery's other products include pale and dark versions of its maltier, stronger (6.4w, 8.0v) Double Enghien and a potent, smooth, spritzy bronze ale called La Divine (7.6w, 9.5v).

This area is noted for its loyalty to the local bières spéciales. "It's the Jeu de Balles that causes the thirst," I was told by the patron at Café Titien, in nearby Bassilly. He was talking about Pelotte, a game that appears in odd pockets and in various rather different forms, along the European seaboard from Friesland to the Basque country of Spain - and, as Jai-Lai, from Cuba to Florida to Connecticut. There was a league-table on the wall. The Jeu de Balles has also led to the practice of long-distance egg-throwing. In 1990, one of the locals threw an egg 63 metres, and it landed in The Guinness Book of Records.

Farther down the road, the municipality of Leuze has two breweries producing Saisons, in the villages of Pipaix (which also has Bush Beer) and Tourpes.

Saison de Pipaix can trace its history back to a farm brewery in the 1780s. The present brewery is still powered by an 1885 steam engine, its piston thumping and exhaling steam as, through a web of pulley-belts, it drives the mash-mixer and rakes. As the mash progresses, the open tun fills the room with steam. Some of the equipment dates from either side of the First World War, and some buildings from the period just after the Second. The brewery remained within one family until the mid 1980s, when the owner became ill and felt he could not continue.

Brasserie à Vapeur is a classic of industrial archaeology. The steam engine featured on the label still drives the brewery.

It was in a very dilapidated condition when it was rescued by two young schoolteachers who were already making beer at home. Jean-Louis Dits taught history, and felt strongly about the traditions of the region. He and his wife, Anne-Marie Lemaire had earlier started an association to promote local products.

Anne-Marie taught biology, which is a good basis for the science of fermentation.

They continued to teach, while putting the brewery back into operation and firing its kettle at weekends, once a month. They called it Brasserie à Vapeur - a true "Steam Brewery". The brewery had made a Saison at the time of its closure, and this was revived. Jean-Louis, working with two or three malts, allowed the mash to gain some lactic

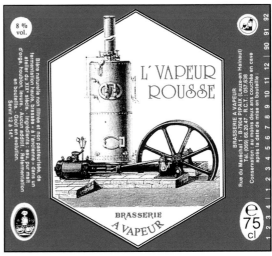

character before a long boil. He used Kent hops, matured the beers for several weeks in mild steel tanks, then bottled them without filtration.

The first time I visited them, they talked of the pleasure of "making something you like". Soon afterwards, I was horrified to hear that there had been an accident at the brewery, as a result of which Anne-Marie had died. Jean-Louis paid tribute to her in a book which produced to tell the story of the brewery. Their two daughters still help in the brewery, and one would like eventually to run it.

In recent years, Jean-Louis has re-married. His wife, Vinciane Corbisier, and her family have a shop supplying materials to small brewers, bakers, cheese-makers and cooks. When I visited them, Vinciane prepared a meat-loaf spiced with coriander, sweet orange peel and cloves. "Jean-Louis is crazy about spices," she laughed.

It sounds like an abbey beer, but Moinette is really a strong Saison.

He has become noted for his use of them. Saison de Pipaix, which has a very fresh, orangey, character contains six "botanicals", including anis, black pepper and a medicinal lichen. We sampled three or four vintages, including the first he ever made. At nearly ten years old, it had a huge orange aroma, a good head, a fine bead, and an almost abruptly dry, herbal, palate (5.2w, 6.5v). Like a cook trying new dishes, Jean-Louis makes a "special" almost every time he brews. Some of his beers contain ash leaves, an ingredient mentioned by the Bénédictine Abbess Hildegarde (1098-1179), whose writings on natural history contain the first definite reference to the use of hops in brewing. Hildegarde was Abbess of Rupertsberg, near Bingen, not far from Mainz, Germany. She did not tell us what ash leaves tasted like, but Jean-Louis reckons they are dry on the side of the tongue, and I agree.

A very round, smooth, beer called La Cochonne had chicory root among its botanicals; all of the beers are primed with fructose made from chicory, a very Belgian ingredient. Later that day, at the nearby Taverne Les Iris, we were served Saison de Pipaix with a magret de canard. The duck was served in a sauce made from the same beer, with cream and shallots. Further dishes were prepared with a variety of styles from the Brasserie à Vapeur, and with beers from the other two breweries in the area.

In his early days, Jean-Louis was greatly helped by the owner of the Dupont brewery. That brewery dates from 1850, and has been in the Dupont family since 1920.

The original Duponts' grandson, Marc Rosier, runs the brewery, and owns it with his two sisters. Immediately opposite is a delightfully basic local café, called Caves Dupont.

Dupont's beers are full of life, and notable for their hop character, with Kent Goldings to the fore. They have a big, rocky, creamy, head; a sharp, refreshing, attack; a restrained fruitiness; and a long, very dry, finish. Once again, I believe these products have lost a little character in recent years, especially since Dupont stopped dry-hopping... but they are still beautifully-balanced, complex, examples of truly artisanal brewing.

The range includes Saison Dupont, subtitled "Vieille Réserve"; an organic version of the same brew; and stronger pale and dark beers under the name Moinette. Mr. Rosier lives on a farm called Moinette. (In French, Moine means monk, and the farm is believed to be on what was once an abbey estate).

Between the hoppy, dry, Moinette Blonde and the perfumy, sweeter, Brune, is La Bière de Beloeil, dedicated to a nearby castle. There was once a brewery at Beloeil, producing a beer called Saison Roland. The Dupont brewery has also made a softer, fruitier, beer, with its grist comprising one third malted wheat, under the Latin name Cervisia. This is dedicated to a Gallo-Roman site in the area. The brewery is forever producing new specialities.

"Taste this," Mr. Rosier would suggest, every time I sought to probe the secrets of his beer. "In your view, just how should a Saison taste?" I would demand. "It must be a good, honest beer. It should have character. It is essential that it has soul," he would reply, with Gallic imprecision.

Du Bocq, of Purnode, in the province of Namur, makes a variety of styles. Its Saison Régal has for its strength (4.8 by weight, 6.0 by volume) a surprisingly light, but firm, body (it is very well attenuated), and a teasing balance between fruitiness and aromatic hoppiness. Similar beers are produced under the names La Bergeotte, Cuvée du P'tit Lu, La Houlette and Val d'Heure.

Like several of its neighbours, this brewery has more labels than beers, and that irritates purists, but no one would deny that it makes some tasty products.

Du Bocq, established in 1854, would have been a sizable brewery in its day. Its chunky, whitewashed buildings, in early industrial style, back on to a small garden that faces the village church. The whole arrangement peeps out of a steep hillside in a valley among the Ardennes. Opposite is the half-timbered house of the owning family. The hillside road winds toward the brewery, crosses another, and that is about the size of Purnode.

In the Belgian province of Luxembourg, Dany Prignon is a beer-lover who works for the local tourist office. Feeling that his area had too few gastronomic specialities (by the rich standards of the Ardennes in general), he started to make beer in Soy (Brasserie Fantôme, 8 Rue Preal) and helped establish a brew-pub in nearby Durbuy (La Ferme au Chêne, 115 Rue Comte d'Ursel) facing the river and Château at Durbuy.

Different beers are made at the two breweries, but their "house" character is to be yeasty and sweetish. Neither brewery has yet made a Saison in the classic style, but Fantôme has used the term

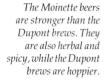

The Moinette beers are stronger than the Dupont brews. They are also herbal and spicy, while the Dupont brews are hoppier.

in a series of beers for summer, autumn, winter and spring. Perhaps a revival is in store.

Fantôme could represent the spirit of revival. It is reminiscent of a Saison, and the brewer has used several locally-grown herbs.

SEZOENS

Flanders has no counterpart to Saisons as a style, but it does produce one beer that is intended to serve the same purpose, and proclaims as much with graphic personifications of winter and summer on the label. Sezoens (pronounced s'zoon) is made by Martens, of Bocholt, in Belgian Limburg. It is a beer of outstanding character and individuality, and its name is, of course, a protected trademark.

It is a bright, golden, top-fermenting beer of remarkable hop character, especially in its palate. It has the taste of fresh hops, wonderfully flowery and lingering. Sezoens is very refreshing, but even better as an aperitif.

I had in the past understood the hop varieties to be Northern Brewer, from Germany, and Saaz. On my most recent visit, I was told that Sezoens was being hopped entirely with Tettnangers, from Germany, but the choice of variety is only part of the story. Sezoens is dry-hopped, not once but twice. That two-handed approach is most unusual. The first dry-hopping is at the beginning of maturation, which is for two to three months, at 0 °C (32 °F). The second dose of hops is two to three weeks before maturation ends. The beer is filtered. Sezoens has a gravity of 12.5-13.5 Plato (1050-54) and an alcohol content of 4.8 by weight, 6.0 by volume. It is very well attenuated. The result is a light, very firm, body; a clean, dry palate; a restrained fruitiness; and that hoppy dryness. There is so much hop flavour that I was astonished to see an analysis rating the bitterness at only 30 units.

The branded glass chosen by Martens for Sezoens resembles a brandy-snifter, but the beer is more of an aperitif.

The brewery first made a seasonal beer in 1860, and at that time it was presumably unfiltered. Sezoens evolved, and has for many years been well known as a filtered brew. This "modern" version found itself being identified as Classic when the brewery recently added a bottle-conditioned alternative. The filtered Classic has its cleanness and firmness; the version with re-fermentation in the bottle is softer, fruitier and spicier. Although they are the same brew, they emerge almost as two products in their own right, and show just what a difference bottle-conditioning makes. In 1989, the brewery launched an amber-red counterpart called Sezoens Quattro. This odd name is intended to suggest The Four Seasons. Again,

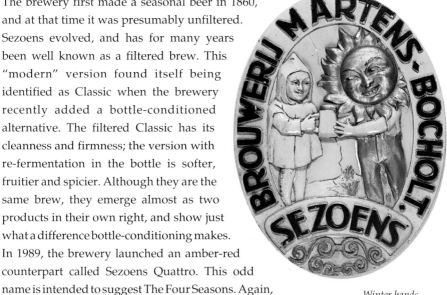

Winter hands over to summer in the charming graphic that has been used on Sezoens labels old and new.

it is a very distinctive beer, with a faintly coffee-ish start; then a clean fruitiness; and finally a quite intense and lingering hoppy dryness. This is a beer with a lot of flavour development. It is well-hopped in the kettle, but there is no further addition during maturation. Less of a refresher, but even more of an appetite-arouser. I have seen it categorised as being in the German Altbier style, but it reminds me more of the beer world's answer to an Italian aperitif.

I once had a memorable meal in which goose-liver pat was served with Quattro; plaice prepared and offered with Martens' Pils; rabbit casseroled in Quattro; and warm cheese pancakes flavoured with Sezoens. This was in Martens' home-town.

The Martens brewery, founded in 1758, has expanded considerably in recent years. It is a very modern brewery, but it also has an astonishing museum on the premises. This collection of discarded equipment was garnered from every great beer-making nation. Each room is devoted to a different stage of the beer-making process, so that the visitor can trace the history of mashing systems, brew kettles, or whatever. Its appreciation requires a serious interest in brewing, but for the enthusiast it is a remarkable sight.

The brewery is open by appointment only (Brouwerij Martens Museum, Reppelerweg 1, B-3950 Bocholt - Belgium; tel. 011-42.29.80).

Martens' astonishing museum faces on to the brewery yard, and just keeps expanding. Museum and brewery are beautifully kept.

For the connoisseur who is more concerned about the end product, Sezoens is the speciality of De Ultieme Hallucinatie, in Brussels (see Drinking Beer in Style).

BELGIAN ALES

Almost all Belgian speciality brews are top-fermenting. In that broad sense, they might all be regarded by an English-speaker as ales, and they are sometimes labelled in this way in export markets. Belgium does, though, have some brews that are instantly recognisable as ales in the more specific sense of the word.

In the Belgian market, some of these have no specific indication of style on the label. Others, even in a country that speaks Flemish, French and German, do use the English word ale.

These are brews of a conventional gravity (usually around 12 Plato, 1048) and strength (about 4.0 by weight, 5.0 by volume), made exclusively or primarily from barley malt (rather than wheat or any less usual grain), seasoned with hops (and not necessarily herbs or spices), fermented with a top yeast, and matured without the use of wood or any other special technique.

An array of ales... relatively conventional by Belgian standards, but some are outstanding brews.

They are amber-red or copper in colour, and usually served filtered. In the European system of units of colour, most are in the 15-25 range; in bitterness, 19-30. They sound ordinary, but some are outstanding brews that no beer-lover would readily miss.

It could be argued that there are four regions of the world where copper-coloured ales of conventional strength are widely made, and that each has a different emphasis of style. Copper-coloured ales in the United States (especially the West Coast) tend to be very aromatic (some American varieties of hop have a minty, perfumy, citric, bouquet); the "Pale" Ale of Britain has more hop bitterness (hence the use of the term Bitter); the Belgian examples are yeasty, spicy-tasting and soft; and the Germans, as typified by Düsseldorf Altbier, are maltier and smoother.

All of these interpretations have sufficient taste to savour, and to demand a second glass, or even a third. Ale is in that respect a sociable style of brew. It is dry enough to be appetite-arousing, yet neither too strong nor too filling for a glass before lunch or dinner.

THE ALES OF ANTWERP

A classic Belgian example, from the city of Antwerp, is De Koninck. That is the name of the brewery and its sole product. The brew is identified simply as De Koninck, without the word "ale". It is the local brew of Antwerp, and widely consumed there as an everyday drink. No other city in Belgium has quite such a familiar relationship with what might elsewhere be regarded as a speciality brew.

In a hotel in Antwerp in the mid 1970s, I inquired where was the nearest spot to be sure of a draught De Koninck. Hotels scarcely ever feature a local beer in their own bars (preferring to offer some less characterful international brand that the guest could have found without leaving home). This was no different, but the lady on reception was clearly pleased to have been asked. "Our famous Antwerp beer... even an Englishman knows it!" she beamed.

The much-loved Bolleke... more masculine than the flute. In Antwerp, take care with your sexual allusions.

The place where she sent me - a tiny, tiled, café on a street corner - had such appetisingly fresh De Koninck that I lost a day there and have never been able to find it again. The visitor who is not quite so feckless should secure a fresh De Koninck among the student drinkers, the mirrors and marble-topped tables at Café Den Engel, on the Grote Markt. Or in the quieter comfort of the city's oldest café, Quinten Matsijs, at 17 Moriaanstraat (corner Hoofdkerkstraat). The café dates from 1565, and is perhaps just a little too well-kept. At Quinten Matsijs, it is possible to play a game called Ton, involving the throwing of discs into holes, on equipment that is 300 years old. If the De Koninck arouses an appetite, there is Gezoden Worst (Antwerp's local pork sausage), and Beuling (black or white puddings). Temptation lurks in every corner. The café even offers a ticket on which glasses of De Koninck are recorded. Buy ten and you get the next one free. Ten? It is a perilously drinkable brew.

I once asked at De Koninck why the brewery had stuck with ale when so many of its rivals had switched to Pilsener-style lagers in the 1920s. Perhaps more interesting, why had it not added a lager at a later stage? "I don't know. Maybe we could never afford it," mused Modeste van den Bogaert, the imposing figure who runs the brewery with his family.

The brewery was founded in 1833, and was originally attached to a beer-garden. It is on the edge of the present downtown area, on a site that was once just outside the city walls. The brewhouse sits amid whitewashed brick buildings set round a courtyard. One, with the appearance of a traditional malt barn, forms the facade of the street.

The beer is made only from malt, with no adjunct of maize or other brewing sugars. The malts are a blend of Vienna and Pilsener types. The hops are all Saaz, mainly grown in the Czech Republic but some from Belgium. The gravity is 11.8 Plato (1047). The hops are added three times to the bricked-in brew-kettle. Most traditional breweries then run the brew through a sieve to remove the "spent" hops. De Koninck's is an especially impressive device which is moved through the

The handsome face of the De Koninck brewery. Take a long, admiring, look... then pop across the road to De Pilgrim for a taste of the product.

brewhouse on a pulley-and-girder system. Such quirks do not in themselves make better beer, but they belong in breweries that have their own individuality and personality.

In 1981, I asked Mr van den Bogaert how long the brewery had used the same yeast. "About 15 years," he said. I should have consulted my notes before visiting the brewery again in 1990, but I didn't. I asked the same question... and got the same answer.

Was the yeast a single-cell pure culture, I asked? "I wouldn't swear to it," replied Mr van den Bogaert, enigmatically. I believe it is, in-

The imposing figure with a beer to match... Modeste van den Bogaert, with a De Koninck. The shot of yeast adds that extra flavour.

deed, a pure culture, though it certainly has plenty of character. Many breweries have had their yeast longer than they can remember. All cultures adapt to their habitat, so every brewery's yeast to some degree develops its own character. Only in recent years have brewers begun to appreciate just how important their yeasts are to the background flavour of their beers. I would say the De Koninck yeast is very important indeed. It imparts a highly distinctive, and delicious, character. Perhaps Mr van den Bogaert does not wish to be too analytical about his yeast: it is like trying to establish why a joke is funny, or how two people come to love each other.

Gift-boxes made from wood are another popular presentation in Belgium. This one contains the soft, spicy-tasting Cuvée Antwerpen 93.

The De Koninck beer spends seven to eight days in primary fermentation (up to 25 °C, 77 °F) and cooling, then has about two weeks' cold conditioning. All of the beer is filtered, but only the bottled product is pasteurised. The finished product has 4.0 per cent alcohol by weight, 5.0 by volume.

De Koninck has a dense, rocky,

head that leaves lacework with every swallow. It is a subtle, soft, ale, with a very elusive fruitiness and spiciness, and a beautiful balance. It begins with maltiness, lightly toasty; then comes the yeasty fruit and spice (one taster was reminded of cinnamon); and finally a most delicate Saaz hop character in the finish.

Many beers taste best on draught, and I feel this is certainly true in the case of De Koninck. For the drinker willing to track the source, the best place to sample it is the café Pelgrim (which may be closed on Sundays), opposite the brewery, at 8 Boomgaardstraat (corner Mechelsesteenweg), Berchem; tel. 218.91.30. This is very much a traditional café, with dark wood dadoes, and sporting trophies on display.

For as long as anyone can remember, the brewery has supplied buckets of surplus yeast from its fermenting hall to the café, where it is served in shot-glasses. Some old people like to drink it "straight" as a tonic. Others tip it into their beer. It looks like milky coffee, and seems to add a bitter, espresso-like, taste. Several other cafés have taken up the practice. Because De Koninck's yeast makes such a magical contribution, there is something especially celebratory about this ritual.

Rustic brewery in the province of Antwerp... open mash-tun at Sterkens.

Other beers have their own glasses - in Belgium, almost every one does - but there is also a special ritual to the serving of

Antwerp's other "Pilgrim" also serves De Koninck... and its restaurant De Grote Gans ("The Big Goose") is known for its beef dishes.

De Koninck. Over the years, the beer has been presented in a number of glasses, but the two most common are a flute and a goblet. Each has its own lore.

The flute, which holds 25 centilitres, is thought suitable only for women. It is ordered in Flemish as a Fluitje, a word that has phallic connotations. A woman announcing that she would like a Fluitje is likely to be greeted with mirth. Fluitje rhymes, more or less, with flout. The -je diminutive adds a "yuh" sound.

The goblet is known as a Bolleke, which is a diminutive of "ball". Bolleke is pronounced boll-uh-kuh, which to an Englishman sounds awkwardly like a colloquialism for a testicle. Antwerpenaars have no such inhibitions, and know that - in their city, at least - this call will bring forth a man-sized glass of De Koninck (which translates as "The King").

After years of renown as a brewery that made only one product, De Koninck launched a second to celebrate Antwerp's year as Europe 's City of Culture, in 1993: a stronger ale, of 6.0w, 7.5v,

175

called Cuvée Antwerpen 93. As a special edition, this was presented in a silk-screened bottle, and served in a new, small, goblet called Prinske. It quickly proved so popular that it may become a permanent offering. Cuvée Antwerpen 93 is slightly darker and redder than the regular De Koninck, and has a distinctively soft, deep, fruity, spicy, character, with a slight suggestion of licorice. It embraces a powerful counterpoint of sweetness and hoppy bitterness, and has a warming touch of alcohol in the finish. The beer is filtered and pasteurised, but invites speculation as to how it would perform with secondary fermentation in the bottle.

In the same year, two ales were launched to celebrate Antwerp as the home of the great painter Peter Paul Rubens (1577-1640). The organisers of the "Rubens' City" commemoration commissioned Jef Keersmaekers, a member of a distinguished brewing family, to create beers bearing the image of Rubens. A heavily sedimented, yeasty, fruity, orangey, dry, Rubens Rood ("red") was produced for Keersmaekers by Brasserie Du Bocq, in Purnode, Namur; and a light but firm-bodied, dry, hoppy, filtered Rubens Goud ("gold") by Maes, of Waarloos, Antwerp.

Rubens Gold is an ale, but the Red is a hybrid. A wheat beer to be dressed in orange?

The red is unusual in that half of its grist is wheat, the remainder being divided between pale and crystal barley malts. Is it a wheaty ale, or a "red" wheat beer? It is hopped with aroma varieties and lightly spiced with orange-peels and coriander. It has a secondary fermentation in the bottle, and has an alcohol content of 3.4w, 4.0v. The gold is produced from spring and aromatic malts, and hopped with Hallertau and Saaz, and has the same alochol content.

The city has only the one brewery, but the province of Antwerp has several. Another noted for its ale is Sterkens, in the village of Meer, in the flat farmlands in the far north of the province of Antwerp, near the border with The Netherlands.

The Sterkens family records in Meer go back to 1654, and there is evidence of a brewery - on the same site - since 1731. At the brewery, I was shown the diary of the great-grandfather of the present principal. One entry, in 1868, read: "The Guild of

Bowmen drank six and three-quarter barrels and eight pints. Price: 100 Belgian Francs and 98 cents." Another recalled: "The doctor bought a quarter-barrel." A month later, the entry was repeated, and again in another four weeks. The doctor seemed to get through a quarter of a barrel each month. That works out at a litre a day, which does not sound excessive. The priest, on the other hand, bought half-barrels, though of a weaker beer, and seemed to have difficulty making them last a month. He paid at the end of the year.

At the opposite end of the province, the south, the historic town of Mechelen (in French, Malines) has a rich brewing history (see Regional Specialities). One of its products is Horse Ale, made by Lamot, better known as a lager brewery. Lamot is part of Interbrew, and there is in the long term uncertainty about the future of this brewery.

Horse Ale has a "warm", soft-fruit, aroma; a distinctively creamy body; and lots of depth of flavour, with rich fruitiness, malty-spicy notes and hoppy aromatics. It is unusual among brews in this category in that it is spiced (Licorice? Grains of Paradise?). It also has a very distinctive hop character. The hop varieties are Belgian-grown Northern Brewer and Styrian Goldings, the latter added to the kettle at a very late stage for their contribution to aromatics.

Equine Ale Number One: from the town of Mechelen, in the province of Antwerp. This is a distinctively spicy product.

A few miles to the west is the Moortgat brewery, at Breendonk. This brewery is best known for its Duvel (see Strong Golden Ales) and Maredsous (see Abbey Beers), but it also has an ale, called Godefroy. This has a rocky head, which is very well sustained, a soft body, and a very definite soft-fruit character in its palate. A suggestion of apricot, perhaps? It is a very complex ale, with a good hop character, and is bottle-conditioned.

A mile or two further south, across the provincial boundary and into Brabant, is a cluster of specialist ale breweries...

Farmhouse turned café... "t Spinnewiel' ('The Spinning Wheel'), at Itegem, in the countryside near Antwerp. The bar will be full when the Sunday strollers are ready for a restorative beer.

The ales of Brabant

There is something of an ale-brewing district, and a strong local following for the style, in the far north-western corner of Brabant. Palm is the name of both a brewery, in the village of Steenhuffel, and its principal product. There has been brewing in Steenhuffel since at least 1597, and the present company traces its origins to 1747. Today, the brewery is the biggest employer in the village, which has a population of about 1,000. The brewery buildings account for about half the village. Palm has three brewhouses, one built in the 1920s, another in the 1970s, the latest in 1990. All of them are fitted with traditional copper kettles. The company uses relatively traditional methods (double decoction, for example) but is very proud of its high-tech quality-control.

Equine Ale Number Two: Brabant horses are the trade-mark of the Palm brewery. The name of the ale itself derives from the palm as a symbol of triumph.

Aerts was originally a Brussels brewery. The "1900" is meant to indicate a turn-of-the-century style.

The trademark Palm, as an emblem of victory, was introduced in the 1920s. In Belgium, the full name of the ale is Speciale Palm. It has been marketed in the United States as Palm Ale.

Either way, Palm has a very fresh, clean, well-rounded character. It has a decidedly toasty malt aroma; a fruity, bitter-orange palate; and a tart, refreshing, finish. This beer has a gravity of 13.2 Plato (1053) and an alcohol content of 4.1 by weight, 5.2 by volume. A stronger version called Dobbel Palm (13.9, 1056, 4.4, 5.5) is produced for Christmas, and sold at the same price.

The two Palm ales also have sister products under the name Aerts. These are drier and hoppier, and made with a different yeast. Speciale Aerts is a little lower in gravity and alcohol, at 12.3, 1049, 3.9, 4.8. Its stronger (17.5, 1070, 5.9, 7.4) manifestation, Aerts 1900, is dry-hopped and bottle-conditioned. Aerts 1900 is not the best-known of Belgian ales, but is a very well-made and distinctive brew. Its hop character seems to grow as a glass is enjoyed. This product is intended to be in the style of an ale from the turn of the century, hence the soubriquet 1900. Aerts was the family name of the owners of a now-defunct brewery in Brussels where these ales were first made.

The Palm brewery also produces a Pilsener-style lager, under the inappropriate name of Bock, but this represents only a small proportion of its output. The brewery's symbol is not a palm but a Brabant horse.

The De Smedt brewery was founded by the family of that name in 1832. The family still runs the brewery, which is in the small town of Opwijk. The town gives its name to the principal product, Op-Ale. There is also a pun in the name, as the word Op in Flemish means "up" (as in "drink up").

The brewery, set round a small garden of acacias and box trees, is old but well run, and the beers are made with a great deal of personal care. The brewhouse dates from the 1950s. In its Op-Ale, the brewery uses three malts, English (Challenger) and Styrian hops, and a yeast brought from Britain just after the Second World War.

Op-Ale has a dense head; a very soft body; a light, dry, fruitiness; and a good clean hop bitterness in the finish. The fruitiness and hop bitterness seem to develop especially well during the warm conditioning at the brewery. The brewery also produces a number of ranges of abbey beers, including Affligem, Aulne and Brogne.

Equine Ale Number Three? Perhaps. Op-Ale remembers its dray-horses on its label.

The western part of Brabant was a very early industrial area, and from the late 1800s until the 1930s, the Ginder Ale brewery at Merchtem was the biggest in Belgium. The brand has nothing to do with ginger ale; it derives from the family name Van Ginderachter.

Ginder Ale has a thick, fluffy, head; a notably fresh, hoppy, and assertively fruity, aroma; a firm body; soft fruit and syrupy notes in a very complex palate; and a gentle, restful, finish. The hops include Kent Goldings, Styrians and Lublins, from Poland, the last perhaps producing the distinctive freshness in the aroma. Or that may derive from the very characterful, estery, yeast used.

It is to be hoped that the individuality of the beer does not diminish now that Merchtem has closed and production been shifted to Interbrew in Leuven.

No, it is not Ginger Ale... that really is a "d". The name comes from a past owner of the brewery.

When the Flemish magazine "Uit" ran a blindfold tasting of ales, Ginder came top among the famous examples, but even it was overtaken by the lesser-known (but stronger, at 5.5) Speciale Stop (a rather negative name?), from Bavik, in West Flanders. Speciale Stop was complimented on its good bead, fruitiness, exemplary bitterness and length.

THE ALES OF WALLONIA

When Pilsener-style lager beers began to spread westward and northward through Europe, the Belgians sometimes responded by designating their own top-fermenting ales as a traditional national style. In the French-speaking part of the country, the simple term "Belges" was sometimes used to identify ales. Or Spéciales Belges. These ales were especially popular in the big industrial cities on the Belgian-French border, notably Charleroi. These terms are still often seen on beer-lists in cafés, and they indicate ales. Although many small breweries in Wallonia continue to produce Spéciales, only one "French-speaking" ale is widely known.

This product comes from the local brewery in the hilly village of Mont-St-Guibert, between Namur and Brussels. The brewery was once known for a bottle-conditioned ale. When it tried to replicate the character of this product in a filtered ale, it sought to sustain the sense of tradition with the brand-name Vieux Temps ("Old Times"). This is the biggest-selling ale in French-speaking Belgium.

Names like "Old Times" worry marketing men in search of eternal youth. The label had a facelift in the early 1990s.

Vieux Temps has a distinctively yeasty fruitiness in its aroma and palate. There is perhaps a suggestion of sweet plums. In palate, it starts sweet, rounds out, then becomes a little drier. It has a sherberty, refreshing, finish. It is an all-malt beer. The hops are the British variety Target and Pride of Ringwood, from Australia.

The brewery was founded in 1858, and Vieux Temps was launched in 1935. The founding family sold the brewery in 1970 to Artois, but remained in the management. It now operates as part of Interbrew.

182

THE BRITISH-STYLE ALES

Although all of these Belgian brews are a part of the country's own tradition, those that adopted the English designation "ale" were inspired to do so by the success of British products in Belgium. Despite having such an astonishing selection of their own brews, the Belgians have over the years found room for products from neighbouring countries, too.

In the course of two world wars, English and Scottish ales and Irish stout became well-known in Belgium. They were once very fashionable, and can still be found. Some are produced by Belgian brewers but given British-sounding names. Others are made in Belgium under licence from British brewers. Some are imported. The most famous importer was John Martin, an Englishman who settled in Belgium in 1909. His imports included Pale Ales from Bass, and later Courage. For many years, Courage marketed in Britain an ale called Bulldog that had been created for John Martin in Belgium. It was known in John Martin's Pale Ale in Belgium. Courage still has Bulldog, but John Martin's Pale Ale is now made in Belgium by Palm. Both are good products, but I definitely prefer the Belgian. When fresh, and especially on draught, it has a hop character, in both aroma and palate, that would be hard to match anywhere.

John Martin was English, but the Anglophone term "pale ale" has been dropped from his label.

Because the average strength of beer is higher in Belgium than in Britain, some English and Scottish products have more alcohol in their imported version than they would in their native countries. In some instances, a strong ale exclusively for the Belgian market, and with its own brand-name, is made by a British brewer.

The Belgians are especially fond of the most traditional type of Scotch Ale: strong (5.2-7.2 by weight; 6.5-9.0 by volume), dark, and very malty. Extra-strong versions of these ales are also marketed as Christmas specials (although the Scots themselves traditionally preferred to celebrate New Year).

Beautiful glasses shaped like the thistle are used to represent "Scotch" ales in Belgium...

Belgium is lucky to have a fine example called Gordon's Scotch Ale, brewed in Edinburgh. While this product is readily available in Belgium (and in France, under the name Douglas Scotch Ale), it is not marketed in its own country. The producers, Scottish and Newcastle Breweries, consider it too strong and expensive for their own local market.

Belgium's brewing industry should take a warning from such myopia. Scotland was once one of Europe's greatest brewing nations, but the arrogance of the people who have managed the industry over the decades, and their failure to appreciate the value of its traditions, have reduced it to a shadow.

MONASTIC BEERS

Five abbeys in Belgium make beer. All are monasteries (that is to say: male, closed, communities). All are of the Trappist Order. They are Orval, Chimay, Rochefort, Westvleteren and Westmalle. Each has its own brewery, within the abbey. There is a further Trappist brewery, called Schaapskooi, just across the border in Dutch Brabant, near the town of Tilburg, at the Koningshoeven monastery. These are the only Trappist breweries in the world. They are also the only breweries entitled to use the appellation Trappist Abbey Beer. Or simply Trappist Beer. Their beers are, of course, also each labelled with the name of the individual abbey. These products are of great interest, and I regard three or four of them as world classics. Without doubt I would accord this soubriquet to Orval, Chimay Grande Réserve and Westmalle Tripel, and others are in contention.

Orval has only one beer, albeit highly distinctive. The others each have a range of two or three, perhaps with the odd further special bottling. Taking into account these special bottlings, the

This brewhouse at Westvleteren has been replaced by something more modern. The brewhouse at Rochefort is shown on the previous page.

186

six Trappist monasteries together have between a dozen and 20 different beers.

Some are dry, like Orval's sole entrant and one of the Chimay range, but most are relatively sweet; most are dark; one or two are golden, such as Westmalle Tripel. For all their differences, they have certain features in common: all are, to varying degrees, strong; all are top-fermenting; all have a second, or third, fermentation in the bottle; and all are fruity. Several, though not all, are made with a proportion of dark candy-sugar in the brew-kettle, and have the distinctively rummy taste that imparts.

In theory, any style of brew produced in one of these six monasteries could be called Trappist Beer. In practice, the Trappists have produced, if not a single style, certainly a recognisable family of beers. This is a major contribution to the world's pantheon of beer-styles, but the Trappists hesitate to take credit for it. Their worry is that, if Trappist Beer is regarded as a style, other breweries might feel free to use the term. ("This is our Trappist Beer, this is our ale, and this our Pilsener...").

The Trappists use the profits from their breweries to fund their monasteries and their work. Inspired by the success of the Trappist brews, several Belgian monasteries or abbeys of other Orders have sought to have their own beers, with similar characteristics. These monasteries may have had breweries in the past. They licence their names to conventional commercial breweries, who produce a range of beers on their behalf. These brews, of course, cannot be labelled Trappist, but they are identified by the less specific term Abbey Beer. There are also commercial breweries that produce "Abbey" beers named after a former monastery, church, or local saint.

The Trappists have their world classics, but several of the Abbey beers are very good brews. Each Trappist brewery is proud of its own beers, and some rather fiercely so, but their bigger concern is that the public should distinguish between those products that are made in monasteries and those which, despite their Abbey names, are not.

BEER AND THE RULE OF ST BENEDICT

People, especially in Protestant countries, often express surprise when I mention beers made by monks. Surely the monastic life of self-denial cannot include beer? When I hear this question, I am surprised, for my part, that it should be asked. No one seems to consider it odd that monks make liqueurs like Chartreuse, give their name to Bénédictine, and have their own wines. Why on earth should they not have beer?

The links between monks and alcoholic drinks are several. In the days when the only travellers were pilgrims (or crusaders), the only hotels were abbeys. Naturally, the guests had to be offered a drink with their meals. In a southern European abbey, the drink would be wine, probably grown by the monks; in the north, it would be beer. In any great house, a brewery was as important as a bakery and a kitchen. Water was often unsafe, but no one was poisoned by drinking beer (nor is anyone today).

This cheery monk was photographed at Westvleteren... could any advertising artist have painted a more telling picture?

Although it was not realised at the time, beer was safe because the brewing water is boiled.

In the days before universal education, the church was a central instrument of learning, and abbeys were havens of study. In a more contemporary moment, a novice monk once excused himself from sharing another beer with me, because he had to complete an essay on Schopenhauer.

In earlier times, the pursuit of medicine, the growing of herbs, the study of fermentation and distillation, were all monastic activities. Several monks made important contributions to brewing science. In more recent times, the production of beer has been a means by which an abbey can support itself. There are famous abbeys that produce cheese, wine, bread, or sweets like nougat.

Life for the brewing monks at Westvleteren has become a little more mechanised since this picture was taken.

In Belgium, the Trappist nuns of Klaarland make yeast tonic tablets. There are other Trappist abbeys in Belgium that grow fruit or vegetables, run chicken farms, or make soap.

Self-sufficiency has been central to the calling since the first holy men retreated to caves, or hermitages, inspired by Christ's contemplation in the wilderness. Modern monasticism began with St Benedict (480-547), and his rule "live from the work of your hands" is one of the foundations of every abbey. St Benedict's own community, at Monte Cassino, in southern Italy, no doubt served wine to its guests, but as monasticism spread, the abbeys that were established further north began to brew beer.

The missionary monk St Columba mentions beer in his rule, which was drawn up in the early 600s. In the 800s, there were no fewer than three brewhouses in the important abbey of St Gallen, not far from Zurich. According to the preserved plan, one brewhouse made beer for the abbey community, another for guests, and a third for pilgrims. St Gallen today has more breweries than any other canton in Switzerland. Austria still has two abbey breweries. One is run by Norbertine brothers;

the other owned by Augustine monks but operated by a secular company.

In the German-speaking world, an abbey is called a Stift (meaning "seminary" or "convent"), or a Kloster ("cloister"). One of these words on a label may indicate that the beer is still made in an abbey - or simply that it was in the past. The abbey breweries in the German-speaking world often have a strong, dark lager as a speciality, but there is no real sense there of a distinct monastic style or family of beers.

Even breweries that still bottle by hand (as some do), have more comfortable arrangements than this.

In Germany itself, but all within the Catholic state of Bavaria, there are half a dozen abbey breweries still run by Benedictine and Franciscan monks (or, in two cases, nuns) and a further two or three that are owned by Orders but leased to commercial operators. There are also in Bavaria several former abbey breweries that are no longer run by religious Orders. Companies like Augustiner, Spaten-Franziskaner and Paulaner, all in Munich, bear testimony to their origins. The name Munich itself, of course, derives from the German word for "monks". The city's monastic history and its growth as a brewing centre are intertwined, and there are similar stories throughout Europe.

In the early part of this millenium, some monks began to feel that the rule of St Benedict was being followed with insufficient rigour. A stricter community was founded at Cîteaux, in Burgundy. The community of Cîteaux became known as the Cistercians. Later, even they came to be regarded by some monks as being too liberal, and a yet more rigorous Order was founded at La Trappe, in Normandy. Thus was born the Order that was to become so influential in brewing.

During the Napoleonic period, many abbeys were sacked. Afterwards, some Trappist monks left France and went north to found communities in Belgium and The Netherlands. In their new homelands, they made the drink of the country: beer.

It is perhaps because they are the strictest of Orders, and therefore the most enclosed, that the Trappists have so effectively retained their tradition of brewing. They are also the strictest adherents to the rule of living off their own land and resources, and these guidelines have no doubt helped to sustain their breweries where other Orders have allowed the craft to die.

With the growth of national brewers, the monasteries have had to become more efficient if they are to compete. This has meant that the monks have over the years enlisted secular workers in the breweries. With hourly calls to prayer or other observances, and a requirement to study, a monk cannot also run a brewery to modern working schedules. It is no longer a matter of fitting in the brewing of beer as though it were the occasional making of jam or pickles.

In every case, a monk still has overall responsibility for the brewery. In some abbeys, there is still a monk as head brewer. In others, monks or novices help on a part-time basis.

Although the Trappist order is silent, monks are allowed to speak when their work requires it. This is a far greater limitation than it may seem. "There is never any time when we can talk

Filling and despatching was no easy observance, either.

191

freely to one another," a monk once told me, taking advantage of his permission to speak to me as a guest. When I stayed in a monastery myself for a few days, I was conscious even of the rattle of the wire coat-hangers as I hung up my clothes at night. I felt as though I was disturbing the whole community.

TRAPPIST BREWERIES OF BELGIUM

ORVAL

The name derives from "Valley of Gold". Legend has it variously that a beautiful princess, or countess, from Tuscany, lost a golden ring in a lake in the valley and said that if God ever returned it to her, she would thank him by building a monastery. When a trout rose from the lake with a ring in its mouth, the princess was as good as her promise.

The first abbey of Orval was founded in 1070 by Benedictines from Calabria, and rebuilt in the 12th century by early Cistercians from Champagne. It was burnt down soon afterwards, rebuilt, then sacked in the conflicts of the 17th century, leaving most of the ruins that stand today. The abbey was restored, and there are records of brewing having taken place in the 18th century, but Orval was then destroyed in the French Revolution. The present abbey is the most visually dramatic of the Trappist monasteries. Its purity of line subsumes Romanesque-Burgundian influences in a design of the late 1920s and 1930s. The visual impact of the buildings is, to beer-lovers, matched by the power of the goût d'Orval.

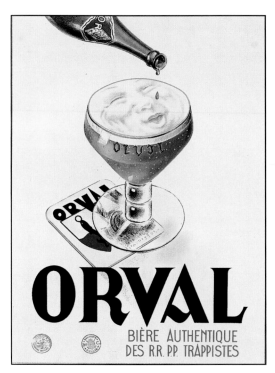

ORVAL

BIÈRE AUTHENTIQUE
DES R.R. P.P. TRAPPISTES

The styles of the 1920s and 1930s have influenced Orval's advertising over the years, and are evident in its architecture (previous page).

The abbey's full name is Notre-Dame d'Orval, though that is seldom used. It stands alone in its valley in the Ardennes, on a bend in the road on the old route from Trier to Rheims, not far from the small town of Florenville, in the Belgian province of Luxembourg.

The address is Villers-devant-Orval, but the hamlet comprises little more than the ruins and the present abbey, a baronical castle, a small hotel, an inn and a post-office.

The abbey's principal buildings overlook an ornamental, reflecting lake set among lawns and topiary. Occasionally, a robed figure will walk by... a monk in his own reflection. In its long history, Orval has been famous for its scholars, its study of pharmacy, surgery, and even of the forging of iron. (Wood from the Ardennes was once turned into charcoal to smelt iron and glass). One of the abbey's smaller structures, looking perhaps like a chapel, turns out to be the brewhouse. There is an hypnotic peace about the place, with its pristine mosaic stairs and beige tiled walls, the 1950s coppers set into decorative mustard-and-redbrick quarry tiles.

At each year's harvest, the secular brewer, Jean-Marie Rock, specifies the varieties of barley to be used by the maltsters. Samples are malted so that he can chew on the grains and make decisions. He is fond of Prisma, from Lower Franconia, but the final choice will depend upon each year's quality. Barley is bought from several countries, and malted in Belgium. The brewery has the malts made to its own unusual specifications. One is somewhere between a pale ale and a Pilsener malt. Another is a crystal malt that helps impart the distinc-

The brewhouse at Orval, with the customary crucifix on the wall. Cleanliness is next to godliness.

195

tively orangey, sunny, colour of the finished beer (21-22 EBC). "I don't want the pale malt to be too soft," says brewer Rock. Let the softness come from the crystal. It's the way the two work together that gives me the beer I want to create. The crystal must not be too red. I want just the right colour, and I have to keep up the pressure on the maltsters to be sure of that.

Orval is one of the world's most distinctive beers, and the malt

character is one element in that unforgettable personality. "Here, try some malt," Rock offers. I eat it as we look round the brewery. The pale is very firm and dry-tasting, the crystal sweeter, crunchy and nutty. Then he proffers some candy sugar, still made by the traditional method of crystallisation on strings. It looks like cracked ice.

From the hoppy boil in the kettle to the foaming fermentation, Orval is a brew full of life.

The water, from the abbey's own well, is high in calcium carbonate. This no doubt heightens the firmness and bitterness of the beer (40 UB).

On my last visit, I must have called just as the hops had been added to the kettle. Even outside the brewhouse I could smell their magically appetising aroma. The hops used at Orval are Hallertau-Hersbruck and Styrian Goldings, as blossoms, one addition at the beginning of the boil and another during maturation. Rock is especially fond of the Styrian Goldings: "That flavour! I like it! That freshness... dry freshness." I remember his predecessor, Roger Schoonjans, rhapsodising about Kent Goldings: "That indefinable special taste... that finishing touch."

The gravity out of the kettle is 13.4-13.7 Plato. The brew has a conventional primary fermentation, at 14-21 °C (57-70 °F), in beautifully-kept, open, stainless-steel squares. The primary yeast is a flocculent, single-cell strain, low in esters, and it is skimmed by hand.

There is then a secondary fermentation, at around 15 °C, in horizontal cylinders of stainless steel. The yeast used here is a symbiosis of about ten strains, which are cultivated together. This secondary fermentation lasts for three weeks or more, and takes place on dry-hops. This secondary fermentation, with its jungle of yeasts, is another formative element in the beer's individuality. The dry-hopping is yet a third.

Without any centrifuging or filtration, the beer is then bottled, with a dosage of the primary yeast and a priming of white candy-sugar. It then has a third fermentation in the bottle, at the brewery, for seven to nine weeks.

At this point, its alcohol content has reached a level of just over 4.1 per cent by weight, 5.2 by volume. A year later, this may have increased as far as 5.7w, 7.2v. The complex nature of this beer's fermentation, and its potential for the development of more alcohol, has at times led even the brewery to under-estmate its strength. A mid-point of 6.2 by volume is now printed on the label.

When the beer is not long out of the brewery, its hop aroma and flavour seems especially flowery, fruity and refreshing. The bouquet can be astonishingly "fresh". At four to five months, the beer pours with a huge head. By six months, its combination of yeasts is beginning to impart some wild characteristics.

The hop, the malt, the colour, the bottle, the label... every aspect is distinctive.

The present brewer likes the beer best at six months. His predecessor suggested one year, at which age I have found it to be very dry and perfumy. Some drinkers like three years. At five years, the "best before" date settled upon to please the bureacrats, it will still be good, but will have lost a lot, especially in its hop character. It should be stored upright, at a good cellar temperature of around 12 °C (53 °F), and poured gently so that the sediment remains in the bottle. It should not be kept in the refrigerator. "People do not want our beer to taste exactly the same every time," Roger Schoonjans once observed to me. "They want the goût d'Orval, for sure, but they want to be able to chat about it: 'I think this one is a little more hoppy... yesterday's was rounder...' In that respect, they treat it like a wine." That is precisely my view about bottle-conditioned beers, but I rarely hear it from brewers. The goût d'Orval is a phrase often spoken among beer-lovers in Belgium. Goût translates as "taste", but the English seems inadequate. It is, anyway, as much aroma as taste. Some gastronomes detect sage, though no herbs or spices are used. Is it, in the end, the malt, the hops or the yeast? It takes all three to make the beer, but those unruly, earthy, yeast characteristics

It's not over yet. From the bottling hall, Orval proceeds to a further period of warm maturation.

seem to me to be fundamental. It is beer with a devoted following. With its intense dryness, it is especially favoured as an aperitif. On another visit, the managing director at that time, Father Bruno, told me: "We like to see our sales rising, but we are not obliged to grow beyond our present capacity. We live simply. The monastery is very attractive, but that was just the style of the time."

As we strolled through the brewery yard, a truck was being loaded by a fork-lift. Father Bruno introduced me to the driver of the fork-lift: "This is Brother Dominic." The driver was visibly wearing his habit under his cover-alls. He smiled, and we shook hands.

Father Bruno was succeeded by a secular managing director, Jacques Petre, an economist. He told me that there were only limited possibilities for expansion. "The monks want Orval to be an abbey, first, not a brewery."

When we took our stroll, we encountered the dynamic young abbot Dom Eric Dion, who was elected to his position on the day he was ordained. Before becoming a monk, he was a jurist. In the brewery one day, the abbot observed: "You keep people happy and I will keep them holy."

On summer weekends, people come from far and wide to have lunch of charcuterie at the auberge "A l'Ange Gardien" (tel. 061-31.18.86), an incongruously 1930s building on the site of the monastery's court of justice. They walk by the lake, visit the abbey ruins, and buy from the gift shop the beer, cheese, bread and honey candy made by the monks. Father Dominic now makes the honey candy. The more devout can buy religious books and the odd volume on beer.

Orval's emblem celebrates the trout that found the golden ring. "Orval" means "valley of gold".

It is not always easy to blend tradition, monastic or not, with the modern world. Years ago, I received a promotional document from Orval describing the monastery and its beer. The text said that the beer could not be exported because its content of living yeast made it insufficiently stable. A year or two later, I received the same material, but this paragraph had been crossed out. The truth is that bottle-conditioned beers can be exported, but must be handled with more care than is common.

The worst Orval I ever had, was served from the refrigerator, and dumped straight into the glass, at a fashionable bar-restaurant in Chicago. I had recommended the beer to the restaurant in the first place. I had then ordered Orval while being interviewed by a local restaurant critic. "What's the best beer in this place?" she had asked. I had tried to show her, and failed miserably. Soon afterwards, the restaurant went out of business.

CHIMAY

The best-known and biggest-selling Trappist beers are produced at the abbey of Notre-Dame on a hillside called Scourmont, near the hamlet of Forges, close to the town of Chimay, in the province of Hainaut. The monastery and its estate of farmland are in wooded countryside, at walking distance from the French border. The official name of the monastery is Abbaye de Scourmont, but the beers are labelled simply Chimay, and they are very widely marketed. Chimay sold its beer commercially from its early days, and was the first Belgian monastery to do so. It was also the first to use the appellation "Trappist Beer", between the two World Wars.

The town of Chimay once smelted glass, and is now a tourist centre for this part of the Ardennes. It has about 3,500 people, and the monastery's brewery, dairy co-operative and farm are important local employers. The brewery makes three beers, but they have some time appeared in two different styles of bottle,

The omnipresent Ardennes watch over the abbey of Chimay. Its beers are celebrated from Toronto to Tokyo.

and it could be argued that this influences their character. One bottle is a standard size, with a crown top. The other is a "wine" bottle, with a wired cork. Recently, the strongest beer was also made available in a magnum. So are there three beers, or seven? Given that the beer is bottled with residual sugar and live yeast, it will continue to develop. The amounts of sugar, yeast and beer in the bottle; the surface areas of beer exposed to the "head space" in the bottle; the disturbance of the contents when the package is shipped, and even a slight porosity of cork, could all be influences. It could be argued that the smaller scale of events in the standard bottle would make for a slower maturation. A counter argument is that the CO_2 in the beer can expel any unwanted traces of oxygen because of porosity in the cork. Either way, there will be subtle differences in the development of the beer. These have not been proven scientifically - and we are all susceptible to aesthetic influence - but I believe the beer in the large bottles has a softer, "fluffier" character. These differences will be most evident in the brewery's strongest beers. One brewer I know (a monk at another abbey) believes that all beers with corks should be opened five or ten minutes before

Three beers, six... or seven? The principal versions, and bottlings, of Chimay.

they are to be consumed, so that the CO_2 that has been in contact with the cork can be vented. This might seem an excessive refinement, but Belgians are serious about beer. Equally, a beer as full of life as the Chimay products will still be plenty lively enough after ten minutes in the glass.

The style instantly associated with Trappist breweries is a

Father Théodore, in the beautifully-kept copper brewhouse where he made some of his favourite beers. The brewhouse went into semi-retirement around 1990.

yeastily-fruity, sweetish, strong ale; soft, full and deep in body, with a dark brown colour and perhaps a reddish tinge. Two of the Chimay beers fit into this style, and are its best-known manifestations. Both have a very emphatic Chimay "house character": a spiciness in which some tasters have found nutmeg and others juniper and thyme. I believe this aromatic tour-de-force arises from a very distinctive and extremely robust yeast, which permits unusually high fermentation temperatures, of up to 30 °C, 86 °F.

One of the two beers with the "house character" is the very fruity (blackcurranty?) Chimay Red. The colour refers to the crown-cork on the standard bottle, or seal on the larger type. This has a gravity of 15.5 Plato (1063) and an alcohol content of 5.5 by weight, 7.0 by volume. The larger bottling of this has also been identified as Chimay Première. Despite its considerable strength, this is the least potent in the range. It does not require laying down, but will round out for about six months.

Port-like beers to accompany a rich cheese. This combination has extended many a Belgian lunch into mid-afternoon.

In the middle of the range comes a beer in a quite different style, Chimay White. This is much hoppier and drier, with a firmer body, slender for its gravity, and a quenching hint of acidity. It also has a paler colour, more of a reddish amber than a brown. Its gravity is 17.35 (1071), with an alcohol content of 6.3w, 8.0v. This was first put into a large bottle to mark the 500th anniversary of the town of Chimay, and was labelled Cinq Cents. Again, it does not require laying-down, but will become drier over a maximum of a year.

A return to a more typical Trappist type is represented by Chimay Blue, at 19.62 (1081), 7.1w, 9.0v. This appears in the large bottle as Chimay Grande Réserve. At this gravity and strength, it has a massive character, especially in its spiciness (a hint of pepper, too?). It is the beer world's answer to a Zinfandel

204

or Port. This beer definitely develops with some bottle age. The monastery considers two years sufficient, but I prefer it older than that. The beer is best stored at 15-18 °C (59-64 °F). In my view it's also best served at that sort of temperature.

All three are most interesting beers. The White seems the most appropriate as an aperitif, and as an accompaniment to the vinegary spiced trout dish "escavèche", which has been popular in the area since the Spanish Netherlands. The monastery also makes a Trappist cheese, which is surely best accompanied by the Grande Réserve. Indeed, I am always happy to pit a Roquefort or Stilton against this beer.

When I first compared it with Port, I was greeted with a raised eyebrow. Later, tests were carried out to monitor Chimay's development in the bottle over a period of several years. After five years, aldehydes began to develop that were similar to those in Port. At the monastery, I have sampled a 25-year-old bottle that was positively "brut".

God clearly smiled on the monks of Chimay when they chose the site for their abbey in 1850. A dozen years later, they decided to establish a brewery, and discovered that the water under their land was perfect for the job. The water is remarkably low in dissolved solids of any kind, and it is clearly an influence in the softness of the beers. For the "husky" texture it gives to the beer, six-row winter barley, typically the variety Plaisant, is used. It is grown in the Champagne region and Gembloux, and malted in Belgium, to a high-enzyme specification. Cara-Munich malt, and wheat, are also used. The hops are German and, perhaps surprisingly, American, though the White has a massively greater "gift" than other two styles.

The beers of Chimay in their present form owe much to the great Belgian brewing scientist Jean De Clerck. After the disruptions of World War II, he came as a consultant to help the monks put the brewery back on to its feet. His counsel proved invaluable to Father Théodore, who was charged with the job of being Brewmaster. When De Clerck died, in 1978, he was buried at the abbey. It is difficult to know who was the most honoured by this, De Clerck or the brewery.

I first met Father Théodore in the mid 1970s, when I was researching the first version of my book "The World Guide to Beer". I nervously asked if my photographer colleague could take a picture of him, standing in front of the gleaming, copper

The new brewhouse earns a shrewd observation from Father Théodore (on the right of the picture) and a characteristically jovial response from Father Thomas. Far right: Professor De Clerck salutes an earlier triumph.

kettles (now replaced by a more modern, but less attractive, brewhouse). With great hesitation, Father Théodore agreed. The photographer took one shot and Father Théodore was striding away, glad that the ordeal was over. The photographer was dismayed: he had intended to take at least three exposures. Fortunately, the sole shot worked out well, and it has appeared widely since.

In the early 1980s, I arrived with another photographer, and Father Théodore was less shy. My assignment was to write an article about the monks' life for "Sphere" magazine. As Father Théodore led us round the abbey's farm and forest lands, he vaulted casually over a tree trunk, unencumbered by his flowing habit. I had to remind myself that he was in his 70s. I stayed in the abbey's guest quarters for a few days, and one evening Father Théodore gave me a tasting of some especially fine "vintages". I was acutely conscious that I was staggering slightly, and banging against walls, as he soberly led me to my quarters. I was also aware that I had kept him up late, and that he would have to rise again for vigil prayers at some unearthly hour.

That, anyway, is my recollection, but it seems that I may have consumed more than was good for my memory. I mentioned the incident in my writing, only to be told years later by Father Théodore that I had got it all wrong. "It wasn't me who saw you back to your quarters. It was Father Robert," he assured me. A few years later, I heard that Father Théodore was no longer enjoying such good health. When I arrived in 1989, to make a film about the Trappists for my tv series "The Beer Hunter", I was concerned as to how I should find him. To my delight, he was as spry as ever, and playing the organ in the abbey church. "I am delighted to see you so well," I remarked. "It's the Chimay beer," he laughed. (His own favourite is the White). I interviewed him for the film, and asked him about the early days, when he had spent long hours isolating the right yeast for the Chimay beers. He recalled: "I worked with Benedictine patience..."

Over the years, it has occasionally been my pleasure to receive a short note from Father Théodore with news of the brewery. As he approached his 80th birthday, he began to communicate by fax, and told me that, in his semi-retirement, he was missing the full activity of the brewery. I heard that he had been unwell again, but he was once more in lively form when I visited the brewery after his 80th birthday, in 1993. He was still acting as a consultant to the brewery, and taking part in the morning tastings that are part of quality control.

With us at the tasting was the monk now in charge of the brewery, Father Thomas, rotund, ruddy-cheeked and jovial. He could have been proposed by Central Casting. The secular head brewer, Marc Habran, was also present. I first met Marc when he worked in the lovely old brewery of Armentières, France.

As each goblet of beer was passed from one person to the next, Father Théodore's was the final verdict. As the tasting ended, he had a glass of White for himself - a daily ritual. The monastic life hardly makes for excessive consumption, but Father Théodore, enjoying his beer with relish at the age of 80, had been told to drink less by his doctor. I had a feeling that God took a different view.

ROCHEFORT

Perhaps the least known of the Trappist breweries is Notre-Dame de Saint-Rémy, near the small town of Rochefort, once again in the Ardennes, in the province of Namur. Its Trappist beers are all of the dark, sweetish, style, and are very typical. I have always regarded them highly, and they seem to have been even better in recent years. In particular, they have a very good flavour development from the first taste to the finish.

In my travels over the years, I had visited every other Trappist brewery at least once before I finally managed to see Rochefort, as it is usually known. The problem was not geographical accessibility.

The cloistered layout of the monastery and brewery at Rochefort is clearly shown in this photograph. Its beers are not the easiest to find.

From Brussels, it is an easy drive south-east even by the scenic route through the barley-and-malt town of Gembloux, down to the rocky gorge of the river Meuse at Namur and Dinant. Then east as the Meuse Valley rolls upward into the middle of Ardennes. As the roads wind into the hills, every bend has a sign

offering farm produce: "oeufs frais, fromage de chèvre, lapin, foie gras..." Like most towns in the Ardennes, Rochefort seems full of charcuteries, bakers and chocolatiers. A few more miles up a country road, with woods on one side and a vista of rolling hills on the other - typical of the Ardennes - is the monastery. Some of the Trappist breweries, knowing that visitors to the region will wish to sample their beer, make sure it is available in a nearby inn, but Rochefort has no such auberge. All of the monasteries are hesitant to admit visitors to the cloister itself. Each abbey has at times had the name for being the most private. The reputation may change in one direction or the other with the election of a new abbot, but Rochefort for many years was known for its shyness. It was some time before I plucked up the courage to seek a visit.

When I finally arrived, I was met by a grey-bearded monk who seemed unaware that I was expected. He fetched Brother Antoine, who was dressed for work in a black sweat-shirt and dark blue drill trousers.

The water does not come out of the "wishing well", nor are barley and hops any longer grown in the grounds... but the beer is distinctive and delicious.

Brother Antoine told me that Saint-Rémy dated from at least 1230, when it was a convent. In 1464, it became a monastery, and in 1595 it began to brew. At that time, barley and hops were grown in the grounds. The oldest parts of today's abbey date

from the 1600s. After the Napoleonic period, the abbey was restored in 1887, and the brewery in 1899.

A plaque of St Arnould, with a mashing fork, overlooks the 1960s brewhouse. This is of a traditional design, in copper, set into beige tiling. There are stained glass windows, and potted plants add a further decorative touch.

The beers are brewed from two Pilsener malts and one Munich type, with dark candy sugar in the kettle. The hops are German Hallertaus and Styrian Goldings, added twice. Two strains of yeast are used. The same two strains are used in primary fermentation and bottle-conditioning. White crystal sugar is used as a priming in the bottle. "Two of the pale malts, two of the sugars, two hop varieties, two yeast strains... two of this and two of that... we like to keep it simple," laughed Brother Antoine.

Some fine beers seem to be made in a complicated manner and others very simply. This is true beyond doubt, but cannot be explained analytically. Brewing is like cooking: there is no "best" way. The brewers who do it their own way do it best. Knowledge is essential whatever the approach, but a feel for beer, and a respect for it, make the best brewers.

Like many Belgian brewers, not only in monasteries, Brother

The "juices" of the malt are extracted from the infusion. The taps enable the brewer to monitor the results.

Antoine had a crucifix watching over his kettles and another in his office. I could hardly avoid noticing that the shelves round his office also accommodated about 400 beer-glasses, steins and bottles.

He suggested that the Rochefort beers were best tasted at 12-14 °C (54-58 °F). Each is distinguished by its gravity in the old system of Belgian degrees, which is now falling out of use. Thus the beers are called simply six, eight and ten. This is handy, observed Brother Antoine, because they are ready to drink at six, eight and ten weeks. The brewery conditions them in the bottle so that they should reach the customer in an optimum condition, some devotees like to lay down the strongest one for a month or two...

Rochefort 6 (which has 6.0 per cent alcohol by weight, 7.5 by volume) has a reddish "autumn leaves" colour; a soft body; and an earthy, herbal palate (a suggestion of Darjeeling tea?), developing to a deep fruitiness. Rochefort 8 (7.3w, 9.2v) has a tawnier colour, a more assertive palate, with an even richer fruitiness (a hint of figs?) and a dash more dryness to balance the finish. Rochefort 10 (9.0w, 11.3v) has a deep red-brown colour; a dense head; a more viscous body; and a profoundly fruity, fig-like palate, with notes of bitter chocolate in the finish.

"Two of this and two of that"... but three Rochefort beers emerge.

If the taste descriptions make some of these beers sound like a meal, that is appropriate enough. The notion of beer as "liquid bread" was apposite not only during Lent, Brother Antoine reminded me. It was absolutely necessary in order to balance the diet. "Trappists would have died without it." Traditionally, Trappists did not even eat cheese or fish. Those rules have been relaxed, but the Trappists still dub the Cistercians "meat-eaters". Today, the brothers at Rochefort do not in general drink the beer except on high days and holidays, though Brother Antoine said there was one member of the community who liked a glass at 10 in the morning. Such abstinence relieved him of the duty of making a weaker "table beer", which some of the monasteries have. Brother Antoine did not exactly say so, but I feel he is pleased not to have to make a table brew. I don't think he really saw that as beer.

211

Always a special experience... Rochefort 8 has a rich fruitiness. Perhaps a hint of figs?

He told me there were 25 monks at the abbey, and four of them had jobs in the brewery, along with five secular workers. For the monks, the important task is the putting in of a new brew each morning. All brewers start early, and those who are monks especially so. At Rochefort, they rise at 3.15, and have the brew tidily under way before heading for High Mass at 7.0 in the morning.

WESTVLETEREN

The smallest Trappist brewery is at the abbey of St Sixtus, in Westvleteren, near Ieper (Ypres) and Poperinge, in West Flanders, close to the border with France. This brewery is so small that it sells its beer only at the abbey and the café next door. Despite its small output, its beers are quite well known.

There could be two, opposite, reasons for this. One is the fact that they are in short supply, and therefore have something of a cult following; this is especially true of one very strong beer.

Another reason is that, in the recovery period after the Second World War, the abbey licensed the name St Sixtus to a commercial brewery ten miles away. The beers made in the abbey were identified as Trappistenbier Westvleteren and those from the secular brewery as St Sixtus. Confusingly, the secular brewery is called St Bernardus, under which name it produces a hearty Tripel. (see p. 50)

In Flanders' fields, near Ypres, the Westvleteren monastery-brewery makes beer with a cult following.

The licensing arrangement has now ended, but the commercial brewer has acknowledged this only by dropping the "Saint". He still produces beers under the name Sixtus.

The monastery's Westvleteren Trappistenbiers and the Sixtus range are similar but by no means identical, especially as different yeasts are used. Both are dark, fruity and sweet. The monastery's beers have suggestions of orange and pear, and a great depth of maltiness. I think they have lost some of their complexity in recent years, but they are still probably the maltiest of Trappist beers. The Sixtus products are orangey, with hints of melon and a spicy freshness.

For many years, the beers made in the monastery had no label, and were identified only by the words Trappistenbier West-vleteren on the crown-top. This artisanal practice of producing beers without labels is gradually ceasing as the European Community festoons brewers with dubious regulations. (What, for example, is the sense of a "best by" date on a beer that may improve for 25 years?).

The old mash-tun made production a head-banging procedure.

Locals cycle up the country lane that leads to the abbey, and load their bikes with beer. French and Dutch come in cars. Sometimes

they will already be parked there, waiting in a queue, in the early hours of the morning. The brewery does not work every day, and releases the beer "when it is ready", so the product is not always available. When there is to be a new stock, especially of the very strong beer, word spreads quickly. The beer is sold by the case from a sales hatch, by a cheery monk. If visitors want a drink, they have to go outside the monastery to the nearby Café De Vrede.

I remember visiting the monastery on one of those days when Flanders looks as though it has been painted in oils on canvas: iridescent light on flat fields dappled with brown cows and pantiled farm buildings. From the lane, the abbey appears the most rustic of the Trappist monasteries: a clutter of styles, with hints of country railway station at one moment and between-the-wars Italianate at another. The starkly modern church is not instantly apparent.

At the bottom of the brewery steps, a figure in cover-alls and green Wellington boots was waiting to greet me, waving enthusiastically to attract my attention. This was Brother Daniel, the brewer.

Horizontal tanks like these can be used for fermentation or, at Westvleteren, maturation.

"Let me change my battledress," he said. He was 33 at the time, a Bachelor of Philosophy who had previously taught French in Zaire. He talked of having felt a "fugitive" in Zaire... of the sense of brotherhood in the monastery. He had been in the monastery ten years and had been concerned with the brewery for about seven. The previous brewer had taught him the job, and he had at first worked in the lab. Despite his familiarity with the place, he managed to bang his head on a pipe as he showed me round. He had just finished reassuring me that he was all right when I banged mine. "This place is a piece of industrial archaeology," he laughed, with a degree of pride and accuracy.

He told me the brewhouse dated from 1900. The kettles, with saucer-shaped tops, were recessed into the brickwork. It was a typical design in old, artisanal breweries in Belgium, but I believe this example has now been replaced with something more modern.

An appreciative sampler... one bottle a day, perhaps a second on religious holidays.

A very rich, sweet, summer malt is used at Westvleteren. The emphasis in the beer is on its malt character, despite the fact that the brewery overlooks a hop garden. These beers really are "liquid bread". They are all warm-conditioned in maturation tanks, for periods ranging from at least two weeks to a couple of months or more, depending upon their strength. Then they are primed and given a dosage of new yeast before being bottled, after which they have a further two weeks' conditioning before being released. At the time, the brewery had four beers, but in recent years it has been offering only three. These are, in ascending order of gravity and strength, known as Special, Extra and Abt (Abbot), but they are also identified by the colour of their crown-top, and their gravity in Belgian degrees.

The Special (red, 6.0 degrees) has an alcohol content of just under 5.0 per cent by weight, 6.2 by volume. It is a characteristically malty brew, with suggestions of vanilla and licorice. The Extra (blue, 8.0 degrees) has 6.4, 8.0, and is fruitier,

Westvleteren for many years licensed the production of St Sixtus. Either the Trappist brew or the secular is well suited to dessert.

with hints of orange, some acidity, and warming note of alcohol. The reverend Abt (yellow, 12) has around 8.8, 11 (I have seen analyses varying from 10.5 by volume to 11.5, but this is bound to happen with beers that are still "alive" in the bottle). It is an immensely full-bodied, rich, creamy beer.

In the monastery, I was served a four-degree beer with my lunch. The monks are expected to restrict themselves to one bottle a day. "Isn't that difficult?" I asked brother Daniel. His answer was simple enough: "Yes!"

Then he told me that a student magazine had reported that Westvleteren Abt beer was an aphrodisiac...

217

WESTMALLE

Although it does make a dark Trappist beer, this monastery is famous for its golden Tripel. This is made exclusively with pale, Pilsener-style, malt, but is a strong, fruity, top-fermenting ale in the Trappist tradition. No other Trappist monastery makes a beer as pale as this, and the style has been widely imitated by conventional commercial brewers. Not only is Westmalle Tripel distinguished by its colour: this is a superb beer all round.

The abbey's full name is Our Lady of the Sacred Heart. It sits behind elm trees and high walls in neat, flat, countryside near the village of Westmalle, north of Antwerp. The monastery was founded in 1794, and is said to have been brewing beer for the brothers' own consumption since 1836, though the product was not sold until the 1870s, and then only in the village. Brewing did not become a commercial business until about 1920. The famous Tripel was developed after the Second World War.

The sense of a self-contained community is captured in this picture of the Westmalle monastery and brewery, which produces the world-classic Tripel.

Most of the present abbey edifice dates from around 1900, but the brewhouse building itself is strikingly 1930s. Inside, the vessels are copper, set into platforms tiled in a decorative pattern of blue, black, red and autumnal colours.

The brew-kettle is heated by direct gas flame, rather than steam, which is more common. This "fire-brewing", as it is sometimes known, produces hot spots in the kettle, and these very faintly caramelise the malt. This produces a hint of a toffee-ish, aromatic, quality that is a traditional feature in some Trappist beers.

The look of the brewhouse did not change dramatically in an upgrade in 1991/2, though a vessel was effectively gained by the addition of a mash-filter to replace a lauter-tun. There are now two brew-kettles, but the system of heating by (gas) direct flame has for the moment been retained. The brewery feels, rightly in my view, that this system may contribute to the malt character of its beers, but worries about the wear on the underside of the kettles. Experiments have been carried out with a steam system.

The brewery produces "Single", "Double" and "Triple" beers. The single, actually known as Extra, is also a golden beer, delightfully delicate in character. It is very dry, and to my palate

There is a fire down below, in the brewhouse at Westmalle. Thus far, the brewery has managed to maintain this tradition.

219

slightly salty. The brewery's water is quite hard, which suits the paler ales. The Extra is usually produced at a modest strength for the monks' own consumption, but it has been made in more than one version, and at a higher potency been marketed outside the abbey. Westmalle does produce the occasional experimental beer.

On the 150th anniversary of its brewery, the abbey issued a commemorative brochure which offered some interesting uses of the beer: "Against loss of appetite, have one glass of Tripel an hour before mealtime; against sleeplessness, drink one Trappist."

The designation Trappist issues loud and clear from Westmalle in this early advertising. In those days, the dark Dubbel was the principal brew.

I particularly liked the precision of the prescription against stress: "two glasses of Trappist will reduce stress by 50 per cent." With the passage of only a few years, it is no longer possible to make such innocent suggestions. (In America, a brewer tried to present a fourteen-point analysis of his beer, including percentages of "negative" elements like sodium and "positive" ones such as protein and three B-vitamins, and was forbidden to do so).

All three of the regular beers contain summer malts from several sources, notably including Lower Franconia and Beauce-Gatinais (the regions south of Paris, in the direction of Orléans). The varieties will vary according to their performance each year. The Gatinais barley malts were especially favoured for their softness by Brother Thomas, when he was technical director at the brewery. In discussing a malt from elsewhere, widely used by other brewers, I asked whether he thought it was perhaps a trifle harsh. "It's brutal!" he replied, thumping the table. I first met Brother Thomas when he was 59 years old. I saw him again nearly ten years later, and he was still thumping the table, permitting himself a laugh at his own excitability. Soon afterwards, at the age of 70, he retired, handing over to his secular colleague of ten years Jan Adriaensens. The specifications of the beers do not seem to have changed.

The Dubbel, with a gravity of 15.7 Plato (1063) also has a dark malt and dark candy sugar. This beer has an alcohol content of 5.2 by weight, 6.5 by volume. It has a reddish dark brown colour;

a soft body; and a palate that is malty and chocolatey, with hints of banana and passion-fruit toward a dry finish. The Tripel has a gravity of 20 Plato (1080), and is made with pale candy sugar. Its famously golden colour registers at 12-13 on the EBC scale. The beer has a dense, white, head that leaves very full lacework. It is very aromatic; creamy in body; with a distinctively clean, orangey, fruitiness in its deep, complex, palate.

The dark Dubbel is a well-loved beer, but golden Tripel is a world classic.

Throughout, there is in the background of the Tripel an appetising hop character. In a beer of such all-round power, 35-38 units of bitterness represent restraint rather than punch. The first time I visited the brewery, they were using English Fuggles, several German varieties, and Saaz from the Czech Republic. On a subsequent visit, Styrian Goldings, German Tettnangers and Saaz were emphasised, "along with others". All are aroma varieties, but Brother Thomas was shy of revealing his precise

The reddish, dark brown (mahogany?) of the Dubbel sets off the bright, golden depths of the Tripel.

hop formulation. Later in our conversation, he mentioned three more varieties. He was also keen to emphasise that the brewery used blossoms rather than pellets. There are three additions, all in the kettle. The finished Tripel has an alcohol content of 7.2 by weight, 9.0 by volume.

After primary fermentation, the beers have a long, slow, secondary of three weeks for the Dubbel and five for the Tripel, at 8-10 °C (46-50 °F). This is a very important part of the production procedure. The beers are then filtered, primed and re-yeasted. The same yeast is used at both stages. There then follows a warm conditioning in the bottle of two weeks for the Dubbel and three for the Tripel, at 21 °C (70 °F).

Brother Thomas told me he felt the beer hit a peak at three to six months. It then became more aromatic after two or three years, and he had greatly enjoyed a sample that had reached a decade.

"Keep some for five or six years, then use it to make a sabayon. It's perfect!" (Bangs table with glass. The vessel is a crystal goblet engraved with a flower pattern, but it doesn't seem to mind). I protested that I might not be able to restrain myself from opening it before then. "All right, drink it with asparagus. Westmalle Tripel is perfect with asparagus. What wine goes with asparagus? That's difficult, eh?!" (Another bang).

Food was on the menu, conversationally speaking. "Getting food right is an art. Just to get potatoes right is an art." (Bang). "Getting beer right is an art. When you can do that, you can call yourself an artisanal brewer. It is the brewer who makes good beer, not the equipment. You have to have a feeling for your beer... know what you are smelling, what you are tasting." (Bang). "It's a question of being there."

"One of the existentialists said: 'Know what you are thinking.' That's important. Sometimes in the modern world we know so much, that we don't know what we are thinking."

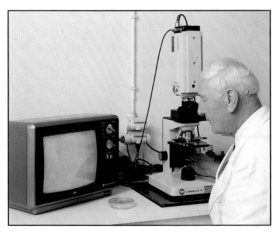

Brother Thomas was the classic example of a brewer who was equally passionate about art and science. Here, he is shown magnifying yeast strains for examination on a monitor screen. Brother Thomas has now retired.

Orval makes a wonderful aperitif... perhaps with artichokes?
Try a Westmalle Tripel with asparagus, or even fish.
Chimay Red goes well with meat, and the Blue with cheese.
Rochefort 10 or Westvleteren Abt are splendid with dessert.

Abbey beers

There are at least 70 abbeys, convents and beguinages in Belgium, and these divide in more or less equal numbers between those that are still inhabited, others that have been deconsecrated and put to different uses, and the remainder that survive as ruins. (A beguinage is an institution found today almost exclusively in Flanders: a sisterhood, ascetic and charitable, but not bound

Abbeys and priories have these beers produced by secular brewers. This community of abbey beers includes some widely-marketed names.

by vows). These various communities were founded by Benedictines, Cistercians, Premonstratensians (also known as the Norbertines) and several other Orders.

It is not always clear which have in the past had breweries, but any sizable community would have probably thought it as necessary as a bakery, kitchen or garden. Several definitely had breweries that ceased when they were sacked by Napoleon, and some continued to make beer until the two World Wars intervened.

Leffe

A good example of a continuing community is Notre-Dame de Leffe. The abbey is close to the Meuse, where it is met by the smaller river Leffe, at Dinant. This is a town of great historic interest and a tourist centre, about 20 miles south of Namur and less than 50-odd from Brussels. The oldest part of the abbey is a garden dating from 1152, with herbaceous borders set round a

The present abbey of Leffe is much as depicted in this engraving of 1740. The river Meuse is in the foreground, with the abbey gardens in the valley rising steeply behind.

fountain. Most of the buildings date from the mid 1700s. The valley of the river Leffe is noted for its herbal plants, and the Premonstratensian brothers still use these to make tisanes. The abbey is believed to have had a brewery from the 1200s until the Napoleonic period, but emerged in the early part of this century without one. At the beginning of the 1950s, the Abbot was chatting to the local brewer and mentioned that the community was having financial difficulties. The brewer suggested that he make beer for the abbey, to be sold under their name as a commercial venture. There were other commercial breweries in Belgum making beers with ecclesiastical-sounding names at the time, but this is believed to have been the first such

Gardening is still an important part of the abbey's life. The Order considers beautiful surroundings an inspiration to religious zeal.

formal licensing arrangement. The local brewery was later taken over by another company, and then that was acquired by a larger concern, but the arrangement has survived and prospered, and the Leffe range are among the best known of the abbey beers.

In 1989, one of the brothers gave me a tour of the abbey. It is older, with smaller, and darker quarters than any I have seen elsewhere in Belgium, but it is the possessor of several very interesting antiques and works of art. Historically, the Premonstrant tradition was to engage the most sought-after artists of the time to produce magnificent works that would inspire religious zeal. The brothers follow the Rule of St Augustine. It is not a closed Order but one that preaches and does pastoral work.

After my tour, I was seated at an old oak table and offered a tasting of the Leffe beers. In general, these are very rounded beers, with a firm fruitiness.

The Norbertine fathers of Leffe during their evening prayers. Will they retire with beer, or tea?

Leffe Blonde is, as its name suggests, golden in colour. It has a dry, spicy, faintly clove-like aroma; a dry, citric, palate (a hint of bitter oranges?); and some hoppy dryness in the finish. In some export markets, it has an alcohol content of 4.0w, 5.0v, but the principal version is 5.5w, 6.6v.

Leffe Brune is a deep, autumnal brown. It has a hint of dessert apples in the aroma, and a good flavour development: from fruity sweetness to brown sugar, then a spicy dryness in the finish. It has a similar alcohol content: about 5.1w, 6.3v.

I have been served both of these beers chilled and found them rather thin. At the abbey of Leffe, they were presented from the cellar, and were full of flavour. There are also three stronger beers, one pale and two dark.

The Leffe range is marketed in Belgium with a parchment-like label.

Leffe Triple is the most delicate and complex beer in the range. It has a rich, golden colour; a clean, light, lemony, appetising, aroma; a fluffy, medium-to-full, body; lemon and vanilla in the palate; and exquisite aromatics in the finish. A lovely, fresh, apéritif beer. Alcohol: 6.7w, 8.4v.

Vieille Cuvée is a stronger dark abbey beer, with a big, very malty, aroma; a full body; gentle hints of roastiness in the palate; and creamy, liqueurish, warming, aromatics in the finish. Definitely an after-dinner beer. Alcohol: 6.24w, 7.8v.

Radieuse (the name referring to the halo that radiates round the head of a saint) is an extra-strong dark abbey beer. This has a rich, earthy, aroma; a very full body; and a whole range

229

This slender, elegant bottle and label has appeared in some export markets.

of flavours: deep fruitiness, sweetness, roasty notes, hoppy dryness... It is a very complete beer, preferably with a book at bedtime (6.8w, 8.5v). The beers are currently made in villages in the same part of the country as the abbey. They all are produced by Interbrew at Mont-St-Guibert, except for the Triple, the sole bottle-conditioned example, which is brewed in Leuven.

GRIMBERGEN

St Norbert (1080-1134) established his Order in Prémontré, near Rheims and just north of what is now Champagne country (500 years later, another monk, Dom Pérignon, played a key part in the development of that drink). St Norbert also founded the abbey that towers above the cherry trees at the village of Grimbergen, now something of a northern suburb of Brussels. Grimbergen is thus one of the handful of abbeys in Europe that were established by the founders of their Orders. The abbey has been sacked four times, and each time rose again. Its emblem is the Phoenix, and this appears on the labels of its beers.

These Norbertine brothers do not seem to be intimidated by the towering church of Grimbergen... but the structure is as powerful as the beer.

In the Norbertine tradition, the abbey has a magnificent Flemish-baroque church, much of which was built during the 1600s. On my two visits, I have found the interior of the church so tall and narrow and rich in carved oak as to be stunning, almost intimidating. No wonder the Norbertines inspire faith. I regained my composure when I noticed that the elaborate carvings in the choir stalls prominently included

231

The abbey rose again, like a phoenix. The born-again bird of classical myth (possibly Phoenician) appears in stained glass.

depictions of hops along with the grapes and cherries.

The present cloister was rebuilt after the French Revolution and restored in the 1920s. Its vaulting and tiling are haughty enough, though they are softened by windows giving onto a garden of tulips. Nearby is a café called the Fenixhof.

Even among abbey beers, those bearing the Grimbergen phoenix tend to be on the sweet, liqueurish side. This sweetness is especially notable toward the finish. There are four Grimbergen beers, two pale and two dark.

Grimbergen Blond (5.2w, 6.5v) is a leafy gold in colour, lightly malty and fruity, with a touch of dessert apples in the palate and aroma. Grimbergen Tripel (7.2w, 9.0v) is gold-to-bronze; more intensely aromatic; with an invitingly soft body; and a big, rounded, assertive, palate. It has a more citric, winey fruitiness, with the warming finish that is characteristic of the stronger Grimbergen beers. These two pale beers share the same yeast in primary fermentation, and gain their perfumy note from it, but the Tripel is bottle-conditioned, and a second culture is used for that purpose. This strain is the one that gave such a nutty complexity to a famous, long-gone abbey-style brew called Tempelier when it was made at the Betekom brewery, near Aarschot.

Grimbergen Dubbel (5.2w, 6.5v), which has a Burgundy colour, is raisiny, chocolatey and toffee-ish, with a finish that is brandy-like. While this version has the customary dosage of dark candy-sugar in the kettle, the stronger, deep amber, Optimo Bruno (8.0w, 10.0v) does not. The name recalls the notion that the finest beer in an abbey was the strong, brown brew traditionally consumed after Lent, at Easter. Optimo Bruno has a drier fruitiness, and again that warming, alcoholic finish.

These two beers have their own yeast, producing a distinctly fruity accent.

All of these beers are produced for the monastery by Alken-Maes. The Maes brewery is not far away, at Waarloos, but its top-fermenting beers are made in the company's charming old brewery Union, at Jumet, near Charleroi.

"Burned but not consumed," says the Latin motto. The beer, on the other hand, most certainly is consumed.

Brewery Union also produces the Ciney range of abbey-style beers, which have different specifications and their own yeast strain. Their house character is to start sweet, but finish drier, and to have a lighter, more expressive, palate.

Ciney Blonde (6.8w, 8.5v) has a bright, golden, colour; a lightly sweet fruitiness; and a crisp finish. Ciney Brune, at the same strength, is soft but dryish, with a hint of cellar character. Ciney Speciale (7.2w, 9.0v) has a dark ruby colour; a "juicy", slightly oaky, palate; and a touch of coriander.

These beers are named after a small town, famous for agriculture and especially for beef cattle, in the province of Namur. Their label depicts the church of Ciney, and there is no link with an abbey. The brand-name is owned by a beer merchant.

MAREDSOUS

This is a Benedictine Abbey, at Denée, south of Namur. It began as a community of Bavarian monks, on land donated by a Belgian ecclesiastical printer, and became an abbey in 1878. The buildings are a good example of the neo-Gothic architecture that flourished in Belgium and France during that period.

The Benedictine of the Belgian beer world? The six-degree is fruity, but the ten is the really liqueurish version.

The Maredsous beers have in general a delicate, perfumy, flowery-fruity character and a very fine, Champagne-like, bead. They all now have a secondary fermentation in the bottle, though this was not always the case. They are each identified by numbers in the Belgian degrees system.

Maredsous 6 has a sunny bronze colour; a spritzy fruitiness in the aroma; a very good, soft, clean, malt character; and a lighty dry, perfumy, finish (4.8w, 6.0v). Maredsous 6 Donker (dark) has an autumnal colour; a firmer body; and hint of tartness in the finish. There is no Maredsous 7. The next beer in the range is Maredsous 8, with a deep, tawny, colour; a body that is light for the strength of the beer (just over 6.4w, 8.0v); a sweeter palate; and hints of chocolate and coffee towards the finish. There was at one stage a Maredsous 9, but that has been dropped. Maredsous 10 has an amber colour; a soft, creamy, well-rounded, body; a beautiful balance of malt and fruit; and a long, warming, finish (just over 7.6w, 9.5v). The last is an especially delicious beer.

These beers are made by the Moortgat brewery, in Breendonk, in the province of Antwerp. This brewery is best known for its Duvel (see Strong Golden Ales).

234

AFFLIGEM

This Benedictine monastery, founded in 1074, played an important part in the religious, political and cultural history of Flanders, and in the hop trade. There are ruins from 1085; a 1665 farm, white-washed and standing round a cobbled courtyard; and 17th-century engravings showing hops and beer barrels.

The abbey once owned gardens in Kent, where the Flemish began the English hop industry. I visited Affligem in the mid 1980s, and photo-

The Affligem beer owes more to malt and yeast than to the region. Nonetheless, the abbey (left) remembers its hoppy history.

graphed the abbey from a hop garden. It is in the hop-growing region of Aalst, between Brussels and Ghent. Sad to say, cultivation in that region has greatly diminished in recent years.

The present abbey is a mix of Renaissance and neo-Gothic. The main structures date only from 1928, though they express in modern building the Benedictine tradition. Brother Stephen took me into the 400-year-old cellars to taste his cherry wine. He told me he bought cherries in Brabant, at auctions, and made 10,000 litres of wine a year, aging it in Port pipes. He said it reached 15 per cent alcohol by volume.

The wine was offered in a Burgundy sampler. It had a deep, cherry, colour; an almost blackcurrant aroma; a soft, smooth, body; a sweetness offset by alcohol; and a hint of sharpness in the finish. When I commented that it perhaps had some Port character, from the wood, Brother Stephen disagreed. To prove his point, he fetched me a glass of Port as a comparison.

Whether Brother Stephen's cherry wine resembles Port is open to argument... but it is a splendid example of the eclecticism of alcohol in Belgium.

Once, at another Belgian abbey - which I shall not mention here - a brother offered me a brandy that he had made on the premises though there was no evidence of any licence for a still. Affligem brewed beer until the Second World War. Today Affligem beers are made by the nearby De Smedt brewery. In general, they have a fruity, sultana-like, aroma; a smooth body; and a finish that is caramelish but nonetheless relatively dry. Several versions have been produced in recent years. The example I have sampled most recently was a Dubbel. It was very lively indeed, with a huge head and dense lacework. The colour was attractively tawny and deep. The beer was very aromatic, with lots of spicy, chocolatey, notes. The palate was spicy (cinnamon?), developing to chocolate and pears. The body was soft, and there was a bitter-chocolate dryness in the finish.

236

De Smedt also produces beers bearing the names of, among others, the abbey of Aulne (a magnificent ruin, near Charleroi) and Postel (an active Norbertine community between Antwerp and the more easterly towns of Turnhout and Hasselt).

CORSENDONK

At the end of the 1300s, the Duke of Brabant's daughter Maria bequeathed her estate at Corsendonk, near Turnhout, to the Augustine Order. The estate became Corsendonk Priory, and gained an international reputation for its scriptorium and library. Erasmus went to the Priory to read the only Greek Bible in the Low Countries, but a few decades later the buildings were sacked during religious and political unrest.

Corsendonk Priory was restored in the 1600s, during which time it is known to have had a brewery. It finally closed in 1784, but the Priory buildings were restored again in 1969-75. They are now used for conferences of heads-of-state and captains of industry.

Corsendonk Agnus Dei is presented chilled (left), as the house apéritif at the Kleine Keizer, on the Grand' Place of Turnhout. That seems a long way from the 1600s Priory shown below.

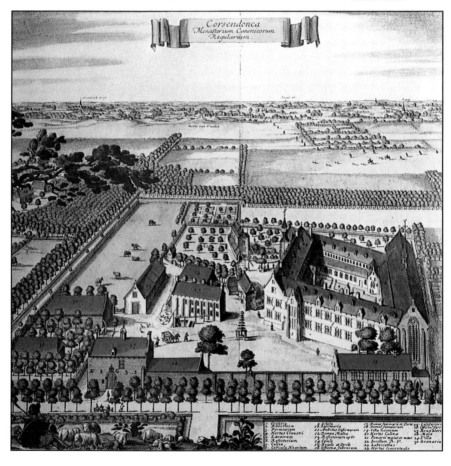

In the dining room, surrounded by original paintings by the pupils of Rubens, and tapestries from the 16th and 17th centuries, I sampled two beers, created in 1982, to which Corsendonk has licensed its name.

Corsendonk Pater Noster (identified in the English-speaking market as "Monk's Dark") has a Burgundy-brown colour; a yeasty, fruity, slightly smoky, bouquet; and suggestions of raisins and dark chocolate in its palate. It has an alcohol content of 5.6 by weight, 7.0 by volume. This beer is produced by the Bios brewery, in Ertvelde, East Flanders. The Pater Noster is available on draught at the astonishingly kitsch Corsendonks Hof, at the end of the lane that leads to the priory. Otherwise, both are bottle-conditioned beers.

Corsendonk Agnus Dei ("Monk's Pale") is of the Tripel type. It has a surprisingly light, fluffy body, and a great deal of finesse: beginning with a dry, lightly citric, fruitiness, and developing to a delicately spicy, perfumy, hoppy, finish. Its alcohol content is 6.5w, 8.1v. This beer is produced by Du Bocq.

The Corsendonk beers are the creation of Jef Keersmaekers, a member of a distinguished brewing family. His grandfather had a brewery making a dark, abbey-style, beer in the northern part of Flanders until 1953, and related families have in recent years been involved in three breweries, including Bios. Mr Keersmaekers, a tireless promoter of his products, makes a point that these beers are produced from an all-malt mash, and that this has been certified in Germany under the terms of the Purity Law - the Reinheitsgebot - though sugar is used in the re-fermentation.

OTHER ABBEY STYLE BEERS

New abbey-style beers are still appearing. In 1993, I found my-self being conducted round the Cistercian abbey of Val-Dieu by Father Joseph: "Those are the guest quarters where the Empress of Austria stayed; that door is a fine example of Liège Baroque; those Cistercian capitals date from 1260..." It was an astonishing march through the centuries, but it was occasioned by that most exciting of events, a new beer. The abbey, which in the distant past produced a hoppy "tonic" beer, had just licensed its name to a range of products from the local brewery three or four miles away in the village of Aubel. The new beer was to be available in the abbey's former stables, now a tavern called the Casse-Croute.

Augustijn does not identify its monastery of inspiration, but some of these abbey beers are more precise.

Aubel, which also grows pears and cider-apples and produces charcuterie, is close to Herve, which gives its name to the region's cheese, pungent and strong-tasting. The two are between Liège and the German city of Aachen (in French, Aix-la-Chapelle).

The brewery was founded in 1850, acquired by the family Piron in 1907, and closed in 1969, at the height of the popularity of mass-market beers. Like many breweries, Piron also had a wholesale-retail drinks business, and this sustained the family for almost a quarter of a century. Joseph Piron, who at the age of 30 had stopped production, decided at the beginning of the 1990s to fit his old building with a brand-new brewhouse, in response to the growing interest in what he described as "authentic" beers. He started to make beer

Tongerlo's six-degree has a dark, russet colour, a syrupy smoothness and a toffee-caramel palate; the golden eight-degree is fruity, starting sweet, but finishing dry. Both have a secondary fermentation in the bottle.

again, using five malts, and three hop varieties, as well as herbs and spices. As chance would have it, I arrived the day before the official opening. He was glad to be back in brewing. "This is my métier!" he exclaimed. "This is my passion!!"

Monsieur Piron told me I was the first person outside the brewery to taste his revivalist beers: Abbaye de Val-Dieu Blonde (5.2w, 6.5v), starting sweet but with a touch of spicy tartness in the finish; a fruity and malty, but surprisingly light-bodied Ambrée (5.6w, 7.0v), dedicated to a mythical Gaul called Aubelus; and a very dark, intense, coffeeish Val-Dieu Brune (6.4w, 8.0v).

In the westernmost corner of Hainaut, at Guignies, the brewery of Allard and Groetembril once made deliciously complex, malty, Saisons and other beers. In recent years, this brewery closed, but the area now has a new beer. Inspired by the need to replace this lost brewery, Guy Valschaerts and his wife set up in business.

Mr and Mrs Valschaerts are both graduates of the Institute of Fermentation Industries, in Brussels. They worked in malting and brewing in Francophone Africa and Haiti before returning to Belgium. In their new, purpose-built, brewery in Rogny, they make two beers in broadly the abbey style, both at 6.5 per cent alcohol by volume, with re-fermentation in the bottle. By naming their beers after the district, they have revived the old brand Brunehaut.

The abbey of Tongerlo was founded nine centuries ago, by clerics from Antwerp and Cambrai. This engraving provides a clear picture of an abbey as an agricultural estate.

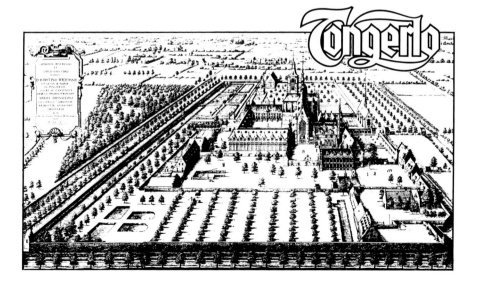

Brunehaut Blonde is bright gold, with a big head; a perfumy (almost talcum-powder) aroma; a light, firm, body; a hoppy palate; and a herbal, dry, finish. Brunehaut Ambrée has an attractively reddish colour; a slightly fruitier aroma; a touch of sweet maltiness in the palate; and lots of flavour development, moving towards an emphatically bitter finish.

I encountered a similar story at Le Roeulx, just north of Mons. Le Roeulx is a hilly little town, full of cafés. It is said to have been founded by a missionary monk known in French as Feuillien and in his native Ireland as Faelan or Foillan (c. 655). The town had an abbey until the French Revolution.

A family that had established a brewery in the town in 1860 later acquired an 1890s brewery nearby, and ran it until 1980. Again, after the brewery closed the family remained in the beer business by running a drinks market. Then, in 1988, a new generation re-opened the brewery.

"When I was five or six years old, I had to work in the brewery during school holidays, and after it closed, I missed it," Benoît Friart told me. "It was our family brewery, and I wanted us to make beer here. I put it to my sister Dominique, and she agreed." I asked Dominique if she now worked in the brewery, and she replied: "Sure! Perhaps not so hard... but I work there. I had it in me. I didn't know... but it was there."

The chunky buildings of Brasserie Friart are alive again, brewing the beer of St Feuillien.

The former maltings and the brewery Friart are handsome, chunky, red-brick buildings, their line softened by smartly-painted woodwork and window-boxes of geraniums. Behind tall, iron gates is a classic tower brewing system, in which the water and malt start on the top floor and the ingredients flow by gravity until they reach the cellar as finished beer.

It is a beautiful brewery, from the beading on the wood cladding of the mash-tun to the tiny, original, mill used to grind spices. Everything has been restored, but not much replaced.

St Feuillien Blonde has a creamy head, a spritzy body and an orangey palate, very hoppy and dry, with a hint of juniper in the long finish; a very good aperitif. St Feuillien Brune has an even richer head; an attractive, deep red, colour; a much softer, smoother, toffeeish, body; and a restrained, bitter-chocolate, palate, with notes of oakiness; a perfect digestif. Both have an alcohol content of 6.0-6.4w, 7.5-8.0v). There is also a slightly stronger Christmas version.

Another Wallonian brewery, Lefèbvre, of Quenast, makes several abbey-style beers. It is especially known for Abbaye de Bonne Espérance, an orangey-coloured brew, robust and assertive, with an excellent malt character and huge aroma and flavour of Styrian hops (5.6w, 7.0v). Bonne Espérance, at Vellereille-les-Brayeux, near Binche, in Hainaut, was a Norbertine semina-ry, then became a secondary school.

The brewery also makes several beers for the Norbertine semi-nary at Floreffe, between Namur and Philippeville. The classic example is called Floreffe La Meilleure ("Best"), and is a ma-hogany-coloured brew with a very soft malt character and a gentle spicing of anis.

In 1991, after a period with no beer, the Norbertine abbey of Tongerlo, between Antwerp and Hasselt, re-entered the market, with products of six and eight degrees, offered by the Haacht brewery. The six-degree has a dark, russet colour, a syrupy smoothness and a toffee-caramel palate; the golden eight-degree is fruity, starting sweet but finishing dry.

Is there any abbey, convent, beguinage, seminary, saint or ruin in Belgium that is not commemorated in a beer? There seem to be at any one time between 80 and 120 Belgian beer-labels that make some ecclesiastical allusion.

In Oudenaarde, the Clarysse brewery's abbey-style beer is called St Hermes, to commemorate the parish saint of the nearby town of Ronse (in French, Renaix). "My husband also liked the name," I was told by Novella Clarysse. "He had a good friend called Hermes who was always full of joie-de-vivre."

The former Dominican abbey of Bornem passed into Cistercian hands... and its name appears on a beer from Bios (who also have a beer simply called Augustijn, with no reference to any abbey in particular).

The abbey of Bornem was Dominican and then Cistercian... and now has a beer from Bios.

The name Witkap clearly alludes to the white cowls of the Cistercians, but again without identifying an abbey. A range of individualistically-crafted beers called Witkap is produced by the Slaghmuylder brewery of Nino-ve, in East Flanders. Among them, Wit-kap Stimulo is a golden, abbey-style, beer with a soft, dense, pillowy, head; a lightly sherbety aroma; a fluffy body; and a palate that develops from fruiti-ness to hoppy dryness (4.8w, 6v). At the other end of the range, Witkap Tripel is much bigger bodied, and more assertive all round (6.1w, 7.6v). These beers were inherited from the long-gone brewery of Brasschaat, in the province of Antwerp, and I believe this was the first golden Tripel, before the style was taken up by Westmalle.

The Cistercians are known as the white friars because of the colour of their cowls.

Abbaye des Rocs is one of several new tiny breweries that have opened in Belgium in recent years. All of their beers are interesting - no one opens a new brewery to make products of a type that are already widely available. Abbaye des Rocs is named after a farm that was once a monastery, near Montignies-sur-Roc, in Hainaut. Its principal product is an abbey-style beer bearing simply the name of the brewery. This has a soft, fruity, spicy, character and 7.2 per cent alcohol by weight, 9.0 by volume. Unlike the Trappist beers, none of the "abbey" brews is made in a monastery, but Des Rocs does have an interesting place of origin. It was created in a tiny weekend brewery in his garage by a civil servant and beer enthusiast. When he started marketing his beer commercially, I asked him whether there were any difficulties with legal requirements, taxes, and so forth. "I know all about that," he told me. "It's my week-day job."

At the gates of the Beguinage, in Bruges, beer-lovers go about their devotion.

247

THE TERM TRIPEL

In the days before widespread literacy, breweries would brand their casks with crosses, diamond shapes, triangles, or other simple marks to distinguish between different strengths, colours

or lengths of maturation. Beers marked, for example, "x", "xx" and "xxx" would certainly have contained ascending levels of alcohol. I am not sure the number of x's would always have re-presented a multiplier, but I have heard it said that in Belgium the words Single, Double and Triple typically indicated three degrees, six and nine. These were the old Belgian degrees of gravity, but

The scene on the label of Brugse Tripel is taken from a miniature in a nearby seminary. It shows the city in the 16th century.

the figures for alcohol by volume would have been similar, perhaps fractionally less.

Today, the term Single is rarely used, but Double and Triple are popular designations in Belgium. A Double is usually a dark brew of 6.0-plus per cent alcohol by volume, and a Tripel often (but by no means always) a pale one of 7.0-plus to 9.5 or more. This is especially true in the case of abbey beers (where the designations are perhaps inspired by the success of the West-malle Trappist products). Elsewhere, a Triple may just indicate a top-of-the line product.

Historically, the term Tripel seems to have been especially widely used by the many brewers that once existed in the Bruges area. This tradition has been strongly maintained by the former 't Hamerken ("Little Hammer") brewery, now known as Gouden Boom ("Golden Tree").

On a site that was once at the edge of town but is now quite central, this establishment dates from the 1500s, and has been variously a tavern, brewery and distillery. It has been in the Bruges brewing family Vanneste since the 1870s. In 1983, the brewery was threatened when one branch of the family did not wish to continue, and at that time it was re-constituted as De

248

Gouden Boom. The name "Golden Tree" is an allusion to a trophy traditionally given to jousters in Bruges. It is now run by Paul Vanneste, in association with the Boon, Moortgat, Palm and Rodenbach breweries. Fifty per cent is held by Rodenbach. In its new life, De Gouden Boom has become best known as a specialist brewer of white beer, but it is also very proud of its abbey-style products, including two Triples. For the abbey of Steenbrugge, with its links to St Arnold, the brewery makes two beers. The amber-brown Steenbrugge Dubbel (5.2w, 6.5v) is full of flavour, with an outstanding malt character and a dry fruitiness in the finish (like biting into a toffee apple). The very pale, greeny-gold, Steenbrugge Tripel (7.2w, 9.0v) has a fruit character more reminiscent of peaches-in-brandy, and lovely citric overlay of Styrian hops. The brewery's own Brugse Tripel is fuller in its golden colour and rounded maltiness, with warming alcohol, a perfumy hop character, and a great complexity of flavours (7.6w, 9.5v).

Behind a façade of 16th-century gabled buildings, through an

A tableful of Tripels, some very old brews. The term has come into even more widespread use in recent years.

Triple Petrus is a darkish example of the style, sweetish in palate, and with 7.5% alcohol. It is from the brewery De Brabandere, in Bavikhove, West Flanders.

arch in which the keystone bears a statue of the Virgin Mary, De Gouden Boom still has its 1902 maltings, though they have not worked since 1976, and the top ten metres (the kiln tower) blew off in a storm in 1986. The 1964 block brewhouse, the first of its kind in Belgium, is softened by the Vanneste family crest and an oak carving of Madonna and Child. In the tiling is a depiction of St Arnold. Whenever I visit the brewery, I am reminded that the present, 58th, abbot of the former Oudenburg and now Steen-brugge monastery is the living successor to the brewers' saint. De Gouden Boom (47 Langestraat) also has an excellent muse-um of Bruges breweries past and present, which is open from Thursday to Sunday during the summer, or by appointment (tel. 050-33.06.99; fax 050-33.46.44).

GOLDEN ALES

Although the designation "golden ale" is not used in Belgium, there are a growing number of beers that fit this description.

The much-admired brewer Anne De Ryck makes an example, which she says has been golden since at least the days of her great-uncle. Mrs De Ryck runs the brewery that bears her family name, in endive-growing country near the hop town of Aalst, in East Flanders.

Her great-grandfather started it as a farm brewery in 1886, and the original buildings still stand, with additions from the 1930s and 40s. He went to Germany to study brewing, as did Anne, before gradually taking over the running of the family business from the late 1970s onwards.

De Ryck is unusual in that it sticks to the German Purity Law, disdaining sugar, an influential ingredient in many Belgian

Going for golden... De Ryck, Rubens, Straffe Hendrik and Flandrien.

The brewer's somewhat mysterious publicity shot seems to suggest age and antiquity...

beers. Its De Ryck Special (spelled the English way after Anne's father spent some time with Newcastle Brewery) has a golden colour with a tinge of bronze; a soft, notably clean, lightly sweet, malt accent; and a delicate hop character. It is brewed from Pils and aromatic malts, with three additions of Belgian Hallertau and Saaz hops and a further gift of Styrians during its four-week maturation (3.4 w, 4.2v). The brewery also has a stronger (4.3w, 5.4v), cherry-red, fruity-malty, ale called Rochus, after the parish saint. There is also an aromatic Christmas Pale Ale.

Opposite a 12th-century castle keep, through a wooden arch, the brewery is set round a cobbled yard. After the Germans confiscated brewing vessels in the two World Wars, second-hand equipment was installed in 1949. The brewhouse, now something of an antique, is well fitted and impeccably clean and tidy. I asked Anne if she had a cleaning day each week, and she reproachfully told me that the place was cleaned after every batch: "Brew-and-clean... brew-and-clean."

Anne's father installed a malt silo, and an auger to move the grain, so that she would not have to heft 160-pound sacks, but she has been known to shovel out the 1800-pound mash-tun.

Anne De Ryck raises her glas to her brewery's centenary... seven years after the event.

Across the courtyard, the brewery's shop sells the beers, which can be ordered gift-wrapped in baskets and cellophane. The bottled versions are unfiltered.

Anne, her husband Omer, and their children, live on the premises. "You can never leave a brewery all alone," she told me. "You must always watch and listen."

It is hard to imagine such pure, clean, beers giving anyone a headache but, should that happen, aspirin is at hand. Anne's husband is a pharmacist, and he runs his shop in the brewery's former stables.

Another well-established golden ale is produced in the Halve Maan ("Half

252

Moon") brewery, hidden in a cobbled yard next to the be-guinage of Bruges. The brewery stands on a canal marking the inner limit of Bruges harbour in the days when the city was one of Europe's greatest trading ports.

De Halve Maan was founded in 1856, though some of its buildings were added in the 1920s. It has been run by four generations of the Maes family (not connected with the Pils brewers of the same name), all called Henri or Hendrik, and a member of the fifth generation delivers the beer. In 1982, the brewery's golden ale was created to be served at a reception to celebrate a new statue of St Arnold in the city. It was slightly stronger than the brewery's regular beer, and came to be known as the Straffe ("Strong") Hendrik.

The Half Moon was an earlier name for what is now the Straffe Hendrik brewery.

After some years as advisers, the De Splenter family, own-ers of the Riva brewery in Dentergem, West Flanders, acquired the brewery in 1989. It has since concentrated on Straffe Hendrik, and developed its own sizable tavern and small beer-garden on the premises.

Visitors can see much of the original equipment as well as the 1968 brewhouse.

The Straffe Hendrik beer (4.3w, 5.4v) is no longer as strong as it once was, but is eminently drinkable. It has a bright gold colour; a hoppy aroma; a creamy, fresh-tasting, start; and a fruity, dry finish. It is brewed from Pils, crystal and pale ale malts, and hopped with German Northern Brewers and Saazers. The beer goes very well with the fish platter that is among the light meals featured. A beer soup is sometimes available. (26 Walplein; tel. 050-33.26.97).

Another golden ale I have enjoyed is the lightly fruity, dryish, but soft, bottle-conditioned, Flandrien (4.0w, 5.0v), from the Louwaege family brewery, in the brick-making town of Kortemark, south of Bruges. A newcomer is the Rubens Gold, discussed with its redder brother brew in the ale chapter.

The use of the typically Belgian aromatic malts, and sometimes

Flandrien, from the Louwaege brewery, is a smaller brother to the better-known Hapkin.

sugar, both distinguish these beers from the golden ales of the city best known for this type of beer: Cologne, Germany. Equally, they tend to be fuller in body than the golden ales traditional in the North-East of the United States.

Strong golden ales

My fellow professionals the wine-writers are always interested in my beery adventures: "What have you brought us to taste?" is a frequent question. "Do you have any Duvel?" is another. No one with a love of good drink could fail to be captivated by Duvel. It is one of the world's most distinctive and individualistic beers, but it requires far less of the drinker than some other classics from Belgium.

It is paler than some Pilsener-type lagers, yet it is technically an ale, in that it is made by top-fermentation. It is soft and seductive,

A devilish display of strong golden ales, among which Duvel is by far the best known.

yet it is a very strong beer (6.8 per cent alcohol by weight; 8.5 by volume). Connoisseurs love it for neither of these reasons, though both are essential to its overall character. They are devoted to it for its complexity and delicacy.

Even by Belgian standards, the presentation of Duvel is something of a ritual. Most top-fermented ales are served at cellar temperature, but Duvel is usually presented chilled, often in a glass that has been kept in the refrigerator.

This reminds me of another drink: Brandies are customarily

served warm, but the "white" eaux-de-vie of Alsace are more often presented chilled, sometimes in a glass that has been treated in the same way. Presented cold, those eaux-de-vie could serve as an apéritif, though they are more often employed as a digestif. Duvel is usually considered to be an apéritif, though it could be served as a digestif. Not only does it resemble an Alsatian eau-de-vie in presentation, it also has a distinct suggestion of Poire Williams in its bouquet and palate.

With its huge, rocky, very white, head; its small, sustained, bead; its satin-smooth body; its distinctive bouquet and palate, especially the "Poire Williams" accent; and the lingering dryness and perfuminess of its finish, it stands apart.

Some individual wines are legends, and the same is true of a handful of beers. This one has a remarkable story. At the height

Duvel is always served in a Burgundy sampler, but surely it is the beer world's answer to an Alsatian eau-de-vie?

of the fashion for Scotch Ales in Belgium, between the two World Wars, a bottle of McEwans was "taken apart" under a microscope by the great brewing scientist Jean De Clerck. It is a scientist's job to study and investigate, and that is what he was doing. Perhaps he was especially interested in flavour characteristics that seemed to derive from McEwans' yeast, which turned out to be a mix of between ten and twenty strains. In those days, McEwans' Scotch Ale was bottle-conditioned, and therefore contained living yeast.

De Clerck did the work together with the local brewery owned by the Moortgat family, in Breendonk, north of Brussels and not far from Mechelen. At the time, Moortgat made dark top-fermenting brews.

BROUWERIJ · **MOORTGAT** · BREENDONCK

Founded in 1871, Moortgat was a classic brewery of the period. Today, it is very modern, with some stylish flourishes.

With cultures isolated from the McEwans yeast, the Moortgat brewery introduced a new dark strong ale. The tale has it that, when the test brew was sampled, a worker at Moortgat expressed the opinion that it was "a devil of a beer!" The brewery decided to call it Duvel, a variation on the Flemish word for devil.

After the Second World War, golden beers of the Pilsener type began to gain ground in Belgium, and this set Moortgat to some more experimentation. In 1970, they unveiled a golden version to replace the dark Duvel. Once again, De Clerck was involved. Even using a Pilsener-style malt, it is hard to produce a truly golden strong ale. The problem is that the wort of the malt needed to make such a strong brew inevitably makes for a fuller colour.

Why did the brewery want such a pale colour? In part, for cosmetic reasons. They wished to produce something that responded to the fashion for paler beers, but did so with its own distinctive flourish. By making the beer with an unusually pale malt, they also gave it a distinctively clean body. They could equally have gone the opposite way, sought a fuller maltiness in the palate, and made a beer that was delicious in that style, but it was not what they were seeking.

The ability to turn barley into malt of a particular colour or natural taste is both and art and a science (like brewing itself). The development of the science has over the centuries had a major influence on the introduction of new styles of beer. The Moortgat brewery was originally able to achieve just the right character because it had its own maltings, at the brewery. This was a floor maltings, and it ceased to operate into the 1980s. By then, free-standing maltings were able to match Moortgat's own, the company felt, and the success of Duvel meant that the space was needed for maturation warehouses. I would swear that the Moortgat maltings gave Duvel an extra refinement, but such memories cannot be proven any more than we can say whether Joe Louis would have beaten Muhammed Ali.

Whether the brewers admit it or not, all beers evolve over the years. Even if nothing else changes, the character of each year's malt is different, and sometimes one variety becomes unavailable and has to be replaced by another. The same is true of hops. Different raw materials will also vary in their inter-action with the yeast, causing it to adapt. Some brewers introduce changes to respond to these circumstances, others to render their lives easier or make their beers less challenging to the consumer. Over the years, Moortgat has refined the yeast in the bottle to make it precipitate and compact better. Brewers of greatly-loved beers have to be careful with such changes: the devotees, quite properly, watch them with eagle eyes.

Two-row summer barley is malted in France and Belgium to a colour of between 2.5 and 3.5 EBC for the production of Duvel, and the finished beer has between 7.0 and 8.0, or 9.0 at the absolute maximum. Pilsener-style beers as a finished product generally vary from 5.0 to 7.5.

The original gravity is 14 Plato (1056). An infusion mash is used, and in the boil hops are added three times. The varieties are Saaz and a particular type of Styrian Goldings. (Final EBU is 29-31). A proportion of dextrose is added before primary fermentation, to boost alcohol and further attenuation. This effectively upgrades the original gravity to 15.5 Plato (1066).

The original McEwans' symbiosis of strains has over the years been narrowed down to two yeasts, and both are used in primary fermentation. The brew is divided into two separate batches, one for each yeast. These two batches are not of equal sizes. This procedure is just one of the many peculiarities that make Duvel such a distinctive beer. Every one, of course, costs extra time and money. Primary fermentation is at between 16 °C (60 °F) and 28 °C (82.4), and the brew stays in the vessels for five or six days.

It is then transferred to cold maturation vessels, where it has a secondary fermentation for three days, during which the temperature is dropped to minus one degree Celsius (30.2 °F). It is then held for three to four weeks' cold maturation before being dropped to minus three (26.6 °F) to complete the precipitation and compacting of the yeast. (The outside walls of the lagering cellars, with inspection ports, make a visually dramatic pattern round the brewery yard. Moortgat is a very modern brewery, but its equipment is all stylishly designed and assembled).

After cold maturation, the brew is filtered and given a priming of dextrose and a dosage of just one of the two original yeasts. The original gravity has at this point been effectively boosted to the equivalent of 17.0 or 17.2 (1073-4).

Such step-by-step increases in original gravity are, of course, not unique to Duvel, and take place in the production of a good many other Belgian beers, but I have set them out here because this regime of fermentation and maturation is one of the most elaborate.

With the priming and dosage, the brew is bottled, and spends 10 to 14 days at 22 °C (71.6 °F) undergoing its third and final fermentation. This takes place in two huge sheds, each about 50 metres long, which together house 175,000 cases at any one time. The sheds have temperature control systems in both the floors and ceilings. These buildings are visible from the main road, and are painted with the legend: "Ssst... hier rijpt den Duvel". The word "rijpt" means "ripens", and the rest hardly needs translating.

Quiet, please... in these temperature-controlled warehouses, Duvel undergoes its bottle-conditioning. But will the passing traffic take note?

Finally, the beer is stabilised in cold storage at 4-5 °C (39-41 °F) for five or six weeks before being released. Some customers then store the beer for a further three to four months, in a cool, dark, place, before serving it. In Belgium, when Duvel is served chilled, it is usually at 7-8 °C (45-46 °F). It also expresses its flavour well at a natural cellar temperature in the range of 12-13 °C (53-55 °F).

Duvel in this bottle-conditioned form is by far the biggest-selling product of the Moortgat brewery. There is also a small sale of a filtered version, which has a green label. Moortgat additionally makes the Maredsous range (see Abbey Beers), Godefroy (Ales) and a Pils.

Duvel is such an individualistic beer that there is no name for the style. Many Belgian brewers have since made similar beers, often using names suggesting devilment or mischief, but none has displaced their inspiration.

Examples I have tasted over the years have included the firm, round Deugniet ("Rascal"), from du Bocq; the big, fruity, assertive, Judas, from Alken-Maes; the aromatic Julius, from Interbrew; and the softer, fruity, darker, Sloeber ("Joker"), from Roman.

One example that seems to have established itself is Hapkin, from the Louwaege brewery, of Kortemark, south of Bruges. The name of the beer derives from Boudewijn Hapkin, a 12th-century Count of Flanders, whose deterrent wielding of an axe is said to have brought peace to his land. Or did he simply use it to cut trees? The region between Bruges and Kortrijk is known as "the Woodland" but trees are today not especially evident. Either way, there is an axe on the label of the beer.

Happiness? Kinship? The name sounds friendly, and perhaps diminutive, in English, but Boudewijn Hapkin was an axeman.

Hapkin has a good Saaz hop aroma; a big, creamy, head; a full mouth-feel; a soft malt character; and big, well-rounded, fruitiness, drying toward the finish. It is made with a decoction mash, has no fewer than four hop additions, and has a two-stage primary fermentation. On the town square, behind a step-gabled house that once accommodated the Louwaege family, the brewery was founded in 1877. Its brewhouse dates from the 1950s, and the company is now in the fourth generation of the family. Hapkin was launched in 1982. Its other products include Flandrien, introduced in 1987 (see Golden Ales) and the long-established Akila ("Eagle") Pilsener.

Another example that has made an impact is the somewhat flippantly-named Delirium Tremens, from the Huyghe brewery, of Melle, near Ghent. The name Delirium Tremens was deemed unacceptable in the United States, where the beer was dubbed Mateen, after an early Flemish brewer in the Americas.

Delirium Tremens is very bright, despite its being bottle-conditioned. It has full, golden colour; a dense head; a very fruity bouquet; a sweetish palate; and a lot of warming alcohol in the finish (at 7.2w, 9.0v, it is slightly stronger than its rivals). The hops used include not only Saaz but also Styrians, and its fermentation demands three different yeast cultures. These are employed consecutively in a two-stage primary fermentation and in the bottle-conditioning.

A Teut is a tinker... this beer was born in the 1980s as a yeasty entrant from a micro-brewery in Limburg.

Huyghe also produces a soft, sweetish, all-malt amber ale (4.1w, 5.2v) called Artevelde. There is also an extremely malty Artevelde Grand Cru (5.7w, 7.2), with re-fermentation in the bottle. The Artevelde brand-name belonged to a long-gone brewery, and was revived in recent years. Jacob, or James, van Artevelde was a Ghent farmer, brewer and merchant who was a central figure in the 14th-century wrangles between Flanders, France and Britain over trade (especially textiles) and political power. His statue dominates the Friday Market in Ghent.

There is said to have been a brewery on the site in Melle since at least 1654, and four generations of the Huyghe family have been involved. The beers are made in a handsome, well-kept, 1930s, brewhouse. For many years, the brewery was known only for its Pilsener-style beer, under the odd name Golden Kenia (this was a variety of barley, long vanished). In 1985, a new generation took charge and the brewery began to develop a wide range of speciality beers, including such oddities as one flavoured with mint.

A classic café restored... 'In 't Oud Wethuys' ('In The Old Law House') offers regional specialities at the open-air museum 'Bachten de Kuppe' (West Flanders).

Regional Specialities

In much the way that France has two or three hundred cheeses, each representing its own locality, so every Belgian speciality beer is to some degree associated with its town, village or district. Almost everyone who makes a speciality would argue that his beer is unique not just to his locality but to his brewery. While some of these beers clearly fit into styles, and others into looser groups, several defy categorisation.

These are sometimes identified in Flemish as "Streekbieren" ("district beers"). In the odd instance, there may be an historical reason why a particular blend of ingredients is used in a certain district. (The hoppy Hommelbier brewed near the growing area of Poperinge is an obvious example). Or a local craftsman may have built equipment that necessitates a particular style of brewing; that happens much more in Belgium than in other brewing countries.

More often, these specialities probably just emerged from the local working habits of brewers, or individuals' preferences and whims. Nor are they all traditional brews. Sometimes, new ones are launched. This is just a selection, first from Flanders, then Wallonia.

Some of Belgium's most individualistic beers defy categorisation... here are just a couple of dozen examples. Any brewing nation would be proud to have such a range.

FLEMISH SPECIALITIES
(from North-East to South-West)

Poorter

This name has nothing to do with the English term Porter, which indicates a beer in a similar style to Stout. In Belgium, Poorter is the brand name of a speciality made by the Sterkens brewery, and dedicated to the community of Hoogstraten, in the province of Antwerp.

The brewery's home village, Meer, is in the municipality of Hoogstraten. The name Poorter, derived from the word for a gate, means "Freeman of the Borough". This beer, which comes in a pottery crock, was first marketed in 1985, to mark the 775th anniversary of Hoogstraten.

Poorter is a top-fermenting, dark, strong beer of 5.5 per cent alcohol by weight, 6.9 by volume that is soft, fruity-sweet and very easily drinkable. It is perfumy in aroma; slightly syrupy in body; malty in palate; with a lightly dry finish. A similar beer is sold as St Sebastiaan Dark. The brewery was originally named after St Sebastiaan. There is also a slightly more conditioned

Beer fit for a free man? Poorter and its brother Kruikenbier look more like Flemish or Dutch gins in their stowy stoneware bottles. The Kruikenbier has a less hoppy brother called St Paul Triple. The Double is a more conditioned brother to the Poorter.

264

version of this beer, called St Paul Double. The same brewery has another speciality that is in my view more distinctive, Bokrijks Kruikenbier. Bokrijk, near Genk, in Limburg, is a town with an open-air museum of agricultural life, including a brewhouse (formerly at Hoegaarden). The beer is available there (Kruik means "crock"). This is a top-fermenting golden strong beer of 6.0w, 7.6v, that is very firm-bodied, fruity-dry and assertive. It has a slightly earthy hop aroma and a splendid aperitif bitterness in palate and finish. It is dry-hopped, with German varieties. Bokrijks Kruikenbier has a secondary fermentation in the bottle. A similar beer in filtered form is available as St Sebastiaan Grand Cru, and in some markets as St Denise. A less hoppy derivative is called St Paul Tripel, and in some markets St Laurent.

Poorter is a speciality from Sterkens... along with a heavenly horde of saints.

Gouden Carolus

An old-established Belgian classic. It is to be hoped that this beer retains its character now that its brewery, Het Anker, of Mechelen, has entered into a trading agreement with Riva. Samples since then have varied from disappointing to reassuring.

The "Anchor" brewery has its offices in a step-gabled building of 1625 that is part of a beguinage dating from the 1400s. Behind the brewery is a courtyard of houses, some dating from the original beguinage, which at one time accounted for about a third of the town. The beguinage seems to have stopped and started in its original function, but the brewery passed into the secular hands of the present family in 1870.

Gouden Carolus is the brewery's speciality. The name means Golden Charles. It could refer to Charlemagne (742-814), who ruled Europe from Aix-la-Chapelle, which is not far away. Or, perhaps more likely, to Charles V (1500-58), who grew up in Mechelen and extended the influence in the Low Countries of the Holy Roman Empire.

The beer is Burgundy-coloured, with a powerful bouquet and a distinctive, extremely complex, sweet-and-sour character. It starts sweet, with suggestions of toffee, raisin, orange and passion-fruit; then becomes quite tart; then the two elements blend into a perfumy, spicy, dryness.

Gouden Carolus begins with a gravity of 19 Plato (1076). It is made from pale and dark malts and a substantial proportion of wheat flour. It has a longish boil (two to three hours), during which Brewers' Gold and Saaz hops, all grown in Belgium, are added. Orange peels and coriander are also used. The brewery was re-equipped after the Second World War, and was at the time a "model" plant. It now has the look of a seasoned veteran. Its most unusual feature is its open cooler, which is effectively a copper trough covering the entire roof. Around the edges are a dozen pillars supporting a canopy, which forms a second roof. Apart from railings, the sides are open. It affords a magnificent view of Mechelen.

Beer fit for an emperor? The Gouden Carolus was also an early European coin, with more romance and personality than the ecu, hard or soft.

I have visited this brewery three times, and on the first two occasions was entertained so assiduously by the principal of the company, Michel van Breedam, that we somehow failed to make the usual tour. This has not happened at any other brewery in the world. On my third visit, I finally got the tour, topped by this remarkable device, the like of which I have not seen anywhere else in the world. At this point, Mr van Breedam told me that the cooler was now being replaced by a modern paraflow.

The open cooler would, of course, encourage a degree of spontaneous fermentation. Would the beer not be different without this? Mr van Breedam thought not, saying that the house yeast was such a mixture, and so habituated, that it was dominant.

The beer has a secondary fermentation in the bottle. It is held for ten days at 25 °C (77 °F) and three months at 14-15 °C (57-59 °F), and emerges with an alcohol content of between 5.6 and 6.2 by weight, 7.0 and 7.8 by volume. Some customers keep the beer for between one and two years, ideally at 14-15 °C. Mr van Breedam likes to keep his own personal stock for three or six months, to let the flavours marry. I once tasted a 22-year-old bottle that had not only the aroma but also the palate of an Oloroso sherry. Gouden Carolus expresses its flavour most fully if served at 12-13 °C (54-55 °F).

The brewery has a fractionally less strong and spicy beer, with a toffeeish smoothness and some dry maltiness, called Mechelsen Bruyne ("Brown"). This little-known beer is one of Belgium's

266

many secret delights. There is also a drier, paler, aromatic, and much hoppier beer called Toison d'Or, broadly in the abbey Triple style. All of these beers are bottle-conditioned.

Pauwel Kwak

There was once an inkeeper called Pauwel Kwak. The first name means Paul and the second is a nickname for someone expansive. Pauwel Kwak brewed his own beer, which was dark and strong. He had a coaching inn on the road from Mechelen to Ghent, and his customers included horsemen who had stopped to water their charges. Kwak would hand them a beer in a glass that they could rest in their stirrup.

Pauwel Kwak's type of beer became a district beer in East Flanders, until it died out with the passage of time. In recent years, it has been revived by the Bosteels brewery, of Buggenhout, East Flanders. The brewery popularised the beer by serving it in a "stirrup cup" rather like a yard of ale. As this has a rounded base, it has to be placed on the bar counter or cafe table in a supporting bracket. The presentation of such an elaborate device leaves no one in doubt as to which beer is being served. It is an imaginative promotional device, if a trifle showy. It works in a country where the serving of food and drink is too serious

Odd name... and unusual glass. The eye-catching stirrup cup did a lot to popularise Pauwel Kwak. It takes an expansive gesture to impress the Belgians.

267

to be hurried, but might not succeed in a less sensitive land. Buggenhout was a manor in the 1200s, and is now a village within commuting distance of Antwerp, Ghent and Brussels. The brewery was established in 1791, and has passed through half a dozen generations of the same family. It is a pretty, whitewashed, brewery in the tower style that can also be found in Germany, Britain and elsewhere. Next door is the elegant family home, with some fine art deco pieces and an impressive wine-cellar.

Pauwel Kwak is a deep amber beer, with an earthy aroma; a body that is full but by no means cloying; a herbal, palate; and a warming hint of alcohol in the finish. It is made from three malts, and white candy sugar is added in the kettle. The hops are Challenger, from England. The original gravity is 18.5 (1074), and the alcohol content of 6.8-7.2 by weight, 8.5-9.0 by volume. The brewery has over the years made a variety of other beers. It has a pils known as Prosit and a "light" beer called Bugg's, which sounds less odd in Flemish than to English-speakers.

The Brigand and the Castle

A speciality that seems to have established itself well in recent years is Brigand, from the family-owned Van Honsebrouck brewery, in Ingelmunster, West Flanders.

Brigand is a strong beer with a bronze-copper colour; a soft body, with an insistent bead (it can be very lively) and some yeast "bite"; and a robust palate, with plenty of fruit but also lots

of hop character, especially in the finish. It starts with a gravity of 20 Plato (1080), is made with Pilsener and pale ale malts, and hopped with Saaz. It is also dry-hopped with Saaz. The final alcohol content is 7.2 by weight, 9.0 by volume. The month and year of bottling are printed in the cork. Brigand expresses its flavour most fully at three to six months after bottling. It should be stored at a natural cellar temperature, and served without excessive chilling.

Van Honsebrouck has over the years produced a variety of speciality beers, and its principal is one of the more colourful figures in Belgian brewing (an industry not short of characters). In 1986, the

Van Honsebrouck family bought Ingelmunster Castle, a 1736 mansion, protected by a moat, on a strategic site once occupied by the Duke of Flanders. In the 1400s, the castle is said to have had a brewery noted for its dark beer. An earlier castle was built in 1075, and there was said to have been an abbey there in 640. The extensive cellars of the present castle are now being used to mature beers from the Van Honsebrouck brewery. A special Kasteelbier has been brewed for this purpose. Except to Flemish-speakers, perhaps its French-language soubriquet as a Château Beer strikes a more immediate chord.

This is a very strong and immensely rich beer, of 25 Plato (1100), 9.6 by weight and 11 by volume. In colour and viscosity, it resembles a dark Port.

Chateau bottles... a beer fit for the Duke of Flanders. But first he has to deal with the Brigands (left).

In aroma, it is very malty, with notes of fresh bread and dried fruit. In palate, it has a smooth, toffee-ish start; a deep, rounded, fruitiness; and winey, Port-like notes in the finish. The beer has at least two yeastings, a second fermentation of two to three weeks at the brewery, at least three months cold maturation in tanks, followed by six to 12 weeks in the castle cellars.

The castle has a park, tea-room and tavern, and the beer is served there, with Belgian cheeses and hams. It may also be bought to take home. Ingelmunster Castle is at 3 Stationsstraat (tel. 056-35.34.91 or 051-30.03.85).

The Mad Brewers

The name is a typically Flemish shrug. The 1840s brewery at Esen, near Diksmuide (and not far from Ostend), in West Flanders, seemed doomed to close, because the owner had become ill. Instead, it was acquired by a family of professional people (an architect, a doctor...) who were keen home-brewers. They used the brewery at weekends only, and developed a range of speciality beers for commercial sale. They called themselves The Mad Brewers (De Dolle Brouwers), and their antique, working, brewery is open for tours at weekends (tel. 051-50.27.81). De Dolle Brouwers has, among several items of historical interest, a remarkable collection of bottles from Flemish breweries of the past. The principal Madman, architect Kris Herteleer, is also noted for his published drawings of breweries and cafés.

I once took a tour, with Kris's mother as a guide. In no other brewery have I met a guide with such knowledge or passion: "Malt, hops and yeast are medicines! We must capture the vivid elements of the hop!! We must be careful of the savage yeasts !!!" The latter was surely a too-direct translation from the French. The Dolle Brouwers' beers, all bottle-conditioned, have rightly won a great deal of acclaim.

The principal product is Oerbier (meaning "original beer"). This is a slightly Scottish-accented, strong (6.0 by weight, 7.5 by volume), very dark ale, made from six malts, candy sugar, and three hop varieties. It has a fruity aroma; a remarkably smooth, creamy, texture; and a sweetish palate with winey undertones. The original version is sub-titled Donker (dark). Oerbier Licht (Light) is very similar to Arabier, the brewery's paler summer product. The name Arabier represents an impossibly convoluted joke, but the brew is serious enough. It is a very well attenuated strong beer (6.4w, 8.0v), notable for its dry-hop bouquet of Kent Goldings.

Boskeun ("Easter Bunny"), at the same strength, is - as its name suggests - a seasonal beer. It has a brassy colour; a yeasty body;

Arabier... the name and illustration derive from an impossibly convoluted joke.

and an interesting balance between sweetness and dryness. It has some cane sugar in the kettle, and is primed with honey for the bottle-conditioning. Different vintages of this beer have varying degrees of honey in the aroma, but all have hints of Sauternes sweetness.

Stille Nacht ("Silent Night") finally is a Christmas beer. It is stronger still:

The "Mad" brewery is well worth a visit. It produces some of the most colourful, tasty, specialities in Belgium.

271

7.2w, 9.0v, with a claret colour; a fruity, apple-like aroma; some dry spiciness (Darjeeling tea?) in the palate; and a sweeter finish.

The passionate guide... Mrs Herteleer, with her family's creations (above). The "Mad Brewers'" range... whimsical names for potent potions (below).

WALLONIAN SPECIALITIES
(from North-West to South-East)

Bush Beer

The strongest beer in Belgium, subject to whichever challenges may arise. The name has nothing to do with the Busch family who make Budweiser in the United States, nor with the small German brewery of that spelling. This beer is produced by the family-owned Dubuis son brewery, whose name is French for "Bush".

The estate Domaine de Guyssegnies gave birth to this brewery, which later crossed a main road and established itself independently on its present site in 1769, but still as part of a farm, with barley prominent among its crops. It has been in the same family since at least the 1890s. The brewery still has something of the appearance of a small château: in a handsome, whitewashed building, in part original, well-maintained, with pantiled roof and green shutters, among oaks, poplars and ash

A small château farm? No, the Dubuisson brewery, producer of Bush.

trees. It is one of two breweries in the village of Pipaix, and three in the community of Leuze, north of Tournai (in Flemish, Doornik) and Mons.

In the past, the Dubuisson made several products, including a strong Saison. At the end of the First World War, the brewery was liberated by a British battalion. When the owning family decided to stop farming, and concentrate on brewing, in 1933, Bush Beer was launched as its flagship product. The beer has an

273

English accent not only in its spelling but also in its style: it is reminiscent of some Barley Wines. Since the 1950s, the beer has been filtered, but it is not pasteurised. In 1981, the brewery decided to concentrate all of its efforts on Bush Beer, and drop its other products.

Soon afterwards, it began to export in a small way. Because of the possible conflict with the name Bush in the American market, the beer has been marketed there as Scaldis, the Latin name for the river Schelde. The river is not especially near, but is as important to Belgium as the Rhine to Germany or the Mississippi to the U.S.

Bush Beer is made from an original gravity of 24.5 Plato (1098), from winter and spring pale malts, and crystal. It is hopped three times, twice with Kent Goldings and once with Styrians. Some sugar is added in the kettle, and there is considerable evaporation in the boil.

Dubuisson has a well-kept, 1950s, copper brewhouse, and its traditionalism has also been evident as it has upgraded its fermentation vessels: retaining the same geometry in the new stainless-steel. After top-fermentation at 24-25 °C (75-77 °F), with a complex, estery, yeast, the brew is skimmed by hand. It is then warm-conditioned for four weeks, and finished cold.

Bush Beer has a deep golden-amber colour; a pillowy head; a soft, creamy-fruity aroma; and a clean, soft, beautifully rounded, palate, chewy and nutty; with a superb balance of clean, dry, spicy hoppiness in the finish (32 EBU). A Christmas beer, Bush de Noël, is made with more crystal malt, hopped slightly less in

Belgium's visual arts have moved on... to the moody images of film-maker André Delvaux. "Un soir, un train" was a famous Belgian movie... Bush Beer makes the connection.

the kettle, but given an extra dosage in the maturation tank. It has an amber-red colour; a delicately leafy, earthy, aroma; a lighter hop character in the palate (27 EBU); and a beautiful balance of malt and fruit. Both have 9.6w, 12.0v.

Cuvée de l'Ermitage

The designation Cuvée is widely used by Belgian brewers. It is presumably intended to suggest a beer that has been matured in the cask in a venerable cellar, though this method is not generally employed by brewers flaunting the term. "Cuvée" is overused, but in this instance the name is very long-established and the beer highly distinctive.

The Ermitage? There were many in the forests of Hainaut in the early Middle Ages, and there are at least two sites that could have inspired the name of this brew, but no one is sure. Whatever the original intention of the allusion, this beer has become more of a regional speciality than an "abbey-style" brew.

Cuvée de l'Ermitage is made in the Union brewery, at Jumet, north-west of Charleroi. This brewery is owned by Maes, for whom it makes the quite different Grimbergen Abbey beers. It also makes some "British-style" beers dating from the period when Maes was owned by Watney's.

Cuvée de l'Ermitage dates from the days when the brewery was owned by the family Duquesnoy. The beer

Monastic mock-up, but the beer has its own heritage... and a very real, distinctive character.

is produced from a gravity of 18.7 Plato (1075), and made with three malts, among which the Pale Ale and crystal types are signatures. The hops, in generous proportion, are an unusual combination of selected East Kent Goldings, Hallertau Mittelfrüh and Saazer (for the aroma) and Northern Brewer (for bitterness). Among the top-fermenting beers made at Union, it has its own yeast strain. This seems to impart a distinctively "warm", "creamy", aroma, and a less fruity palate than might

275

be expected in a strong (6.8 per cent by weight, 8.5 by volume), top-fermenting beer. The beer has one month's maturation, and is filtered and pasteurised.

Cuvée is very dark, with garnet highlights. It has a smooth start, with hints of sweetness, then a surprisingly assertive dryness in the finish (52 EBU) - almost the sappiness of an Armagnac.

La Chouffe

The name comes from the hamlet of Achouffe, in a spectacular valley in the Ardennes, near the small town of Houffalize, just north of Bastogne, in the Belgian province of Luxembourg. Is there, though, such a thing as a Chouffe? Yes, the Chouffe is the bearded gnome, wearing a red hood, who is the emblem of the brewery.

An 1805 farmhouse became the first home of the brewery, in 1982. Set into the building is a statue of St Joseph, the parish saint. The founders of the brewery added a painting of their Chouffe on the gable end of the whitewashed building. The founders are brothers-in-law. One was a food engineer in an ice-cream factory and the other worked for a food company. They brewed at home before setting up in business.

An early grist mill was a machine formerly used to mash beets at a farm, and a temperature gauge was salvaged

The "Chouffe" is the gnome on the label. His painting on the first brewery became a local landmark. (see also p. 277)

from a steam locomotive. Their first kettle, which could brew two hectolitres, was made from a wash-copper found in an antique shop. (This is not as eccentric as it may sound: the first Carlsberg lager and Coope Pale Ale were brewed in similar vessels). A couple of years later, a seven-hecto kettle was built, then the size went up to 22. Finally, or probably not, the brewery moved across the farm track, on the same site, and increased in size to 70 hectos, in a purpose-built, chalet-style structure.

The beers are brewed from piney Ardennes water, Pilsener and crystal malts, candy sugar in white and dark forms, Styrian and Saaz hops, and coriander. Bog myrtle was used for a time, but the brewery has moved away from some such elaborations.

There are two principal products, both with a clean, soft, lightly malty fruitiness. La Chouffe (19 Plato; 1076; 6.4w, 8.0v) has a golden-to-peachy colour and a sweet, fruity, aroma and palate,

276

with citric notes, becoming tarter, winey and more complex with bottle-age. It is intended to be a refreshing strong brew. While La Chouffe has become slightly paler over the years, the darker McChouffe has gained a little in colour. This beer was inspired by a Scottish friend of one of the partners.

McChouffe is yet more aromatic, with a dense head, and is more robust in both its sweetness and winey dryness, with a touch of warming alcohol in the finish. Other specialities are produced on occasion.

After fermentation, the beers have a period of cool maturation in tank before being filled into Champagne bottles, dated on the cork, and conditioned at

the brewery. There is also a magnum, called Big Chouffe (the English word is used). Customers are recommended to lay down the bottles for three months to a year. A farmer in the Ardennes makes a crusty, semi-soft cheese flavoured with La Chouffe, and a charcutier produces a pork and beef sausage seasoned with coriander and the beer.

Overlooking the brewhouse is a dining room serving dishes prepared with the beers. Adjoining this is a less formal tavern. The brewery also has a gift shop (tel. 061-28.81.47).

SPICED BEERS

Several Belgian classics are spiced, but in recent years a number of new brewers have made a speciality of this technique. Their activities have constituted a minor revival in the production of spiced beers. One of the first revivalists was Antoine Denooze, the owner of one of the best speciality beer cafés, De Hopduvel, in Ghent. In an upstairs room, he brewed a very spicy beer, with a notable anis character, called Stropken, and this was later put into commercial production at the Slaghmuylder brewery, at Ninove, in East Flanders. This beer was subsequently replaced with a less assertive, more delicately flavoured, brew called Stropken Grand Cru.

Café owner and collector of breweriana Antoine Denooze also created a beer called Stropken. The name is an ironic reference to the halters that the Lords of Ghent were obliged to wear by Emperor Charles in the 16th century.

Another revivalist, a home-brewer, created Houten Kop: very dry, with suggestions of anis, bitter orange and honey; and a less flavourful beer made with a large proportion of unmalted barley, and called Vlaskop. The names mean "Wooden Head" and "Flaxen Head". The beers are produced commercially at the Strubbe brewery, at Ichtegem,

in West Flanders. In the same province, the Steedje micro-brewery, at Ettelgem, makes a Trippel that suggests kiwi fruit, though that is not actually used. In the same province, at Westouter, the new Roberg micro-brewery makes a dark, sweet, spicy beer.

In Hainaut, another new micro, La Binchoise, makes a soft, syrupy, medicinal-tasting, product called Réserve Marie de Hongrie, and a honeyish brew known as Le Pavé de l'Ours.

In the city and province of Namur, the micro-brewery La Caracole makes soft and delicious beers, including an Ambrée spiced with bitter orange peel and a Brune seasoned with sweet orange and licorice.

Elsewhere in Wallonia, in the province of Luxembourg, at Soy, the micro-brewed Fantôme contains both coriander and strawberry juice. It is a soft, honeyish, beer with a dash of alcohol in the dryish finish. The Fantôme brewery has produced a number of one-off, or seasonal, brews using different seasonal and locally-grown spices.

New small breweries continue to open. They do not all survive, but some do. With them come new "Streekbieren".

Belgian Pils

Once, all beer was either dark or cloudy and yeast-sedimented, and many classic styles still are. Only when techniques of temperature control made it possible to kiln a very pale malt, and yeasts could be bred and trained to precipitate in an orderly fashion, could a golden, clear, beer be produced.

The world's first such beer was a pale lager produced in the town of Pilsen, in Bohemia (then a province of the Austrian Empire, now one of the two components, with Moravia, of the Czech Republic) in 1842. In brewing, that is recent.

At the time, Bohemia's language of government and trade was German. In German, a town of origin becomes adjectival when the suffix -er is added. The new style of beer was identified as "Pilsener". Sometimes this is spelled "Pilsner", with only one "e". Or abbreviated to "Pils".

This Pilsener type of beer was not better than other styles, but it was different, and visibly so. Its brightness was a dramatic asset at a time when mass-produced glass was taking over from stoneware or pewter drinking-vessels.

The beer made in Pilsen was very good, thanks to the sweetness of Moravian barley and the extraordinary delicacy of Bohemian hops, not to mention the skills of the brewers there. It could be made in large quantities, because steam-power was enabling breweries to work on a larger scale. By the middle of the century, steam railways were beginning to revolutionise distribution. The Austrian Empire was a single, German-speaking market, soon to be joined in a trading bloc by Bavaria and Prussia.

Pilsener beer became fashionable throughout German-speaking Central Europe, and was widely copied by local brewers. They made lager beers to the same gravity (around 12 Plato, 1048), in a golden colour, with a delicate hop bouquet and an "elegant" hoppy dryness, or bitterness, in the finish. This has become the definition of a classic Pilsener-style beer, along with an alcohol content of around 4.0 per cent by weight, 5.0 by volume (though this may vary by a few decimal points to either side).

Not every city followed suit, though. Some stuck to their own styles, and others devised local versions of golden lagers. Munich, for example, already had dark lagers, and now introduced a golden type with a distinctively malty accent. Dortmund began to produce its own, slightly stronger and bigger-bodied, style of golden lager.

In 1883, at the Carlsberg brewery in Copenhagen, the first pure culture, single-cell, lager yeast was isolated, making for a much more reliable production of clear, golden, lagers. In 1886, Heineken, of Amsterdam, began to use a pure culture yeast. These two breweries - in small, maritime nations - did much to popularise a Pilsener derivative as the most widespread style of beer.

Although these techniques were soon known everywhere, they have never totally triumphed in the nations with a deep brewing tradition. Even in Germany, many other styles continue to be brewed, and westerly cities like Düsseldorf and Cologne stay with top-fermentation. In

Pilsner Urquell is Bohemian and Czech... most definitely not to be claimed by Belgium. Its style, however, became universal, and it inspired some interesting products in Belgium.

Belgium and the British Isles, older traditions have survived especially well. In the second half of the century, Belgium was a newly-independent nation, preoccupied with establishing itself; Britain was busy ruling the world: neither country had much time for foreign ideas. In Belgium today, about 75 per cent of beer is broadly of the Pilsener type; in Britain, about 50 per cent.

Meanwhile, Europeans who emigrated to the New World in the middle of the last century opened up Middle America and established the new brewing technique there. With their central position, and the spread of the railways, they soon had national brands. Golden lagers, often identified as "Pilsener" beers gradually spread in this way throughout the world.

In Belgium, the abbreviation Pils is widely used. In Britain, because of the early success of a brand of low-sugar Pils for diabetics, the term is often misunderstood to mean some kind of diet beer. The British also misunderstand the term "beer" to indicate only ales, and not to include lagers. The North Americans often use the term "beer" to mean only golden lagers. In most parts of the world, when a drinker orders "a beer", he is thinking only of a golden lager, and his brand is probably a distant derivative of the Pilsener type. A golden lager looks refreshing but, outside the most traditionalist brewing nations, many are no more than bland thirst-quenchers.

Martens Pils... a Belgian beer evoking a Bohemian appellation. Stella Artois is a Pilsener-style beer, too. Both are advertised here outside a student café in Leuven.

The brewery in Bohemia that made the first Pilsener beer is still operating. Its beer is called Pilsner Urquell ("Original Source"), and is still a product of outstanding character. The town of Pilsen has a second brewery, next door to Urquell, and making

282

a very similar but very slightly less elegant beer. This is known as Gambrinus. The Czechs thus seem to have chosen a Belgian name (though there is a less widely-recognised theory that Gambrinus was derived from a medieval Germanic word meaning "germination of grain").

The Czechs argue that only Urquell and Gambrinus can be regarded as Pilsener beers. They are the only two made in Pilsen, after all, though the Czech Republic has many other breweries producing similar beers. Outside the Czech Republic, the closest interpretations of the Pilsener style are in general those made in Germany, followed by the slightly less hoppy, lighter, examples from Belgium. The Dutch and Danish examples are usually milder, and they have influenced the international interpretation. Britain's golden lagers are generally lacking in character, and those from North America very light in both palate and body.

Like the Czechs, the Germans make all-malt Pilseners, at least for their

Belgium's famous Pils-brewing city, Leuven, crowns a Beer King every five years. He then "rules" over a Whit weekend of beery events evoking the Burgundian era.

domestic market, though some export versions are lightened with corn, rice or other fermentable sugars. German Pilseners' hop character is reflected in units of bitterness ranging from the lower or mid 30s to lower 40s. Belgian Pilseners are usually 80-95 per cent malt, and units of bitterness are customarily in the range of mid 20s to 30s. Many of the international Pilsener types have 80 per cent malt or less, with bitterness in the lower 20s. Some North American examples have 70 per cent malt, or less, and 12-15 units of bitterness.

Continental Europeans in traditional brewing nations tend to mature their Pilsener-type beers for between one and (in rare cases) the classic three months. Those elsewhere often mature their pale lagers for a maximum of three weeks.

Such comparisons cannot tell the whole story, but they provide some measurable indications of a beer's likely character. Because most other Belgian styles are so distinctive to their home country, only the Pils beers easily compare with those from other nations.

283

STELLA ARTOIS AND INTERBREW

With alumni like Erasmus and Mercator, the university town of Leuven already held a central place in Flemish life, but the opening of the canal in the mid 1700s made it an inland port, too. "Among the distinguished guests," say records, "was Mademoiselle Artois, of the brewery..."

Internationally, by far the best known Pilsener-style beer from Belgium is Stella Artois, made in Leuven, a city conveniently placed near the middle of the country and the border between Flanders and Wallonia. The brewery traces its history to at least 1366. At that time, the existence of a brew-pub called Den Horen was noted in local records. The inn's sign was a hunting horn. Nearby was forest land in which wild boar and deer were hunted.

In 1425, Leuven became a university town, after which its

importance grew. A century later, it had 42 breweries. In 1708, Sébastien Artois, who had been an apprentice at Den Horen, graduated as a master brewer there. Less than ten years later, he had bought the business. Through siblings, marriages and inheritances, Artois remained in the family for more than 100 years and its shares are still privately held.

Sébastien Artois brewed in the days before lagering was widely practised. The brewery first made lager in 1892, and introduced Stella in 1926, as a Christmas beer.

In 1892, Artois began making a golden lager, called Bock. In Germany, the term Bock indicates a strong beer. In Belgium and France, it was in the past widely used for a golden lager weaker than a Pilsener. (Perhaps because such a beer could be consumed in the lager mugs favoured by the Germans?). In 1926, the brewery introduced a Christmas beer which was a golden lager of a typical Pilsener strength, with a spicy hop character. Taking the Christmas sign as its symbol, this was called Stella (Latin for "star").

Loburg is Belgium's answer to the milder premium lagers of Denmark.

Stella Artois became Belgium's best-known beer, both inside and outside the country. Artois grew into Belgium's biggest brewing company, and bought competitors not only locally but also in The Netherlands, France and Italy.

Barley from France, the British Isles and Denmark is used in Leuven. The French barley is brought by barge. Leuven is an inland port on a canal, linked in the other direction through Mechelen to the Schelde and the sea. At the canalside, the various Artois buildings dominate a section of the town.

The barley is steeped and spread on the six floors of the famous maltings at Artois. In the company's new, 1992, brewhouse - stainless steel, but with vessels in the traditional shape - the malt has a decoction mash. It is then boiled with Saaz Hallertau and Northern Brewer hops, from the Czech Republic, Germany and Belgium, in two additions.

In 1989 a marketing campaign was launched to highlight the traditional qualities of the product.

The end product has a distinctively Czech hop character in its aroma, and a faint hint of new-mown hay; a crisp, dryish, malty middle; and a nice dash of hoppy dryness in the finish (27 units of bitterness).

In recent years, it has become very slightly more aromatic and malty, and fractionally less dry.

Artois also has a stronger (4.6 by weight, 5.7 by volume), maltier, sweeter golden lager called Loburg, which is actually intended to compete with some "super-premium" entrants from Denmark. Loburg has its own yeast culture.

The company also produces Pils under several local labels, including Wiel's and Safir.

These were originally breweries in Brussels and Aalst.

At the end of the 1980s, Artois and its major rival Jupiler, who already had some cross-shareholdings, merged to form Interbrew. Jupiler had its origins in a company making brewery equipment. That company was founded in 1812, and the brewery went into business in 1853. The founding family was called Piedboeuf, and that was the name of the company for many years. Its beer was named after its location, at Jupille, near Liège, one of the biggest cities in Wallonia. The Pils called Jupiler, which is still brewed there, is Belgium's biggest-selling beer. It is light in taste, dryish, with a touch more of the new-mown hay and fractionally more maltiness. There is also a non-alcoholic beer from Jupiler.

Traditional kettles at the Jupille brewery, which makes Belgium's biggest-selling beer.

With its touch of post-modernism, Artois' new brewery is a landmark in Leuven. It faces Artois brewhouses from the 1960s and 1970s, which may now be turned to the production of specialities such as ales.

Interbrew also makes Pils and a number of other products under the name Lamot, at an old-established brewery in Mechelen. This brewery traces its history to 1627, and was for a time in the 1970s and early 1980s owned by Bass, of Britain.

The group has a number of other brands and breweries, and several well-known specialities, which are discussed elsewhere in this book.

ALKEN-MAES

In Belgium, devotees of Pilsener-style beers have long had a special regard for Cristal-Alken. This beer is made in the village of Alken, in the province of Limburg, in the north-east of the country. Possibly because Alken is close to Germany, or perhaps because the brewery was established to cater for the robust tastes of the coalmining industry that grew up in Limburg during the 1920s and 1930s, Cristal has traditionally been brewed to be more assertively hoppy-tasting than other Belgian Pilseners. Its signature is Saaz, though German and Belgian hops are also used. The beer is also notably pale in colour, and very clean in palate. Its yeast was originally obtained from König Pils brewery, of Duisburg, Germany. There were fears for the integrity of Cristal when Alken was acquired by Kronenbourg, of France, in 1979-81. When I mentioned these anxieties in a book, I received a surprise phone call inviting me to Alken, and was flown to Belgium by the brewery and shown how specifications and procedures were being maintained. The brewery was very anxious indeed to reassure me on this point, and to show me that members of the two founding families were still in key positions on the production side. Alken's view was that it would protect Cristal as a local product, while also making Kronenbourg, an international brand, for a wider market. Aside from the particular merits of these two products, Belgian Pilseners are generally fuller in flavour, especially hop character, and smoother, than those from France.

The flowery "white wine" among Belgian Pils... with its distinctively Czech touches.

Since that visit, Alken-Kronenbourg has linked with Maes. There is now a company called Alken-Maes which is half owned

289

The kettles of the handsome brewhouse of Maes are visible to passers-by on the road between Antwerp and Mechelen.

by Kronenbourg. (Maes, a common name in Flanders, is pronounced "Marse").

It, too, has a strongly regional base in the Flemish half of the country. In its case, the locality is the north-west, Maes is between Antwerp and Mechelen, at Waarloos. This is an area where the clay soil of the Schelde delta gave rise to a brick-kilning industry, and no doubt some hearty thirsts. Waarloos is believed to have had a brewery since the 1300s, and in the 1800s a brick-maker who had too many sons to absorb into his own business saw one of them turn to making beer. The oldest building today is the handsome 1935s brewhouse (one of two) visible from the main road. After the Second World War, the company became especially known for its Pils.

The company's principal, Theo Maes, has guided the brewery through a period of ownership by the British company Watney, and now partnership with Kronenbourg, while retaining his own reputation for having strongly Belgian views about the making of good beer.

For one reason or another, I have visited Maes three or four times. On each occasion, I have been given an extremely detailed tour, with stops for thorough explanations at every point. Maes is known for contracting a maltings in the Czech Republic.

"The Chapel", where the brew is slowly cooled. Maes Pils is made in a gentle, slow, manner, and the result is a delicately appetizing beer.

When I first visited Maes in 1983, I was told that the Czechs provided 50 per cent of the malt for the company's Pils. In 1990, I heard that this practice had ceased, and raised the question. A few days later, I received a fax saying: "Our Czech maltster will be in Belgium next week. Would you like to meet him? Perhaps he can arrange a visit to the maltings..." I was unable to take up the offer, but I have visited four or five maltings in the Czech Republic, and been deeply impressed with their product.

Maes employs the classic double decoction method of mashing; uses Saaz hops throughout in its Pils; allows the brew to cool naturally in an open vessel in a room known in the brewery as "The Chapel"; follows a classically cold (5.5-8.6 °C, 41-47 °F), slow (12-day), two-stage, procedure of fermentation; and matures the beer for between two and three months. The result is a Pils with a distinctively flowery, "white wine" bouquet and palate. It is clean-tasting and light-bodied, but with plenty of soft texture.

Haacht

Within the scale of Belgian brewing, Haacht is the one further large producer of Pils. It also distributes Pilsner Urquell in Belgium. Haacht's own entrant is identified as Primus, and sub-titled Haacht Pils.

This is an easily-drinkable Pils, deliberately restrained in bitterness. It starts sweetish, and quickly moves to a dry, crisp, quenching finish. The malts are from The Netherlands and France. Saaz hops are used for aroma, and German varieties for bitterness.

Haacht also makes a golden lager in the Dortmunder style, called Adler. This is very smooth and malty, with a sweetish palate and a balancing dryness in the finish. Adler has a gravity of 15.5 Plato (1062), 5.3 per cent alcohol by weight, 6.6 by volume.

Its other products include a "White" wheat beer, a very distinctive regional speciality called Gildenbier (see Brown Beers) and the Tongerlo abbey beers. Haacht also sells a mineral water from its own wells.

The "brewery and dairy of Haecht" soon decided where its priorities lay. The company's name has over the years been spelled in both French and Flemish styles.

The company began in the 1800s, as a dairy. The Belgians drink a lot of milk, but perhaps prefer beer, so a brewhouse was added

in 1898. A maltings from that period still stands, though it is now used as a warehouse. The present principal buildings date from a major expansion in 1923. The following year, this was the subject of a royal visit that is still remembered in prominently-displayed photographs. The gathering of moustachioed men in greatcoats looks over a handsome brewhouse with a hint of Art Nouveau. The 1930s tasting room, with walnut panelling, leaded windows and chandeliers, is reminiscent of a hunting lodge.

Primus and Gambrinus: the stained glass is one of those decorative touches beloved of proud, old, breweries. Nor have architectural flourishes been forgotten in the façade of the new offices (below, centre of picture).

293

Opposite the brewery, a handsome pub and terrace dispenses Primus unfiltered, the way it was served in the days when people came and filled their own stoneware jugs. The brewery is close to woodlands, near the village of Boortmeerbeek. Across the main road is the village of Haacht itself. The location is in a triangle formed by Leuven, Brussels and Mechelen.

INDEPENDENT PILS BREWERS

By no means every Belgian brewery makes a Pilsener-type beer, but a great many do, and some have more than one. Belgium has just under 100 brewers, but about 125 Pilseners.

I have not tasted every one, but I have sampled many. If, among those from independent brewers, there is one that stands out head-and-shoulders above the others, I have yet to find it.

Several independents produce Pils in a greater volume than any other style, but none really makes a speciality of it. The style began to establish itself in Belgium in the 1920s and 30s, especially after the Second World War. It grew during the post-war period, when people wanted to forget nationalism, and espoused tastes that were "international", "modern" and unchallenging. It still enjoys a good 70 per cent of the market,

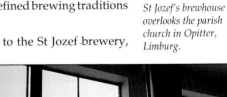

Pax Pils has a touch of regional character, and a rather retro label.

but its share has in recent years been eroded by the revival of interest in traditional specialities. Although Pils is the everyday beer in most parts of the country, its greatest loyalists are perhaps in the eastern provinces of Limburg and Liège, away from metropolitan tastes or the more defined brewing traditions of some other regions.

St Jozef's brewhouse overlooks the parish church in Opitter, Limburg.

In Limburg, a farm gave rise in 1804 to the St Jozef brewery, in the village of Opitter, near Bree. The present brewhouse dates from the 1930s, and overlooks the parish church. The company is in the fourth generation of the same family. Its Pax Pils is an example I have enjoyed recently.

Why give a beer the Latin name for peace? Perhaps the period of its origin, and the brewery's location near to two national

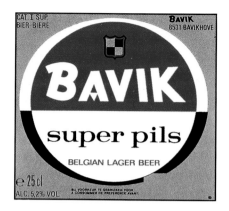

*Three good present-
day examples.*

frontiers, give a clue. It might be a good beer with which to toast European Union if its European competitors in Maastricht do not get there first.

Pax has a light, clean, malt character that I have found in other Pils from this region, and a firm, crisp, finish. It has a high malt proportion: 94 per cent, with the remainder maize. The brew is hopped three times, with Northern Brewer, Hallertau and Saaz, and the flowers are chopped in a mill (an unusual, though by no means unique, process, intended to get the most out of the hops). The yeast is of German origin, by way of another Belgian brewer, and the maturation is for four to five weeks.

The brewery also makes a fuller-tasting golden lager with the misleading name Ops-Ale. This is not to be confused with Op-Ale, from Brabant.

St Jozef also has an amber, maltier lager, in the Vienna style, called Bokkereyer, after the brigands that once roamed Limburg.

I have also appreciated the hoppy Pils made at another Limburg brewery, Martens, of Bocholt, and I have quenched my thirst with many in other parts of the country, from Akila, Bavik and Cara, to Vera, Wieze and Zweden Premium Pilsener.

What I would love to find, though, is a Belgian brewery bringing the country's robust sense of individuality to a Pils bursting with hop aroma and uncompromisingly bitter in the finish. I know such a Pils, in Limburg - called St Christoffel - but it is made on the Dutch side of the border, at Roermond.

For all their own great skills, Belgian brewers have always been willing to take inspiration from others. One or two Belgian brewers make firm-bodied, Dortmunder-style, lagers, and several confusingly use that city's term, "Export", for a lighter-tasting golden lager.

296

Some of the great old names of Belgian brewing decorate the walls of the beer-garden at the Hopduvel café, in Ghent. Most Belgian brewers promoted Pilsener-style lagers after the Second World War.

DRINKING BEER IN STYLE

Europe's "federal capital", and Belgium's, has some of the world's most elegant places in which to drink beer. Small wonder that they are described by three flourishes of French: Belle Epoque, Fin de Siècle and Art Nouveau.

No visitor to Brussels should fail to see some of its turn-of-the-century interiors, nor to sit down in such surroundings and enjoy the art of the Belgian brewer. To do so is a part of the ritual of Brussels. Perhaps there should be a winter visit to admire the decorative arts and a summer one to sit on the terrace and watch the pavement life.

The expansive visitor should probably stay (and the less extravagant merely pop in for a drink) at the de luxe Hotel Métropole, built in 1895 on the Place de Broucquères. Its Café Métropole is a chandeliered extravaganza, within which you may be offered the speciality of the house, a Campari-based cocktail called an Italiano. Nice drink, but wrong place. When in Brussels, do as the Bruxellois do: at the tables around you, people will be drinking a Duvel here, a Radieuse there, a Hoegaarden White across the room. This is by no means a

Fin de siècle extravaganza at the Métropole (below and previous page).

299

The service turns out to be friendly at the more rustic Vossegat.

speciality beer café, but nonetheless it has about 20 brews on its list, most of them Belgian. Even one of the decorative glass panels depicts beer being decanted from a cask into stoneware jugs.

If you prefer somewhere plainer, pop over the road to the 1884 Brasserie Vossegat (54 Boulevard Adolphe Max), which restricts itself to stuffed animals in glass cases and dominating waitresses in white aprons. They sit by the bar with the look of tricoteuses, but turn out to be quite friendly.

Along the main thoroughfare, the Boulevard Anspach, stand and face the Stock Exchange (in French, Bourse). Down each side is a small street, and on each is a classic period café.

Medal-winning service is showcasted at Cirio... there is even an insouciant stylishness to the prominently-positioned arrangements for personal comfort.

On the left side, Rue de la Bourse has Taverne Cirio (1886), with panels - outside and in - advertising Vermouth Bellardi, of Torino, Champagne Jacot, of Epernay, Ferroidas Royal Port, of Oporto and London, and McEwan's Scotch Ale on Draught. The customers are drinking Palm ale and Hapkin (a spicy, fruity, sweetish, strong beer somewhat darker than Duvel). Again, it is

not a beer bar, but it offers about 45 from which to choose. The old lady nursing a Bush Beer looks as though she should be drinking absinthe. An elaborately carved back bar has five shelves of glasses gleaming expectantly. There are three rooms, partially divided by carved wooden screens and swirly mirrors into half a dozen chambers. In an inner chamber, 50 medals, awarded to Francesco Cirio for services to the drinker, are displayed in a frame.

On the other side of the Bourse, in the Rue Henri Maus, is the most famous Art Nouveau café, Falstaff. This is in two houses built in 1883 by Baron Allard, with 1903 interiors by a designer

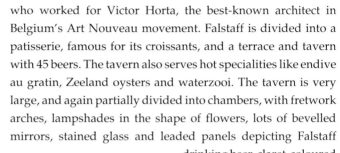

who worked for Victor Horta, the best-known architect in Belgium's Art Nouveau movement. Falstaff is divided into a patisserie, famous for its croissants, and a terrace and tavern with 45 beers. The tavern also serves hot specialities like endive au gratin, Zeeland oysters and waterzooi. The tavern is very large, and again partially divided into chambers, with fretwork arches, lampshades in the shape of flowers, lots of bevelled mirrors, stained glass and leaded panels depicting Falstaff drinking beer, claret-coloured walls, and a couple of recessed corner areas at the back for those intent upon a tête-à-tête.

Falstaff, a fictional fifteenth-century Englishman, announces himself in the Franco-Belgian Art Nouveau style.

I had always simply used the Stock Exchange as a landmark to find Falstaff, and when I finally took the trouble to note the street name, a thought struck me. Was Henri Maus not the man who coined the term Art Nouveau? No, I had apprehended the wrong mouse. It was Octave Maus who, with Edmond Picard, also a Belgian, founded the magazine "L'Art Moderne", in 1881. Their publication is credited with having first used the expression. The term later established itself in Paris, too, with the opening of a shop there called Art Nouveau in 1895. When we talk of Art Nouveau, we should probably think of Belgian cafés rather than Paris Metro stations. In fact, some of us do.

The movement argued that a man who designs buildings, decorations or furniture can be an artist. It recognized the craftsman - the artisan - for his cultural contribution, and that has passed into Belgian consciousness. It is no accident that "artisanal" is the word with which so many small brewers choose to describe themselves.

Belgium's tradition of handicrafts and technical skills goes back to the hermitages and abbeys in the forest of the Ardennes, the charcoal-burners, iron-melters and makers of glass, and to the tapestry-weavers of Flanders. When the Industrial Revolution came, and the brief colonial era, Belgium's privileged enjoyed a period of great prosperity and creativity. It was the "Belle Epoque", the good times before the First World War. It was during that period that a group of middle-class and wealthy intellectuals developed "the art of the people" as a design theory. It is still there for us to enjoy when we have beer.

Or was Falstaff really a Fleming? Shakespeare's second Globe Theatre was in Southwark, an area where Flemish immigrants had established many breweries and beer-houses. Falstaff is said to have been based on a local entrepreneur and publican, Sir John Falstolfe.

Follow Henri Maus, and keep walking until you reach the Grand' Place. Everyone visiting Brussels goes to the magnificent Grand' Place, with its 17th-century Guild Halls (among which the only one used for its original purpose is the Maison des Brasseurs, the Brewers' House). At numbers 24-25, you can take the weight off your legs and have a beer at La Chaloupe d'Or, dating from 1900.

Not every historic café in Brussels is fin-de-siècle, and a good few are older. There are several hidden in alleys off the streets around Grand' Place: La Bécasse (11 Rue de Tabora) serves Gueuze; l'Image Nostre-Dame (Impasse des Cadeaux, off Rue

Marché aux Herbes) has Bourgogne des Flandres as its speciality; and Vieux Temps (12 Grasmarkt) has the beer of the same name.

If you would like a beer in a café where Max Ernst once exhibited, and René Magritte was a customer, look for La Fleur en Papier Dor (55 Rue des Alexiens).

One of Brussels' favourite cafés is Mort Subite ("Sudden Death"), at number 7 Rue Montagne aux Herbes Potagères. This is from the 1920s, but it still has very much that turn-of-the-century ambience. With its bench seats against the cream-painted walls, its ceiling-high mirrors, and the row of tables in the middle, it has something of the feel of a railway station brasserie. Its name derives from a dice game that was played by regulars from offices in the area. If they were called back to work, the rules of the game would be revised to end in "sudden death". It was thus that the name Mort Subite attached itself also to the house beer (see Lambic).

Visitors to the Brewers' House (with horseman on top) may enjoy a beer as they tour its small museum. The Brewers' Confederation are justifiably proud that their Guild House is still used for its original purpose. In no other country do the brewers have quite such a grand home.

What was once the Bakers' Guild House, on the Grand' Place of Brussels, is now a magnificent tavern, called Le Roy d' Espagne.

The Gilded Flower (above) and the Ultimate Hallucination (below)... the names, teasing the human spirit, are typically Belgian.

Still in the city-centre, but more of a stretch of the legs (and well worth the effort) is the Ultieme Hallucinatie (316 Rue Royale), built in 1850 and restored in 1904. This has a classic Art Nouveau interior, with its marble staircase, brass peacocks and bench seats worthy of a train. One part of the Ultieme Hallucinatie is a studenty caf, which serves snack meals, and the other is a very good restaurant, with prices to match (tel. 02-217.06.14).

All of these cafés are interesting for their interiors, and each has what anyone but a Belgian would probably regard as a wide range of beers. With the possible exception of the Ultieme Hallucinatie, none would regard themselves as specialising in having a large selection.

The true specialist beer café is a Belgian and Dutch phenomenon, and it is not possible in a book such as this to do much more than give a list of some well-established favourites.

*Dirk Van Dyck's café
'Kulminator' is
a hidden delight
in Antwerp...
a collector's corner
for the inveterate
beer-taster.*

Specialist Cafés, Bars and Shops

While most of the cafés discussed elsewhere in this book are featured for their ambience or the availability of a particular beer, there are other establishments that specialise in offering a large range of brews.

What follows is only a small selection. A fuller listing of Belgian beer cafés is published in "Bier Jaarboek", by Peter Crombecq, published by Kosmos, of Antwerp and Utrecht. Although that Year Book is published in Flemish, its listings are relatively easy to follow. A very informative and regularly updated newsletter, a "Selective Guide to Belgian Bars", is published by the country's branch of Britain's Campaign for Real Ale, Postbox 5, 67 Rue des Atrébates, 1040 Brussels, Belgium (fax 02-299.02.86). CAMRA in Britain also published a paperback "Good Beer Guide to Belgium and Holland" (32 Alma Road, St Albans, Hertfordshire, England, AL1 3BW; fax 0727-84.87.95).

My thanks to Stephen D'Arcy, Vanberg and Dewulf, Derek Walsh and Drew Ferguson for their suggestions.

IN BELGIUM

Antwerp

* Het Elfde Gebod (the 11th Commandment), Torfbrug 10, just behind the cathedral. A collection of religious statues and icons, with about 30 beers, both ecclesiastical and sinful. Good Flemish snack foods. Opens 10.0. Tel. 03-232.36.11.
* Kulminator, Vleminckveld 32. More than 500 beers. Patron Dirk can appear abstracted, but he and his wife Leen have created one of the world's great beer-bars. Monday, evenings only (opens 8.0). Other weekdays, from noon. Saturday, from 5.0. Closed Sunday. Tel. 03-232.45.38.
* De Groote Witte Arend, Reyndersstraat 18. Has its own chapel, sometimes live chamber music in the courtyard, and about 40 beers. Opens 11.0. Tel. 03-232.08.80.
* Taverne Bierland, Korte Nieuwstraat 28. More than 450 beers, on a well presented list, in a former newspaper office. Opens 12.0. Closes Sundays.
* Shop: Belgium Beers, Reyndersstraat. Tel. 03-233.15.38.

Bruges

* 't Brugs Beertje, Kemelstraat 5, in a narrow alley near Simon Stevin Plein. Famous beer-bar with knowledgeable owners. More than 200 brews, and beer seminars by arrangement. Opens at 4.0. Closes on Wednesdays. Tel. 050-33.96.16. A couple of doors away is the beer-and-gin bar 't Dreupelhuisje.
* Taverne Erasmus, Wollestraat 35. A beer bar in a hotel. Tel. 050-33.57.81.
* Staminee de Garre, de Garre Passage 1. A beer café conveniently near the tourist office. Classical music. Tel. 050-34.10.29. The same proprietors have Den Dyver, in the street of the same name, offering cuisine à la bière. Opens 12.0 (11.0 weekends), closes Wednesdays. Tel. 050-33.60.69.
* De Schaere, Hooistraat 2. Noted for excellent service, good beers, and speciality teas. Tel. 050-33.20.67.

Brussels - *City centre*

* Beer Street, Boulevard Anspach 119. More than 70 Belgian speciality beers on tap at an impressive counter. The owner is also the patron of "Chez Moeder Lambic". Open every day at 9.0.
* In 't Spinnekopke ("Little Spider"), Bloemenhofplaats 1. Has an extremely extensive list, and serves classic Belgian dishes, the majority prepared with beer. Spanish-born owner Juan Rodriguez is author of Cuisine Facile à la Bière. Open 11.0-3.0 and 6.30-11.30. Saturday, evening only. Closed Sunday. Tel. 02-511.86.95.

Brussels - *Districts*

Elsene/Ixelles

* Les Brassins, Keienveldstraat 36. Has a good selection of brews and blues, against a background of old posters. Evenings only (from 5.0). Closed weekends. Tel. 02-512.69.99.
* Le Chatelain, Kasteleinsplein 17. About 50 beers and hearty Brussels "folk foods". Opens 10.30. Closes Sundays. Tel. 02-538.67.94. There is a market on the square on Wednesdays.
* Chez Moeder Lambic, Boondaalse Steenweg 441. Draught beers - more than 50 - are its speciality. Also more than 100 bottles. Tel. 02-649.72.41.
* La Houblonnière, Londenplein 4. Old favourite. Opens 11.0. Tel. 02-511.14.23/502.15.97.

St Gillis / St Gilles
* Chez Moeder Lambic, Savoiestraat 68. This one has a mere 10 draughts, about 30 vintage beers, and a total of about 700 brews on the card. Studenty café. Opens at 4.0 in the afternoon. Provides comic books (a Belgian speciality). Tel. 02-538.09.38. Try also the nearby Beulemans, on P. Dejaerlaan.

Jette
* Le Miroir, 24 Place Reine Astrid. Brewpub (see 'White' beers) and very large bar-brasserie. A favourite among serious beer-lovers. Tel. 02-424.04.78. Opposite Sunday morning market.

Marollen / Marolles
* Estaminet Les Tritons, 18/20 Rue de l'Epie. About 40 beers, including the Boon range. Quite high prices. Opens 10.0. Tel. 02-513.10.27.

Schaarbeek / Schaerbeek
* 't Narrenschip, Rogierstraat 185. Student café with about 30 beers and modest prices. Closed Friday evenings, weekends, and during July-August college vacations. Tel. 02-217.22.27.

Ukkel / Uccle
* Au Vieux Spijtigen Duivel ("The Poor Old Devil"), Alsembergsesteenweg 621, Ukkel. More than 700 beers, including the hard-to-find Oud Beersel Gueuze and unsweetened Kriek, in the 16th-century building. Opens noon. Closed Sundays. Tel. 02-344.44.55.
* Shop: Bières Artisanales, 174 Chaussée de Wavre. Tel. 02-512.17.88.

Charleroi
* Beau Lieu, 3 Rue du Commerce. More than 100 beers. Opens during day. Tel. 071-32.89.69.

Ghent
* De Hopduvel, Rokerelstraat 10. Famous café, with good selection of vintage brews and spontaneously-fermenting beers. 150-200 beers in all. Hot food (not Tuesdays) and Belgian cheeses. Garden. Open every day. Tel. 091-25.37.29.

* Ghent has a good selection of beer cafés. After De Hopduvel, the two best known are: De Dulle Griet, Vrijdagmarkt 50, tel. 091-24.24.55; and Het Waterhuis aan de Bierkant, Groentemarkt 9, tel. 091-25.06.80.

Hasselt

* 't Hemelrijk, in the street of the same name, at number 11. 100-150 beers. Hours vary. Tel. 011-22.28.51.

Leuven

* Gambrinus, Grote Markt 13. For its ornate 1890s interior and fresh local brews (including Hoegaarden and Leffe on draught), this café is a Leuven favourite, even if it is not strictly a speciality beer-bar. Open every day. Tel. 016-20.12.38.
* Domus, Tiensestraat 8. Brewpub, whose own beers include a subtle, complex honey ale. Nine draughts and 60 or 70 bottled beers. Studenty clientèle. Open every day. Tel. 016-20.14.49.

Liège

* La Vaudrée, 149 Rue St Gilles. Almost 1,000 beers, 40 vintage brews, more than 40 draughts. Restaurant. Open 24 hours every day. Justly renowned.

Mons

* L'Alambic, 25 Place du Marché aux Herbes. About 80 beers. Snacks. Tel. 065-34.60.07.
* La Podo, 43 Rue de la Coupe. Traditional "brown" café. More than 100 beers. Snooker, billiards. Tel. 065-34.70.77.

Namur

* L' Eblouissant, 27 Rue de l'Armée Grouchy. Excellent specialist beer bar, with hard-to-find Wallonian specialities. Hearty sausages. Ice-cream flavoured with beer. Opens noon; 7.0 on Saturdays. Closed Sundays, except for performances of folk-music, often Irish. Tel. 081-73.71.39.
* Shop: La Table de Wallonie, 6 Rue de la Halle. About 300 beers, and spirits. Closed Sunday and Monday. Tel. 081-22.06.83.

Oostende

* Taverne Botteltje, Louisastraat 19. Beer-café (more than 200 brews), restaurant (sometimes with beer dishes) and small

hotel. Ostend is a main port for ferries from Britain. Taverne Botteltje's hotel is a good place to begin a visit. Tel. 059-70.09.28.

* 't Ostens Bierhuis, Kapucijnestraat 48. 150 beers. Closed Tuesday. Tel. 059-70.67.01.

OUTSIDE BELGIUM

FRANCE

Lille

* Le Pub McEwans, 143 rue Gustave Delory, Lesquin (near Lille airport). A Belgian-accented bar, with branches in other French towns. Tel. 20-96.06.30.

Paris

* Taverne St Germain, 155 boulevard St Germain. Tel. 42-22.88.98.
* Le Mazet, 61 rue St-André-des-Arts, St Germain. Tel. 43-54.68.81.
* Le Gueuze, 19 rue Soufflot, near boulevard St-Michel. Tel. 43-54.63.00.
* Au Trappiste, 4 rue St-Denis. Tel. 42-33.08.50.
* La Taverne de Rubens, 12 rue St-Denis. Tel. 45-08.14.59.
* Taverne-Restaurant Gambrinus, 62 rue des Lombards. Tel. 42-21.10.34.
* Hall's Beer Tavern, 68 rue St-Denis. Tel. 42-36.92.72.
* Le Sous-Bock, 45 rue St-Honoré. Tel. 40-26.46.61.
* L'Abbey, 1 Place de la Bastille. Tel. 42-72.16.39.
* L'Oiseau de Feu, 12 Place de la Bastille. Tel. 40-19.07.52.
* Au Général La Fayette, 52 rue La Fayette. Tel. 47-70.59.08.
* Taverne Kronenbourg, 24 boulevard des Italiens. Tel. 47-70.16.64.
* L'Entre Siècle, Avenue de Lowendal, 15e, features cuisine à la bière, highlighting Belgian brews. Tel. 47-83.51.22.

THE NETHERLANDS

Amersfoort
* Mariposa, Valkestraat 10. Ten draughts, 175 bottled beers, including many Belgian specialities. Opens 4.30 on weekdays, 2.0 Friday, Saturday, Sunday. Tel. 033-611.176.

Amsterdam
* Belgique, Gravenstraat 2, near the Dam square. Belgian beers and jenever gins. Opens 11.0. Closed Tuesdays. Tel. 020-625.19.74.
* In de Wildeman, Nieuwe Zijdskolk 5, off Nieuwendijk shopping street. Renowned beer café in former gin distillery. A delightful place in which to drink, with a separate room for non-smokers. Els Van der Linden presides while her partner Henk Eggens is more often at his whisky bar nearby. Opens at noon, closes Sundays. Tel. 020-638.23.48.
* De Zotte, Raamstraat 29. Specializes in Belgian beers. Noisy and smoky. Opens 11.0 weekdays, 4.0 weekends. Tel. 020-626.86.94.
* Shops: De Bierkoning, Paleisstraat 125 (just behind the Royal Palace), central and friendly, tel. 020-625.23.36; D'Oude Gekroonde Bier- en Wijnwinkel, Huidenstraat 21 (next to Leidsestraat), a handsome, canalside, shop, but more expensive; Berts Bierhuis, Hugo De Grootstraat 3, has some esoteric selections; also a branch in Utrecht. Tel. 020-684.31.27.

Arnhem
* 't Moortgat, Ruiterstraat 35. Keen promotors of Belgian beer. Open 12.0, except 4.0 on Sundays. Tel. 085-45.03.93.

Breda
* De Beyerd, Boschstraat 26. At 500 or 600 meters from the railway station. A pioneering establishment, very highly regarded, run by the family De Jong, who have played an important part in the beer café movement. No connection with the similar-sounding cafés De Beiaard, in Amsterdam and other cities. This Breda café opens at 4.0. Tel. 076-21.42.65.
* De Dulle Griet, Reigerstraat 6. In the heart of the city. Describes itself as a "Burgundian" café. Opens at 4.0. Tel. 076-21.27.76.

Delft
* Locus Publicus, Brabantse Turfmarkt 67. Opens 11.0 weekdays, 12.0 Sundays. Tel. 015-13.46.32.

Deventer
* De Heksenketel, Brink 62-63. Opens 11.0 weekdays, 12.0 Sundays. Tel. 05700-13412.

Dordrecht
* De Tijd, Voorstraat 170. Opens 2.0 Friday and Saturday, 3.0 other days, except 5.0 on Tuesday. Tel. 078-13.39.97.

Enschede
* De Geus, Oude Markt 2. Opens 10.0 weekdays, 11.0 Saturdays, 2.0 Sundays. Tel. 053-31.05.64.

Haarlem
* Bruxelles, Lange Wijngaardstraat 16. Sometimes loud music, but lots of Belgian beers, and an occasional offering of cuisine à la bière. Opens at 5.0. Tel. 023-31.45.09.

The Hague
* Den Paas, Dunne Bierkade 16a. Cosy café in the old town. Opens 3.30. Tel. 070-360.00.19.
* Shop: De Wijn en Bier Boetiek, Leyweg 803-5. Tel. 070-366.70.92.

Hengelo
* 't Pleintje, Burgemeester Janssenplein 25. Opens 11.0 weekdays, 12.0 Saturdays, 2.0 Sundays. Tel. 074-91.24.25.

Leiden
* Shop: De Man van Drank, (previously In De Gooie Mie), Hartsesteeg 13. Many Belgian beers, and speciality spirits. Tel. 071-122.28.13.

Middelburg
* De Mug, Vlasmarkt 54-56. Serious beer café, which also takes pride in its food. Opens 4.0. Closed Monday. Tel. 01180-14851.

Nijmegen
* 't Pumpke, Molenstraat 65. Opens 12.0. Closed Sundays. Tel. 080-22.92.55.

Rotterdam
* Cambrinus, Blaak 4. Near the old harbour, the library and the Blaak metro station. Some Flemish dishes and cuisine à la bière. Opens 12.00 weekdays, 2.0 Saturday and Sunday. Tel. 010-414.67.02.
* Locus Publicus, Oostzeedijk 364. Student café. By tram or metro to Oostplein ("East Square"). Opens 5.0 weekdays, 9.0 pm Sundays. Tel. 010-433.17.61.

Tilburg
* Zomerlust, Oisterwijksebaan 15. Beer dishes on Fridays. Opens 7.0 Wednesday and Thursday, 3.0 Friday and Saturday, 11.0 Sunday. Tel. 013-42.52.92.

Utrecht
* Jan Primus, Jan van Scorelstraat 27-31. Pioneering beer café through two decades. Friendly clientèle. Opens at 3.0, closed Sundays. Tel. 030-51.45.72.

GREAT BRITAIN

Pubs
Belgian beers remain a connoisseur's taste in Britain, and few pubs offer them, though the odd one has taken an interest. These range from, in the south of England, The Canterbury Tales (tel. 0227-76.85.94), opposite the Marlow Theatre, in Canterbury, Kent; to, in the north, The Mason's Arms (tel. 05395-68436), Strawberry Bank, Cartmell Fell, Windermere. In Scotland, the café-bar Negociants (tel. 031-225.63.13), in Lothian Street, near Edinburgh University, is another example.

Restaurants
* Belgo, 72 Chalk Farm Road, London, NW1. Open evenings only. Tel. 071-267.21.79.
* The Market Restaurant, 104 High Street at Edge Street, Manchester, M4 1HQ. Evening only. Tel. 061-834.37.43.

Shops

* Leeds, The Ale House, 79 Raglan Road (tel. 0532-45.54.47).
* Lincoln, Small Beer, 91 Newland Street West (tel. 0522-52.86.28).
* London, The Beer Shop, 8 Pitfield Street, near Old Street (tel. 071-739.37.01).
* Preston, The Real Ale Shop, 47 Lovat Road (tel. 0522-52.86.28).
* Sheffield, Small Beer, 57 Archer Road (tel. 0772-20.15.91).
* Surrey, Hog's Back Brewery, Tongham, between Farnham and Aldershot (tel. 025-278.23.28).
* York, The York Beer Shop, 28 Sandringham Street, off Fishergate (tel. 0904-64.71.36).

Mail Order

* The Beer Cellar, Unit 10, Thame Park Business centre, Wenman Road, Thame, Oxforshire OX9 3XA (tel. 0844-26.05.00).
* Belgium Bière, 23 Monarch Way, West End, Southampton, Hampshire SO3 3JQ (tel. 0703-47.02.77).
* The Elite Beer Company, Jubilee Estate, Foundry Lane, Horsham, West Sussex RH1 5UE (tel. 0403-26.15.54).

UNITED STATES

Boston area

* The Sunset Tap & Grill, 130 Brighton, Allston, Mass. About 75 draught beers and 325 in bottle, including some Belgian classics. Tel. 617-254.13.31.
* Marty's (specialty food shop), 675 Washington Street, Newton, Mass. Tel. 617-332.12.30.

New York City

* Burp Castle, 41 East 7th Street (off 2nd Avenue), in the East Village. Specializes in Belgian beers. Next door to Brewsky's beer-bar. Tel. 212-982.30.06.
* Café de Bruxelles, 118 Greenwich Ave (W 13th Street). Bar and restaurant, with cuisine à la bière. Tel. 212-206.18.30.
* Dean & Deluca, 560 Broadway, Soho. Gourmet food store that carries Belgian beers. Tel. 212-431.16.91.

Suburban New York

* Katonah Beverage Barn, 24 Woodbridge Road, Katonah. Tel. 914-232.78.42.

New Jersey

* Baumel's Liquors, 30 Westfield Road, Clark, N.J. (liquor store). Tel. 908-388.19.05.
* Grand Opening Liquors, 1058 High Mountain Road, North Haledon, N.J. (liquor store).
* Stage Left, 5 Livingston Ave, New Brunswick, N.J. Does gastronomy beer dinners. Tel. 908-828.44.44.

Pennsylvania

* Brigid's, 726 North 24th Street, Philadelphia. Small restaurant, owned by a Belgian, with cuisine and beer to match. Tel. 215-232.32.32.
* The Farmhouse, 1449 Chestnut Street, Emmaus, Pennsylvania. Beer-tasting dinners. Tel. 215-967.62.25.
* Kunda Beverage, 349 S. Henderson Road, King of Prussia, Pennsylvania. Distributor and retail by the case. Tel. 215-265.31.90.

Maryland

* Sutton Place Gourmet, 10323 Old Georgetown Road, Bethesda, (speciality food shop). Tel. 301-564.31.00.

Washington D.C.

* The Brickseller, 1523 22nd Street, N.W. A famous speciality beer bar.
* Chevy Chase Wine and Spirits, 5544 Connecticut Ave, N.W. Store with a good selection of Belgian beers.

Virginia

* Belgique Gourmand, 302 Poplar Alley, Occoquam (restaurant). Tel. 703-494.11.80.
* Schneiders of Capital Hill Gourmet, 3117 Duke Street, Alexandria (specialty food shop).
* Total Beverage, 13055-C Lee Jackson Highway, Chantilly (beer supermarket). Tel. 703-817.11.77.

Florida
* Rendez Vous, 106 St George Street, St Augustine (restaurant).

Chicago
* Quencher's, Fullerton and Western.
* Sam's Wine Warehouse, 1000 W North, at Clybourn (liquor store). Tel. 312-664.43.94.
* Whole Foods, a shop at the same shopping complex, with a great selection of Belgian beers. Tel. 312-587.06.48.

Texas
* The Dog and Duck, 406 West 17th Street, Austin. American-Belgian beers of the Celis brewery. Tel. 512-479.05.98.
* The Gingerman, 5607 Morningside, Houston, with a branch in Dallas.

Colorado
* The Wine Company, 5910 South University Boulevard, D-4 Littleton (liquor store). Tel. 303-795.13.13.

California
Perhaps because of its wine industry, and its consequent industry in drinks and gastronomy generally, Northern California makes an especially good job of stocking and serving Belgian brews. This is just a small selection of outlets, all in the San Francisco area.

* Le Petit Café, 2164 Larkin, San Francisco. Bistro featuring Belgian beers. Tel. 776.53.56.
* Toronado, 547 Haight Street, San Francisco. New Wave Rock music and Belgian beer. Tel. 415-863.22.76.
* Cannery Wine Cellars, 2801 Leavenworth, San Francisco. Good beer selection, including Belgian beers.
* Mrs Coffee's Belgian Bistro and Pub, 3004 Pacific Avenue, Livermore, East Bay. Tel. 510-449.19.88.

For information on sourcing Belgian beers in the United States contact Vanberg & Dewulf, 52 Pioneer Street, Cooperstown, N.Y. 13326. Tel. 607-547.81.84, fax 607-547.83.74. They import more than 15 authentic Belgian speciality beers.

CANADA

Francophone Canada has taken Belgian beers more strongly to its heart than the English-speaking provinces, but some of the more famous brews are becoming widely available in liquor stores (which are state-controlled).

Montreal
* Le Bistro des Bières Belges, 2088 rue Montcalm, St Hubert. Tel. 514-465.06.69.
* Le Houlinsard, 139 St Paul. Tel. 514-843.74.32.
* La Maison des Bières Importées, 1418 Cartier. Tel. 514-522.05.06.
Restaurants
* Witloof, 3619 rue St Denis. Tel. 514-288.01.00.
* L'Actuel, 1194 Peel Street. Tel. 514-866.15.37.

Québec City
* Thomas Dunn pub, 369 St Paul. Tel. 418-692.46.93.
Restaurant
* Mon Manège à Trois, 102 boulevard René Levesque. Tel. 418-649.04.78.

Québec Province
* Auberges des Douceurs Belges, 121 des Falaises, Pointe-au Pic (four to five hours North of Montreal, beyond Québec city). Tel. 418-665.74.80.
* Restaurant Le Bruxelles, 150 boulevard St Madelaine, Trois Rivières (between Montreal and Québec City). Tel. 819-376.85.36.

Toronto
* Allen's, 143 Danforth Avenue. Belgian beers among the good features of this New York Saloon in a Greek neighbourhood. Tel. 416-463.30.86.
* C'est What, 67 Front Street East. Belgians and Canadian microbreweries. Tel. 416-867.94.99.

Calgary
* Buzzard's, 140 10th Avenue SW. Bar- restaurant, with some Belgian beers among an international selection. Tel. 403-264.69.59.

Vancouver
* The small chain Fog'n'Suds has some Belgian beers among its international selection.

JAPAN

Some important Japanese supermarkets offer Belgian beers, either in the food and drinks department, or in the gift shop. In Tokyo, there is a small chain of cafés named Beer Bar Brussels, with a central subsidiary in Yarai-Cho 75, Kagurazaka (tel. 03-3235.1890).
At Asaka 2/13/21, in Tokyo, Masahura Yamada serves Belgian beers at the Bois Céreste (tel. 03-3588.6292) and remembers the times he was a piano player in Brussels.

Every effort has been made to ensure the accuracy of this list, but readers are asked to check by phone before travelling to visit an establishment. Policies and opening hours can change without notice.

INDEX

Affligem Dobbel   *Gordon Scotch*   *Haecht Witbier*

Petrus Triple   *Belle Vue Kriek*   *Duvel*

Chimay   *Hoegaarden Grand Cru*   *Leffe Brune*

Jupiler   *Timmermans Witte Lambic*   *Rodenbach Alexander*